T0311789

Office Lean

Understanding and Implementing Flow in a Professional and Administrative Environment

Office Lean

Understanding and Implementing
Flow in a Professional and
Administrative Environment

Ken Eakin

A PRODUCTIVITY PRESS BOOK

First edition published in 2020

by Routledge/Productivity Press
52 Vanderbilt Avenue, 11th Floor New York, NY 10017
2 Park Square, Milton Park, Abingdon, Oxon OX14 4RN, UK

© 2020 by Ken Eakin
Routledge/Productivity Press is an imprint of Taylor & Francis Group, an Informa business

No claim to original U.S. Government works

Printed on acid-free paper

International Standard Book Number-13: 978-0-367-19665-3 (Hardback)
International Standard Book Number-13: 978-0-367-19664-6 (Paperback)
International Standard Book Number-13: 978-0-429-20381-7 (eBook)

Visit the Taylor & Francis Web site at
http://www.taylorandfrancis.com

Contents

Preface: Caring for People

I started my professional career in an entry-level job in the glamorous world of container shipping. Having avoided the real world during most of my twenties with unprofitable adventures like earning a graduate degree in film theory in Wisconsin or trying my hand at being a photojournalist in South America, I finally had the desire to settle down and purchase furniture. I took a job as documentation clerk in the local offices of a large, international container shipping firm. I typed out bills of lading for exporters in a "green screen" software program on big, chunky computer terminals. Noticing that I could spell the names of faraway ports like Nhava Sheva or Tanjung Pelepas, management soon promoted me to being an Export Customer Service Representative.

I soon found out that I had been right all along in avoiding the reality of full-time work for all those years. I felt like I was working at the lost luggage counter at the airport: the only time a customer would contact us was when they were angry. Something had gone wrong and they needed me to fix it. If they were simply placing a booking or submitting documentation, they did so via email or fax (this was the early 2000s). But if they needed a problem fixed right away, they wanted a real-live human being to abuse verbally. I was one of the unlucky few whose job it was to pick up the phone, absorb their rage, and then try to find a mutually agreeable solution with them.

The shipping industry's main goal was to fill its ships with paying cargo. Thinking in economies of scale, the shipping lines kept building bigger and bigger ships with the rationale that the cost per container would go down the more they could put on the same ship. As soon as one giant shipping line announced plans to build the world's then-biggest ship, another competing line would, a year later, build one just a little bigger. Currently the biggest ships are as long as four football fields and can carry the equivalent of over 19,000 20-foot containers. This problem is, this "bigger-is-cheaper" logic only works if there are enough paying customers to fill every voyage.

The worst thing you could hear around the office was that a ship sailed "light". As a result we, like every other shipping line, regularly overbooked our ships to ensure they were fully utilized at sailing time. Customers, predictably, would place "buffer" bookings with more than one carrier, and then choose which one to go with based on which was cheapest or most conveniently scheduled. It was a vicious circle of mistrust for everyone involved.

The industry, like global trade, goes through boom and bust cycles. During my 13 years in the industry, I saw both sides of these cycles a couple times. In boom times, the lines charge high prices and leave a lot of cargo on the dock due to overbooking. In bust times, they drop their prices to nearly nothing. Even if the customer pays $1 to ship a container of lumber to Hong Kong, it is $1 more to offset the cost of financing the $300 million ship carrying it. It is $1 more not lost to the competition and one less empty space on the ship. Nonetheless, the low prices were not sustainable. The layoffs inevitably arrived. And then the offshoring of operations. Hiring and salary freezes. Those still left in the office started rationing the post-it notes.

Customer service had the delightful job of telling customers that we "rolled" their booking to next week—meaning that we cut it from this week's sailing. I remember hearing: "F---ing [name of my employer]! You guys are the worst … the absolute *worst*!"; "You guys totally *suck*! I need you to get that container on that ship NOW or I'm gonna call up _____ [name of sales person, or CEO] and have you fired!"; "You can't do this to me. You're killing me. How can you do this to me? You really want to kill me like this? You know what my customer's gonna do to me when he hears this? You better get that container on that ship TODAY or I'll come over there and beat you with a baseball bat!"; or the all-time favorite: "Let me speak to your supervisor!"

After a few years as a customer service representative, I was promoted to that supervisor. When the calls got really ugly, they were all escalated to me.

> *Unfortunately, sir, there is no alternative ship we can put your cargo on.*
>
> *I'm so sorry, but the only other departure to Dubai this week would have to transship in Melbourne, Australia, and that has a transit time that is, at minimum, three weeks longer than if we wait until next week's sailing.*

I agree it's totally unfair. No, I am not trying to give you a heart attack. Still, I'm afraid we can't airfreight your 350 tons of steel to Kuala Lumpur. I truly wish there were something more we could do. Sir, if you'd like me to continue to help you, please do not threaten my staff with violence.

This was my job for five years. I appeased angry customers as best I could, even though I could offer them nothing in compensation for our company having screwed up their shipments in its desire to fully utilize their ships. My staff and I were told how bad our company was so many times a day that it was hard to feel proud of who we worked for and what we were doing. We were all deeply demoralized. We worked hard and really cared about our customers, but it is hard to constantly offer "service with a smile" when you are being cursed at all day, and are essentially powerless to help customers. Leadership would complain (behind our backs) about our sullen attitudes, and, to our faces, encourage us with empty boosterism about being more upbeat and cheerful. They believed this was motivating. I found myself working long hours, only being able to turn my attention to the unread emails once the phones stopped ringing around 5 or 6 pm. I frequently stayed until 7 or 8 pm. One of the unfortunate things about working in an international business like shipping is that the emails from overseas would start pouring in just as the domestic ones subsided. It is a 24/7/365 business.

Our company's operations were almost as bad as our customers said they were. I do not think any of our competitors were any better, but that did not exactly make us good. We had archaic and inflexible IT systems that often caused operational nightmares when they did not interface correctly with the port's IT systems. Our transshipment hubs were frequently congested, and containers would sit for weeks with no notification from anyone. We had to track and babysit our customers' shipments as they moved around the world because the company could not provide such a service (at that time) in any reliable electronic way. No one in any of our 125+ offices around the world seemed to care about anyone's cargo but that of their own domestic customers (just as we did not really care about theirs). The global operations machine that was our company was not about caring for customers. It was about filling ships up with steel boxes to make profits or, at least, minimize loses.

When we were not being abused on the phone, we would send frantic and urgent emails across all sorts of time zones in hastily written

English—and English was our *first* language, at least for many of us. English as a second language and cultural differences in our overseas offices exacerbated email communications. Sometimes we would make phone calls in the middle of the night asking transshipment ports to please not overlook our customers' most urgent containers in Manzanillo, Singapore, or Rotterdam. There was rarely a dull moment. We always had some issue going on with customs holds, rail delays, container shortages, stormy weather at seas, longshoremen's strikes, trucker shortages, port congestion, plagues of locusts (seriously, they can shut down ports in West Africa), trade sanctions, and the like.

As more and more functions were offshored in the early 2000s, it took longer for customers to reach customer service, in large part because the "front office" was substantially reduced in number to realize the "savings" of offshoring. Offshoring turned the front office customer service into the middleman. Imagine wanting to hold a conversation with Person A, but, instead of being able to speak directly to Person A, you can only ask Person B to write down what you want to say and then Person B would hand the written note to Person A on your behalf. Person A would then, after a few days, misinterpret your note, dictate a nonsensical series of clarifying questions back to Person B, who would then tell you that, while a response from Person A was received, it was full of questions and would need to be clarified before giving you an answer at some indeterminate time in the future. Now multiply that by thousands of customers wanting to talk to customer service at the same time and you have an idea of how effectively offshoring worked for customers.

Work friendships with my colleagues were what made work bearable. Another good thing about working in the shipping industry was that there were many repeat customers. You could build a relationship with them. I came to know many of our regular customers quite well. Once I had built some trusting relationships, they did not get quite as mad at me. Some of them came to understand that we were trying our best, even when the Byzantine system of the shipping business did not work in their favor. And I genuinely wanted to help them. We all did. We just felt powerless.

It was not realistic to think we could influence dock workers in Algeciras or Dar es Salaam to prioritize our customers' containers, but what really annoyed me was how the overbooking practice was, ostensibly, within our control. The trade and marketing team was right down the hall, and yet there was extraordinarily little teamwork between them and customer service. The trade and marketing team sat closer to the President's office, were more highly paid, and generally regarded customer service and operational logistics employees as lowly order takers. (We were, in fact, very creative problem solvers).

The typical service cycle that customers went through was that sales people would promise them the moon and the trade analysts would overbook the ship. When the customers were informed by customer service that their bookings were cut and their containers were sitting on the dock rather than onboard a ship, they would call up their salesperson in anger: "you promised me that I would be guaranteed to load that ship!" and the salesperson would say something to the effect of, "oh, I'm really sorry to hear that. You'll have to speak to customer service to get that fixed. They must have screwed up the load list again. I'll put you through to our export supervisor." And my phone would ring again.

At management meetings the salespeople would complain how many calls they had to handle from customers who were upset about operational issues. It was not *their* job to handle the menial and shabby operational issues. Why couldn't our customer service people simply get their act together and handle these calls? It was taking time away from their noble selling activities!

When I got a chance to become a Process Improvement Manager in 2006, I jumped at it. Here was my chance to make things better! Better for our employees; better for our customers; and better for the company! I was incredibly naïve about what sort of real change I could really bring about, as one individual up against the entrenched culture of the container shipping business, but I was super passionate and willing to try. We did have some local successes. We shortened lead times for documentation, created better inventory management, and automated a lot of manual, tedious work that customer service reps were doing.

I have since lost my naïveté but still have the passion to improve the working lives of people. My process improvement journey started with wanting to help our customers, as well as the terribly underappreciated customer service agents who took all the blame and were powerless to do much about it. I continue to believe that my work's purpose is primarily to help people. It has never been about cutting jobs. Lean, to me, is (and always will be) about ending the suffering that our dysfunctional management systems are creating. It is about wanting to make work better for people, *all* people.

Acknowledgments

First and foremost I need to thank François Villeneuve, who gave so much of his time to read the manuscript and provide honest, direct feedback. Thank you to Joe D'Appollonio and Mona Draper for starting me on the LSS journey. Ken Miller inspired me to write a book and Karyn Ross encouraged me to approach CRC Press. Additionally, Marcel Schlueter, Michelle Huang, and Jacob Stoller gave me some very valuable feedback on early drafts.

EDC has provided me a great place to work, learn, and improve myself over the last five years. The amazing people I get to work with every day provided a real-world laboratory for testing out many of my ideas. There are too many people at EDC to thank individually, but I do want to call out Ken Kember and his staff in the Finance and Technology group: Marsha Acott, Sue Love, Stephano Carrera, and Marc Gervais, all of whom treated me with the utmost respect and kindness, even when I was expounding at length about all sorts of abstract Lean concepts. (Even better, they actually tried some of them!). Kevin Harris, Ken Shulha, Jason Bedard, Dave Rowsell, and Dan Mancuso all generously reviewed some chapters. A special thanks is also due to Scott Powell and the OpEx team—I learned a lot from my colleagues Sue, Elaine, Sassan, Sarah, Bern, Adam, Joe, Sylvie, Allison, Mike, Hafsa, Sherri, Dominique, and the many, many others in the wider Lean/Agile/BPM community at EDC. If it had not been for Scott and EDC, I would not have had the opportunity to learn from great Lean practitioners and thinkers like Jake Raymer, Mike Stoecklein, Mike Orzen, Tracey and Ernie Richardson, Richard Sheridan, and Tim Healey.

Craig Szelestowski is owed a special shout out for providing great conversations, insights, and the opportunity to hone my thinking and public speaking at conferences.

Finally thanks to my wife, Janie, and our two beautiful children who endured long periods of my being a somewhat absentee husband and father while I wrote on nights and weekends. My first priority is now to make it up to them with as much of my time and love as I can.

Author

Ken Eakin is currently a Senior Advisor of Operational Excellence at Export Development Canada (EDC), a government-owned export credit agency that is self-financing and operates on commercial principles. Based in Ottawa, Ken has been a Lean coach to leaders at all levels, including senior executives, in the areas of Lending, Insurance, Finance, IT and Corporate Services. Prior to working at EDC, he worked as a Process Improvement Manager in the container shipping industry in Toronto, where he earned his certification as a Lean Six Sigma Black Belt. He holds an MA in Cinema Studies from the University of Wisconsin–Madison, and an MBA from the Rotman School of Business at the University of Toronto. He teaches a course on Lean to MBA students at the University of Ottawa's Telfer School of Management.

Introduction: We Don't Make Widgets

I was initially inspired to write this book back in 2015 when I was trying to explain the benefits of value stream[1] mapping as a means to finding and eliminating non-value–adding activities to a woman who is an investment portfolio manager. She sells bonds and commercial paper to raise funds for all of her corporation's short-term liabilities: primarily loan disbursements, but also all operating expenses and capital purchases. Her teammates also invest surplus cash in liquid financial instruments to maximize the use of idle cash. Their main job responsibility is to ensure the firm has enough cash or cash equivalents (in the right amount, at the right time, at a reasonable price, in the right currency) to cover all the company's obligations each day, without incurring the undue cost of carrying too much idle cash (a type of "inventory" in the banking world). Her daily tasks include monitoring market price fluctuations and cultivating favorable relationships with investment dealers who buy bonds and commercial paper. While she has no influence over market prices, she has to use her judgment on how much cash to raise, in what quantity and at what price. She also has influence over the "relationship" aspect of the job. But she feels it is fuzzy and intangible "thinking" work, not something that can be codified and standardized into explicit rules and standard procedures. She says to me, "Sure, this may work in manufacturing, but we don't make widgets around here."

What was a Leanster like me to say to that comment?[2] It turns out there is lots to say, but at the time I only spluttered out something to the effect that Lean concepts were "universal" and valid in any industry. She did not buy it. I moved her attention over to the whiteboard we were trying to design and dropped the value stream mapping subject.

As I ruminated over this afterward, I berated myself for not having a snappier and more convincing answer. I felt like I had let her down. I have encountered resistance (as all Lean practitioners have) to Lean ideas many times in over a dozen years of doing this kind of work in office environments, so I am hardly surprised each time skepticism comes to visit. But this incident made me realize that I believed too much in the benefits of Lean as an unexamined article of faith. I would become so caught up in explaining the tools and methods that I would too often lose sight of the fact that others do not share my degree of zealotry. I did not get why they did not "get it". So, I started to examine my faith in Lean, trying to understand why some people might not embrace it with quite the same enthusiasm I did. Maybe I am not explaining it right, I thought. This skepticism led me on a journey of learning that made me realize how counterintuitive some of Lean's fundamental concepts can be. Now I have written a book about it.

A number of exceptional companies all over the world have achieved amazing results (for their customers/patients, their investors, and their employees) by implementing Lean practices. Most of the big, enterprise-wide Lean success stories are in the manufacturing and healthcare sectors. Yet many of the local teams I have worked with in industries like financial services or transportation have also typically experienced real, meaningful, and measurable benefits like improved business performance, better customer satisfaction, and higher employee engagement.

So, while I was talking to the portfolio manager, it only seemed logical for me to believe, given my personal experience of having seen Lean's repeated success on the "frontlines" in many different teams and in different types of industries, that most frontline employees would want to embrace all this cool improvement stuff. I mean, who does not want to improve? *It is self-evident*, I had mistakenly assumed. *It should sell itself!* While I have come to expect some executives to be quite resistant to Lean, I had, in that moment, become so enthusiastic about its benefits that I had foolishly forgotten that sometimes the frontline employees will also resist it.

I am older and (perhaps) wiser now. Let's face it, Lean does not sell itself. Many people see Lean as some faddish Japanese thing, like Manga and Anime, and receive its zealous promoters with as much warmth as they do robocalls and door-to-door salespeople.

The so-called "white-collar" professions, based in offices and producing only intangibles like money and information, perhaps resist it most of all because there are no stellar benchmark Lean companies to point to, unlike the way manufacturing can point to Toyota and healthcare can point to ThedaCare. Yes, there are plenty of good success stories in teams or even entire departments of many service/office companies (particularly smaller, entrepreneurial IT firms). There are plenty of inspiring anecdotes and blog postings. Yet without any industry-leading benchmarks to point to, many employees and leaders have concluded Lean is just another variant of a three-letter, flavor-of-the-month improvement program—Total Quality Management (TQM), Theory of Constraints (TOC), Just in Time (JIT), Business Process Reengineering (BPR), Business Process Management (BPM), Six Sigma, etc.

To make things even harder, Lean (and its three-lettered cousins) has acquired a bad reputation over the last 30 years or so of its existence because it has been used unscrupulously as a crude cost-cutting tool in many companies, causing many to say that "Lean is Mean" or that it stands for "**L**ess **E**mployees **A**re **N**eeded"[3]. It does not help that westerners tend to think of Japanese society as one where people work themselves to death[4]. While one could argue that this is not the "real" application of Lean, it is still guilty by association in the minds of those who have not yet experienced first-hand its transformative benefits.

Executives are also skeptical because they have seen these sorts of programs come and go before[5]. They know that if you throw a bunch of new tools and methods with enough enthusiasm into any area of a business, you are likely to get some gains … for a while. But does it stick? Does anyone like it? Does it really make a difference? Will it make me change my own behavior? Before jumping into the deep end, executives want some reassurance that Lean has produced real, bottom-line results, and, furthermore, not just at a couple of Japanese car companies, but at other companies just like theirs. After all, they do not make widgets.

The Lean community has the problem of not quite yet having the compelling evidence the skeptics are looking for when it comes to professional office/service work. There are plenty who are experimenting successfully with it. To name only a few: TD Ameritrade, Mass Mutual, Euroclear, Xerox Business Services, the State Government of Washington—have definitely moved it well beyond a superficial "flavor-of-the-month" status. A lot of major banks and insurance companies across the world have tried to deploy Lean in one way or another[6], especially after the financial crisis of 2008–2009 forced them to look at their operating models very differently. Many new and established firms (and even many government institutions) are now in a committed relationship with some aspects of Lean. Many call it "Agile" or "Lean Start-Up", which are essentially Lean ideas applied to new product development. Some of these firms have achieved financial success, but it is hard to attribute Lean as the sole cause—in fact, it could be entirely coincidental, especially since Lean has only taken hold in pockets. None has yet to harness the full benefits of Lean at the enterprise level because almost all are still stuck in what Bob Emiliani calls the "Tool Age"[7]. That is, they are still overly focused on how the relatively superficial tools and methods can bring them short-term results, rather than on how deeper, principle-based behavior can ensure their success over the long-term.

The resistance and skepticism found in professional firms these days is the same kind of resistance and skepticism that Lean manufacturing faced in its early days as well. Yet some amazing and exceptional companies like Danaher, Wiremold, Lantech, and quite a few others overcame it, and continue to enjoy tremendous, undeniable success because of their Lean transformation[8]. So, what is holding back some exceptional professional, office-based firms from having the same breakthroughs?

Clearly, time is a factor. Deep Lean transformation of an entire organization is, by definition, not a quick fix—it takes many years, if not decades, to achieve and sustain Lean gains at a high level. Corporate culture generally takes a long time to change[9]. Even the revered Toyota—from whose business system[10] Lean is derived—started on their own journey in the 1950s and they did not perfect their business system in the first decade or two (in fact, they will tell you they are still perfecting it, and that it will never be perfect).

I am optimistic that time will not hold Lean back for very much longer in the professional world of work. The traditional model of management, a product of the industrial age, is struggling to adapt to the digital age. Mature, established companies in mature, established industries are discovering (often the hard way) that our digital age requires different management competencies and capabilities in order to thrive and succeed. Lean offers a progressive, humanistic alternative[11]. Amazon, one of the digital age's biggest financial success stories so far, is, in some ways, a Lean company[12]. In fact, all five of the most valuable firms in the world (by market capitalization, as of this writing)—Google (Alphabet), Microsoft, Apple, Facebook, and Amazon[13]—are all experiencing the benefits of Agile practices, which is basically Lean software development. And many smaller, tech-enabled firms like Netflix, Uber, Spotify, and Airbnb, to name just a few of the well-known ones, are doing the same thing[14]. As many more companies follow their lead, perhaps because consultants are making them scared of missing the "digital disruption" bus, Lean/Agile concepts are happily being introduced into both small start-ups and large bureaucracies more widely and rapidly than ever before.

All of the firms outside of manufacturing and healthcare currently pursuing Lean/Agile are discovering, just as manufacturers pursuing Lean did in the 1990s and early 2000s, that *sustained* excellence requires more than the mechanical implementation of tools or blindly copying methods. Ask a seasoned Agilist, for instance, what it takes to sustain Agile at scale, and they will tell you that it is much, much more than a project management methodology—just like anyone who has been practicing Lean for more than a few years will tell you that it is much more than a set of operational tools to make the assembly line run better. Both Lean and Agile require a radical rethinking of management and value creation. It has to become a philosophy, a mindset, a set of principles that consistently guide thinking and behavior in the face of ever-changing business conditions and emerging technologies, at least if the enterprise is serious about sustaining it. But with so many embracing the technical (tool-based) aspects of Lean in the way they organize and deliver their work, it is probably just a matter of time before a company in the world of professional business will emerge to become the first great, fully-fledged, Toyota-level Lean benchmark for office-based businesses around the world.

A second, and more important, factor that is holding back those who think for a living (what is generally referred to as "knowledge work") from obtaining the full benefits of Lean, is that the concepts and methods have not been well-translated and adapted from their successful application in manufacturing into simple, relevant, and meaningful concepts for those who work in a professional office environment[15].

Since the vast majority of Lean success stories come from physical production environments (i.e. manufacturing), extracting the relevant lessons and then finding appropriately analogous situations in the intangible, electronic, and largely invisible environment of complex knowledge work is too steep a hill to climb for most. The mental gymnastics required to translate Lean practices from the factory floor into useful applications in an office are simply too demanding and time consuming for most professional workers.

Even if one leaves out the Japanese terms, consider the vocabulary found in most Lean books: scrap, defects, run ratios, takt times, tool calibration, the exchange of dies, scrap materials, pack-out quantities, inventory turns, safety and OSHA[16] incidents, shipping stocks, water spiders, hourly operators, and supermarket withdrawals. Lean articulates its financial benefits in terms of reducing inventory turns or reducing scrap and defects (including returns) as percentage of sales. All of these terms, while perfectly meaning-ful in a manufacturing environment, mean absolutely *nothing* to professional office workers. Nor do more examples that involve activities like milling, stamping, painting, grinding, lathing, deburring, mitering, welding, painting, cutting, bending, washing, or assembling. Office workers just cannot relate to this language of work.

If you ask most Lean manufacturing pundits how Lean applies to the office, their go-to response might be that Lean principles are universal and apply to all types work, just as I had tried with the investment portfo-lio manager. The universality of the principles is true, but also completely impractical: people cannot take "universal principles" to the bank. They are just not specific enough. If its wider adoption beyond the factory is going to succeed, Lean's practicality matters. Lean has to convincingly promise to solve actual business problems that leaders can relate to if they are going to "buy-in" enough to try it. Lean has to use a vocabulary that is relevant to its audience, and, unfortunately, Lean has thus far limited its audience mostly to manufacturing and healthcare.

The poor translation of Lean into office contexts means there is a lot of misunderstanding about it—and humans do not generally want to do things that they do not understand[17]. Yet we can only truly understand Lean (or almost anything, for that matter) by learning through first-hand experience. In other words, we have to *do it* in order to understand it. But why would you even try it if you have never before experienced Lean's benefits, and neither have any of your industry peers, and, moreover, it seems hard to understand? Unfortunately, leaders too often resolve this chicken and egg dilemma by oversimplifying and "dumbing-down" Lean into something far more appealing but also far more akin to the status quo, thereby preordain-ing its lack of real impact to a company's culture or results. When the Lean "program" then yields disappointing outcomes, it causes everyone to con-clude that Lean "can't work here", that it is only a "manufacturing" thing (or a "Japanese" thing), or that it was "poorly executed" by whichever suitable scapegoat was responsible for the Lean program[18].

The few books about Lean that do try to explain how it applies to office/ service work often use too crude of a cut-and-paste approach, taking Lean manufacturing tools and methods from the "shop floor" and jamming them into the non-manufacturing world without much regard or appreciation for the complex and highly variable nature of the work that happens there (and the distinct professional culture that surrounds it). For instance, one very accomplished Lean author, whose thinking and writing I generally admire a lot, in an article about applying a Lean tool (*kanban*, in this case) in an office environment, writes:

> Is office work that complex? The actual act of building a car and the act of ordering a car to be built cannot be compared. It is much easier to say something than to do it. Giving instructions is much easier than building a car[19].

So, immersed in (and enamored with) the car industry are the minds of many of the best Lean thinkers that conceptualizing office work requires them to invoke an analogy to automobile manufacturing. To make matters worse, there is an implicit assumption that all office work is comprised of simplistic and transactional data entry, electronically "giving instructions" to the shop floor to make something. Certainly, office work is *physically* easier than any sort of factory labor, but I cannot think of a surer way to alienate an audience of professional businesspeople than to say that the work they do is simpler than assembly line work.

While some of the existing "Lean Office" books have some very valuable teachings, they are almost all written by industrial engineers[20] who have worked most of their professional careers in manufacturing settings, and who have then gone on to apply Lean successfully in their factory's "back office", the very label suggesting that the work that happens in the office has a subordinate role to production operations (it is all just clerical order entry, right?). In these "back office of the factory" scenarios, the essential and difficult work of convincing senior leadership to embark on a Lean transformation in the first place had already been accomplished. The organization's Lean journey of struggle, resistance, fear, and setback, followed by periods of learning, discovery, and eventual progress was already over in the production area before the back-office implementation even began. Lucky for them. But what are the rest of us, without a shop floor or supportive executives or industrial engineers, to do?

The office-as-factory-extension approach diminishes the broader potential of Lean in two ways: 1. it misleadingly gives the impression that it is just a collection of tools that can be transplanted "as is" from the factory floor into any work environment, in any industry; and, 2. it largely avoids the topic of how Lean principles and systems can be used successfully to improve not only low-variation administrative work (i.e. repeatable tasks with shorter cycle times, like order entry), but also highly customized and variable knowledge work that frequently comprises the bulk of activities in today's professional offices.

I have come across very few books or articles that explain clearly and simply how to implement Lean successfully where the "production operations" of a company happen exclusively inside an office environment—i.e. where there has been no prior Lean transformation somewhere else within the company; where there are no tangible/visible raw materials or inventory; and where all the value-producing and revenue-generating "production" work is performed in cube farms, not on factory floors. Yet this is precisely how insurance, education, banking, law, PR, journalism, government, accounting, electronic media and entertainment, advertising, real-estate management, consulting, travel brokerage, software development, market research, telecommunications, and IT security firms—in short, most of the economy in the developed world—provide all or most of their value to their customers.

80% of US workers now work outside of the manufacturing and agriculture industries[21], and at least half of them work in an office (when you exclude healthcare, retail, and hospitality, 40% of the population works in the financial, professional, or business services, IT, real-estate management, education, or government sectors—i.e. the so-called "white-collar" professions). Manufacturing, it should come as no surprise, is in decline. Manufacturing used to provide 65% of all US jobs in 1965, and has, sadly, diminished to as low as 8% in 2014[22]. Even if the successful spread of Lean were to help manufacturing make a comeback in North America, it will likely not overtake office/service jobs' proportion of employment in OECD countries any time in the near future[23]. It seems important, then, given how strong a case there is for Lean's ability to increase prosperity and create value in our society, that the Lean community does more to help bring the full value of Lean to professional, office-based businesses. This book is a contribution toward that effort.

This book is divided into four parts. Part I sets the foundations. I explain the need for a more progressive management system in our bureaucracies. I explain how to distinguish traditional management and Lean management from one another, from a technical point of view, primarily through the way we think about efficiency. I assert that Lean management forces us to think about efficiency in terms of how a firm's operations or projects improve the flow of value to a customer. I also touch on the social or "people" side of Lean and how fixing work systems, not people or technology, is far more effective in bringing about positive, respectful Lean changes to one's office culture.

Part II explains the two fundamental design principles, continuity and balance, that help us design our work to achieve better flow.

These principles help frame problems and envision new and effective (but often counterintuitive) approaches to solving common organizational problems. I provide some real-life examples of implementing Lean practices in office environments in the areas of accounting, insurance, lending (commercial loans), and software development.

Part III gets into the structure and nature of problem solving and the (reviled and misunderstood) notion of standard work, two cornerstone practices of Lean thinking, and how flow both supports problem solving and standardization, but also depends on it. One particular problem that every company seems to want to solve these days is how to innovate with technology faster and better, especially now that larger, older firms are struggling to become "digital" lest they be "disrupted" by smaller and more nimble companies with better technology. I explain how Lean thinking can help us integrate digital technologies into our operations more effectively so that we can capture more customer value with them.

Part IV closes out the book with some new ways to think about leadership and strategy—topics which have been overly written about from a traditional management perspective. Lean can offer us a different perspective on our well-worn mental models. At the end of the book, I come back around to how vital and central caring about people is in a successful Lean enterprise.

Notes

1. See the Appendix for a definition of the term "value stream".
2. This was before I had discovered Ken Miller's excellent little book: Miller, Ken. 2013. *We Don't Make Widgets: Overcoming the Myths That Keep Government From Radically Improving.* Washington, DC: Governing Books.
3. See Dan Riley (aka Employee X)'s *Look Before You Lean* for an amusing diaristic account of an employee who had a bad experience with external consultants tactlessly imposing Lean on him and his colleagues. Employee X. 2013. *Look Before You Lean: How a Lean Transformation Goes Bad—A Cautionary Tale.* Vista, CA: The Nobby Works.
4. See for instance: Adelstein, Jake. 2017. *Forbes*, October 30, 2017: www.forbes.com/sites/adelsteinjake/2017/10/30/japan-is-literally-working-itself-to-death-how-can-it-stop/ (accessed May 19, 2019).
5. There are many good economic, social, political, philosophical, and historical reasons why most executives—especially in large, publicly-traded companies—resist Lean. Bob Emiliani's *The Triumph of Classical Management over Lean Management* (2018) discusses this in much further depth.

6. See, for instance, many of the companies that are mentioned in McKinsey & Company. 2011. *Lean Management: New frontiers for financial institutions.* Also, Swank, Cynthia Karen. 2003. *Harvard Business Review,* October 2003: https://hbr.org/2003/10/the-Lean-service-machine (accessed May 19, 2019).

7. Emiliani, Bob. *REAL Lean (Volume 2): Critical Issues and Opportunities in Lean Management.* Wethersfield, CT: The Center for Lean Business Management, LLC, 2007.

8. Wiremold was acquired by the French firm Legrand in 2000, and, from what I have read, its Lean culture has, unfortunately, not survived very well.

9. There are, of course, some exceptions to this, like the rapid and remarkable turnarounds that happened at Wiremold or NUMMI. The Wiremold story is detailed in Art Byrne's book *The Lean Turnaround* (2012). NUMMI stands for New United Motor Manufacturing, Inc. and was the famous joint venture between GM and Toyota that lasted from 1984 to 2010. A fascinating podcast of the cultural change story is available on NPR: Langfitt, Frank. 2015. *NUMMI 2015*: This American Life (NPR podcast) www.thisamericanlife.org/561/nummi-2015 (accessed May 19, 2019).

10. See the Appendix for a definition of the term System.

11. Lean, ironically misunderstood as being associated with "old" modes of industrial mass production, is a model of a new, progressive management capability entirely relevant to the digital age. And Toyota is nothing if not a "disruptive innovator": how else did a small, nearly bankrupt Japanese automaker, over the course of 50 years, displace the American Big Three auto giants and become the world's most valuable car company (more than four times the value of Tesla) in such a highly competitive industry?

12. Admittedly, Amazon has a long way to go in terms of showing greater respect toward its employees (the people side of Lean), but it's supply chain system has benefitted from the technical application of Lean practice: Onetto, Mark. 2014. When Toyota met e-commerce: Lean at Amazon. *McKinsey Quarterly,* February 2014: www.mckinsey.com/business-functions/operations/our-insights/when-toyota-met-e-commerce-lean-at-amazon#0 (accessed November 17, 2018); Amazon's current CTO, Werner Vogels, also blogs about companies of the future being "data factories" and that data factories can learn a lot about running a successful factory operation by studying Lean: Vogels, Werner. 2017. *All things distributed,* December: www.allthingsdistributed.com/2017/12/rethinking-production-of-data.html (accessed November 17, 2018).

13. Amusingly, the French came up with the acronym GAFA (Google, Amazon, Facebook, Apple) as shorthand for "America's evil internet empire": www.macmillandictionary.com/dictionary/british/gafa (accessed November 17, 2018).

14. For a good overview of how widespread Agile has become, see Denning, Steve. 2018. *The Age of Agile: How Smart Companies Are Transforming the Way Work Gets Done.* New York: Amacom.

15. Even though there are good economic, social, political, philosophical, and historical reasons why most executives might resist Lean (see note 3, previous), I am not convinced that most executives in white-collar professions even understand Lean sufficiently well to know what they are resisting.

16. OSHA stands for Occupational Safety and Health Administration, under the US Bureau of Labor.

17. I am paraphrasing Bob Emiliani here, who writes, "Leaders do not do what they do not understand". Emiliani, Bob. 2018. Supplement to the book *The Triumph of Classical Management Over Lean Management*: https://bobemiliani.com/wp-content/uploads/2018/07/Supplement_TCMv1.3.pdf p. 27 (accessed September 12, 2018).

18. The UK government's failed experiment with "Deliverology" (based on the book by the same name by Michael Barber) is a good example of failed improvement efforts based on oversimplification. In this case, only one aspect—the measurement of results—of a larger, complex system was substituted for the whole. Its disastrous effects are chronicled in Seddon, John. 2014. *The Whitehall Effect*. Charmouth: Triarchy Press Ltd.

19. Ballé, Michael. 2018. Is Kanban Relevant to Office Work? *The Lean Post*, March 19, 2018: www.lean.org/balle/DisplayObject.cfm?o=3612 (accessed May 18, 2018).

20. Let me make it clear that I have nothing against engineers. I respect engineers very much and have often been mistaken to be one myself (and I take it as a compliment!). I am suggesting only that their highly analytical and detail-oriented ways of thinking could well be producing an overly narrow and homogenous body of literature.

21. Bureau of Labor Statistics. 2017. Employment by major industry sector. www.bls.gov/emp/ep_table_201.htm

22. Morley, Robert. 2006. The Death of American Manufacturing. *The Trumpet* (February): www.thetrumpet.com/article/2061.24.80.0/economy/the-death-of-american-manufacturing (accessed May 20, 2019); Bureau of Labor Statistics. 2017. Employment by major industry sector. www.bls.gov/emp/ep_table_201.htm. The healthcare (including social assistance) and manufacturing sectors (including mining and construction), taken together, represent barely 20% of the labor force. Sadly, this means that Lean is mostly unknown (and seemingly irrelevant) for up to 80% of the workforce.

23. Even if more manufacturing were to be "reshored" back to developed countries (eliminating the waste of transportation) in the future, the rapid advances of automation in this sector mean that the number of jobs returning would not be the same as in previous times. See, for instance, Buttonwood. 2017. The manufacturing jobs delusion. *The Economist* (January 4, 2017): https://amp.economist.com/buttonwoods-notebook/2017/01/04/the-manufacturing-jobs-delusion (accessed November 23, 2018).

GRASPING THE SITUATION

Chapter 1

The Legacy of Industrial Management

Bing! The elevator signals that it has arrived at your floor. Its doors open. You step in, turn around 180 degrees, press the button corresponding to your destination floor, then step back slightly, everyone doing a little shuffle to try to accommodate everyone's personal space as best they can. You notice in your peripheral vision that Bob is in the elevator. You worked with Bob on the initial phase of Project X last year and have not seen him in a while.

"How's it going Bob?" you ask.

"Oh, you know, busy."

"Project X?"

"Yeah, it's launching next month and it's feeling a little crazy these days. How are you?"

"Busy. Volume has gone up 35% since last year, and with Sylvia on vacation we're really struggling."

"Yeah, I can imagine."

Have you ever noticed how everyone at your office, during small talk in the elevator, or at the cafeteria, or in the break room, says they are "busy"? Or when asked why they cannot deliver their projects on time, it is because they have "too much on their plate" or "over capacity"? Do ever you think to yourself that it is a freaking miracle that anything ever gets done at all in your office because everyone is so busy with 100 different things going on all the time?

Chaos

Competing priorities, unread or misunderstood emails, too many projects on the go, unclear expectations, preparation of unnecessary reports and presentations, unplanned work, staffing shortages, badly designed software, poorly thought-out corporate metrics, politics, favoritism, turf warfare, information overload, long hours, endless meetings, smartphone addiction, and an utter lack of coordination between different functional areas of the business. Everyone is constantly busy (see Sidebar), yet so little ever seems to get done. Does this sound like your workplace?

HOW MUCH WORK IS THE RIGHT AMOUNT OF WORK?

Saying one is busy sounds like a complaint, but it is often a bit of boast. Being "busy" signals to yourself and others that you're "in demand", that your boss shows she appreciates you by giving you more work, and that you have job security. The odd thing is that if your work was moving along at a healthy, reasonable pace—in that rare sweet spot between boredom and stress—you would *still* tell your overburdened co-workers you were busy, lest they think you are not as appreciated or valuable as they are. In fact, if you were in an even rarer moment of slack, where your workload allowed you some spare time to breathe and think, you would *still* tell your co-workers you were busy, wouldn't you? Because not only would you be feeling underappreciated, you would also be inwardly panicked that if word got out that you were not so busy, someone higher up might start thinking, "Hmm, if we're not so busy in department X, could we reduce headcount to save some money?" In this perverse state of affairs, we are stressed when we have too much work, and also when we have too little! But do we truly know how much work is just the right amount? And if we did know, how could we ensure that our work remained at such a level?

Unfortunately, this example describes many office workplaces. It is a dysfunctional system, and, sadly, it is the norm. There is widespread burnout, demoralization, and lack of engagement: according to Gallup's 2013 *State of the Global Workplace* report, 87% of employees worldwide are "disengaged" or "actively disengaged"[1] at work. In the US, 80% of employees say that they suffer from high levels of stress in their job, and more than half do not take their full vacation entitlement (and when they do, 59% check their emails)[2].

In such a dysfunctional system, heroism, fire-fighting, and workarounds prevail[3]. People resort to heroics simply because they have multiple deadlines and insufficient time to meet them all. Since everyone is waiting on someone else, work moves at a tortoise's pace. Waiting employees amplify their multitasking, creating the conditions where they will very likely have to work long hours under high stress to meet their deadlines at the last minute. Management, also often working heroically long hours, often makes things worse by recognizing and rewarding such behavior.

When problems arise, or a boatload of unanticipated work suddenly appears (because an important customer or high-ranking executive just asked for something), people resort to fire-fighting: they douse the flames of a problem to make it go away as fast as possible for the sole purpose of moving on to the next most pressing fire as fast as possible. People are usually so busy putting out fires that they do not have the time or inclination to pause and think about how they might prevent the fires in the first place. In fact, they would much rather have their bosses appreciate them as fire-fighters than go unnoticed as fire-preventers.

Workarounds emerge when people feel powerless to change their chaotic reality for the better. They resort to working outside the formal system: the folkloric tips and tricks, tribal knowledge, and political maneuvering that allow them to get things done faster than others. Often you can find all three dysfunctional behaviors at once: someone finds a workaround to put out the fire and meet the customer deadline at the last minute. This employee becomes the heroic "fire-fighter" of the month. The greatest fire-fighters of all are often promoted, rewarded with larger staffs, larger budgets, and larger salaries. And so, the dysfunctional system propagates.

Is this really the best that contemporary management can do? Since, as Bob Emiliani writes, "better management of organizations is so important and consequential to people's lives and livelihoods, and to society"[4], why can we not do better?

Industrial Management

The origins of our current management system date back about 250 years. It is a product of the Industrial Revolution. By the mid-19th century, craft production had been almost entirely supplanted by mass production, and many commercial firms had grown so large in size, wealth, and complexity that their owners simply could not manage them on their own, especially if they were geographically dispersed (like the railroad companies). These growing firms needed new roles and organizational structures as a form of governance.

At the time, the Church and the military were the only existing models of large-scale organization. Following these models, business owners divided up the work into functional specializations and organized the reporting structures hierarchically. It may come as a surprise, but the standard, pyramidal org-chart that we are all so familiar with today has not existed since the dawn of time. It originally came about in the mid-19th century because many companies had simply grown too large (and, in the case of railroads and banks, geographically dispersed). Employees and owners needed a diagram to keep track of (and enforce) who did what in which part of the company. For the same reason, companies created a new role: someone who was paid to oversee the work of others, but who had no ownership stake in the company—they called them "managers". Prior to the Industrial Revolution, workers reported directly to the owner of the company (or the owner of the land). During the Industrial Age, as the size of firms grew larger in the mid-1800s, workers became narrowly specialized in their designated tasks (often simple and repeatable), and were overseen not by the owners directly, but through a vertically organized chain of command of intermediate managers and supervisors[5].

Business owners were, for the first time in history, removed from direct supervision of the work, and came to rely on their hired managers to report back to them the status of their business. Because of their growing size, 19th century firms organized themselves in ways that structurally altered the relationship between owners and the work being done. Previously, in the era of craft production, owners monitored both the *process*[6] of producing widgets and the *results* of their sale. This was now split in two. Lower-level managers, not owners, were now responsible for running operational processes successfully, while the business results—the numbers of sales and expenses; profits and losses—became the exclusive purview of the owners and higher-level executives. (Not coincidentally, modern financial accounting arose during this period of business history too). The advent of the joint-stock company and the formation of large, limited liability ownership associations further diffused the relationship between owners and the daily operations of the business.

What has resulted from the advent of the large company is a mechanistic, top-down, disconnected (aka "siloed") model of organizing and running a business. This industrial model of management has endured into the present because it has served the financial interests of business owners quite well for much of the 19th and 20th centuries. While working conditions have certainly improved, the fundamental philosophy of management has not.

Yet this old industrial model of management appears now to be far less useful (even to owners) than it once was. Many giant (and formerly very successful) corporations are now struggling, as technology companies have displaced the old giants of industry and have become giants themselves. Silicon Valley firms are generating a lot more buzz in the business press, as well as value for their shareholders, than the old stalwarts like General Electric, Procter and Gamble, or ExxonMobil.

Developing countries perform much of the world's industrial manufacturing, and that which remains in the developed world is highly automated. Developed economies are becoming increasingly service- and office-based. Most of the highest-valued public companies today produce few, if any, physical goods. They produce instead things like operating systems, information and data sharing platforms, e-commerce platforms, predictive algorithms, and cloud computing capabilities. In professional businesses, employees are often experts in their fields, with high levels of education and knowledge. The computer has become the dominant technology of professional value creation, and information and money move easily and quickly within and between firms globally, through vast electronic networks. Meanwhile, the internet has given customers much more choice—and much more power over the sellers of goods and services in many markets. In short, times have changed.

Compliance Machines

Given that the nature of business has changed so much in the world's developed economies since the late 1800s, and increasing digitization only appears to be accelerating the cycle of "creative destruction" in our current moment, it is perplexing that most companies today persist with a traditional, industrial model of management that was developed in an era when companies mass-produced physical goods in labor-intensive factories. The nature of office work has become much more complex, inter-connected and fast-paced, yet it is still organized into narrow areas of expertise, and employees are still organized in vertical, hierarchical silos, much like an assembly line.

"The corporate bureaucracies we've built are compliance machines", writes the great Lean author, consultant and thinker Michael Ballé[7].

While most leaders are usually laissez-faire ("hire smart people and leave them alone") in professional offices, when the big decisions have to get made, industrial age command-and-control (or its politer cousin "review-and-approve") is still the pervasive management style. Executives of these compliance machines, under intense pressure to please boards of directors and shareholders, sequester themselves in closed-door meeting rooms to create grand plans about how the work they do not understand should be performed by people whom they have never met. Frontline workers begrudgingly follow the top-down plans, then surreptitiously find work-arounds to please their customers when the well-intentioned plans from on high inevitably fail to do so. Middle managers then must "blame and explain" their way out of the mess of missed targets and dissatisfied customers. Could our current system of management be causing the widespread epidemic heroism, fire-fighting, and workarounds that we see in our offices every day?

LEAN IS NOT MASS PRODUCTION

Contrary to popular opinion in professional office settings, Lean is *not* about mass production. Toyota, from whose management system Lean derives, distinguished itself from (and has now surpassed, in every measure) its rival auto-manufacturers like General Motors, Chrysler, and Ford, by adopting a system of production that moved them *away* from many of the practices of traditional mass production. The "Big Three" American automakers, on the other hand, have been, until recently, the epitome of large-scale mass production (under competitive pressure, they have slowly come to imitate many aspects of Toyota's production methods over the last 20 years).

Back in the 1950s, amidst the bleak economy of post-war Japan, Toyota could not compete with the Big Three (or any other auto-maker) on the same playing field—they simply didn't have the money or space—so they created their own distinct industrial production and management system. In so doing, they changed the game forever: producing cars in smaller lot sizes, using less space, with less cost, in less time, and with higher quality. Furthermore, Toyota employees are some of the most loyal and engaged employees you could ever imagine. Toyota has seemingly found the holy grail of the business world: long-term, *sustainable* competitive advantage. And, importantly, it achieved this not through predatory take-overs to achieve transient market dominance, but through its remarkable business system. Its business system is not a static program that can be simply purchased or copied. It is a dynamic, ever-evolving system that allows the company to adapt better and faster to change than its competitors. Such a system allows Toyota to deliver more value and innovation to its existing and future customers, year after year, consistently building customer loyalty and growth. Currently Toyota enjoys a market value that is more than that of Ford, Chrysler, General Motors, and Tesla combined. Toyota is a "disruptor" if ever there was one.

Everyone is constantly busy, yet so little ever seems to get done. Employees *and* management are equally frustrated by this state of affairs. So are customers. Lean offers us a proven alternative to the legacy industrial, mass production management model, and allows employees to get lots more done in their day while working at a healthy pace. But to take advantage of Lean, we first must learn to think somewhat differently. And this all starts with how we think about efficiency.

Three Main Takeaways

1. Our offices are organized and managed much like 19th century mass production industrial enterprises were: in vertical hierarchies and with narrow, specialized roles.
2. Our outdated bureaucracies do not work very well. Everyone is busy, but it takes forever to get things done. Research shows that most employees are not very engaged at work.
3. From a financial perspective, many of our traditional companies are struggling to adapt to the digital era. In an era when much of what our economy "produces" is made up of the intangible goods and services of technology and information, our management model is outdated.

Notes

1. Gallup, Inc. 2017. The State of the Global Workplace: http://news.gallup.com/reports/220313/state-global-workplace-2017.aspx (accessed May 20, 2019).
2. Bartleby. 2018. The Stress That Kills American Workers. *The Economist*, July 21, 2018: www.economist.com/business/2018/07/21/the-stress-that-kills-american-workers (accessed May 20, 2019).
3. I am indebted to Jacob Raymer of the Institute for Enterprise Excellence (IEX) for inculcating in me these three symptoms of dysfunctional systems.

4. Emiliani, Bob. 2018. Supplement to the book *The Triumph of Classical Management Over Lean Management*. https://bobemiliani.com/wp-content/uploads/2018/07/Supplement_TCMv1.3.pdf (accessed September 12, 2018).
5. See Scholtes, Peter R. 1998. *The Leaders Handbook: Making Things Happen, Getting Things Done*. New York: McGraw-Hill, pp. 2–4 for a succinct history of how railroads created modern management.
6. See the Appendix for a definition of the term Process.
7. Ballé, Michael. 2018. The Depth of Lean Thinking. *Planet Lean*, August 14, 2018: http://planet-lean.com/the-depth-of-lean-thinking/ (accessed May 20, 2019).

Chapter 2

Two Types of Efficiency

It is tempting to think that the way out of our dysfunctional work systems—where everyone is busy and yet so little ever seems to get accomplished—is to simply focus on increasing efficiency. Indeed, ask anyone for the first word that pops into their head when they hear the word "Lean" (in a business context) and you will likely hear "efficiency". But we do not often pause to think about what we mean, exactly, by efficiency.

It can often turn out that efficiency is not the solution but the problem. Just as our model of management (as top-down hierarchies) originates in the Industrial Age, so too does our notion of efficiency. And both concepts are deeply ingrained our business psyches—not just the psyches of rich, powerful CEOs, but of everyday workers like you and me.

Much of our traditional thinking about efficiency is basically the logic of economies of scale, which is a concept that originated with Adam Smith, the father of modern economics, in the early days of the Industrial Revolution. We believe we are being more efficient when we, as individual workers, accomplish more tasks (i.e. we analyze more data, develop more features, close more deals) in less time. And we believe that if everyone, ourselves included, became more efficient at finishing the tasks that we are all individually responsible for, the more cost-effective our company's operations would be. And the more cost-effective our company's operations are, the better our overall company's business results will be. Hence working faster = more tasks in less time = lower cost per task = better financial results.

But what if this were not the only way to think about efficiency? Niklas Modig and Par Ahlstrom, in their brilliant little book *This Is Lean*[1], offer a very interesting and useful distinction between two *different* kinds of efficiency. One is from the inside of a company, looking out at its customers; and the other is from outside the company looking in, from the customer's perspective. Modig and Ahlstrom call these two types of efficiency, respectively, "resource efficiency" and "flow efficiency". Understanding these two types of efficiency is a useful way to understand how Lean companies differ from traditionally managed companies.

From the company's perspective, it is "efficient" when its internal resources (people, property, and machines) are busy and well-utilized. All its employees (and the technological tools used to do the work) are working hard and getting a lot of stuff done. A company pays a lot of money for salaries and overhead, so it naturally wants to get its money's worth from its employees and tangible assets. It does not want people sitting around with nothing to do, it wants Return on Investment, or ROI. To the extent that the company can keep everyone busy, it is considered "resource efficient". When it comes to managing operations, most leaders believe that achieving greater resource efficiency is the key to better ROI.

In contrast, from the outside customer's perspective, a company is "efficient" only when it delivers exactly what the customer wants quickly. In a flow-efficient company, the customer is boss. The customer does not really care how busy or idle the company's employees or machines are. The customer does not really care how much it costs the company to produce the good or deliver the service, so long as the price is appealing enough for the customer to be willing to pay it. The customer simply wants the goods or services they ordered to "flow" to them as quickly as possible. When you go into the pharmacy to buy some toothpaste, you really do not care if the staff is standing around talking about the latest flavor of Doritos or busily restocking shelves. You just want to quickly find your desired brand of toothpaste at a fair price, have a hassle-free check-out experience, and get on with your busy life. Similarly, our desire for flow efficiency (as consumers) drives us to shop online—do we care how hard the company worked to deliver our UltraMegaMixer2000 to our door on time, or how much it cost the company to do this, or do we just care that it was delivered on time? This is not just applicable in retail scenarios: to the extent that *any* company can provide its customers with exactly what they want, when they want it, in the right quantity, at the right price, such a company is considered "flow efficient".

In an ideal world, of course, a company would have high amounts of *both* resource and flow efficiency. What company does not want to please its customers *and* manage its costs? So, all companies pursue both resource and flow efficiency … to some degree. Yet in practice, companies find it difficult to maximize both types of efficiency and tend to favor one type of efficiency over the other. In fact, these two types of efficiency, as Modig and Ahlstrom argue, can work in opposite directions from one another—as you gain more of one, you can lose some of the other. You can have low-cost *or* high-quality, but not both[2]. Hence most managers operate with this assumption that they have no choice but to make trade-offs, believing they cannot truly lower operating costs (through greater resource efficiency) *and* increase customer satisfaction (through greater flow efficiency) simultaneously. They either must hire more people (and/or invest in more technology) to offer better service or provide lower prices. They cannot have it both ways.

Lean, in contrast, to paraphrase Modig and Ahlstrom's definition, is as *an operational strategy that resolves the tension between these two types of efficiency to achieve a higher degree of both.* While traditional economic thinking is about short-term win–lose trade-offs, Lean thinking is about long-term, win–win solutions.

Assuming there must be trade-offs, traditionally managed companies (that is, most companies) tend to pursue an operational strategy of *resource* efficiency over flow efficiency. Most companies choose to pursue resource efficiencies (with profitability being the main goal of this type of efficiency) in their operations, and, then, secondarily, try to optimize customer experience (so long as this does not erode profit margins). Lean (and Agile—see Sidebar) companies operate differently: they pursue a mix of both resource and flow efficiencies, but *with a much greater and deliberate emphasis on flow efficiency and customer value.* They consciously strive for the uninterrupted movement of goods or services in such a way that it creates faster delivery, better quality, *and* lower costs ... for *customers.* ROI and profitability in a Lean worldview are not ends in themselves, but a natural consequence of achieving greater flow efficiency in its operations.

LEAN AND AGILE: WHAT'S THE DIFFERENCE?

Less than you would think. Lean and Agile practices share many features, but Lean tends to be applied more in ongoing operations, where there are more repeatable processes that can be documented and improved upon; and Agile tends to be more for new product development (R&D or "innovation"), where there is more ambiguity about outcomes and the customer is more likely to change his or her mind frequently.

Agile is the consolidation under one moniker[3] of a bunch of similar software development methods (RAD, XP, UP, Scrum, etc.) that arose in the 1990s, that loosely resembled Lean manufacturing ideas (which were gaining popularity in the West at the same time). The primary commonality is the focus on flow efficiency: rigorously prioritizing and focusing on handling fewer units of work at once (i.e. in smaller batches, or "sprints") to deliver faster value to the customer with less effort. Both Lean and Agile also embrace problems, solving them in a similar manner, rapidly and continuously.

Agile, in fact, builds and improves upon Lean's focus on learning. Where Lean focuses on first learning about customer wants and needs while engineering a product, and then helps employees learn how to improve the process of producing it, Agile tends to focus on learning about customer wants and needs as it builds the product. Agile—as well as other disciplines like Lean Startup and Design Thinking—uses rapid iterations of product development to learn faster what the customer does and does not want. Assuming both that market conditions and customer desires will change unexpectedly, Agile firms are able to react with *agility* to these changing demands.

As Agile becomes more recognized and popular in mainstream businesses, it is branching out of software development and evolving to be understood as more of a philosophy—a principle-based mindset—much like the understanding of Lean evolved when it branched out of manufacturing. And Agile, just like Lean, has the same challenges: as it expands as a practice into other functional areas of a business, across a variety of economic sectors, it bumps up against a traditional culture of inveterate resource efficiency.

Agile practices also become easily watered-down, misunderstood and misapplied, quickly devolving into a narrow and technocratic use of tools, rather than the adoption of a wider set of principles and behaviors that respect and develop people. So, there are good and bad applications of Agile, just as there are with Lean.

The Agile movement is learning, just as the Lean movement has, that a humanistic, respectful corporate culture is a necessary precondition for its successful adoption as a widespread business system.

The Persistence of Resource Efficiency

In the "gilded" years of the Industrial Age[4], many companies enjoyed a monopolistic or oligopolistic market position. Differentiating from the competition in terms of quality or speed of delivery was not that important, because there was very little competition. What mattered most was price. If you could produce your widget more cheaply, you could sell it more cheaply, and gain more customers. If you gained more customers, you could then negotiate lower prices with suppliers, which allowed you to produce your widget even more cheaply, and gain even more customers. Competitor firms would find it difficult to enter markets since they could not match the prices of the incumbent firms, who enjoyed the cost advantages created by economies of scale and having a large share of the market. Without much competition, it was a largely self-sustaining system of wealth generation for business owners. Hence resource efficiency—getting one's money's worth from employees and capital machinery—was important to maintaining market dominance and profitability.

Even as more competition arose in many industries throughout the 20th century—in part due to stricter regulations around monopolies and other anti-trust activities—most companies did not radically change how they managed their operations to be more competitive. Instead, they simply did more of what had worked in the past: they doubled-down on resource efficiency. The mental model of how to run a business profitably had already been embedded into the thinking of industry leaders from over a century of traditional Industrial Age business practice. Alfred P. Sloane, head of General Motors in the 1930s and 1940s, with his hyper-rational, "by the numbers" approach to management[5], is perhaps the most iconic representative of a 20th century industrial manager's "resource-efficient" mindset.

In the 21st century, the growing amount of consumer choice, global competition, and digital automation has been causing more companies to either consolidate their market power and gain transient competitive advantage, with acquisitions and mergers reducing market competition and taking choice away from customers[6], or increasingly focus on customer satisfaction to create (and constantly recreate) new markets. Some of the most highly-valued firms today are exceptionally innovative and customer-centric (e.g. Apple, Amazon, Google) and are using digital technology as a way to deliver to customers what they want, when they want it, in the right amount, at the right price. Essentially, these latter firms are becoming more competitive than their rivals by increasing flow efficiencies.

Yet most companies today persist with a belief that resource efficiency is better than flow efficiency. This is not because they all mistrust their customers, employees, and suppliers, and greedily pursue profits above all other considerations. It is simply that the industrial model of business management has become so deeply embedded in our consciousness and business culture that most of us cannot imagine managing business operations in any other way. Our conventional methods of business and management thinking and practice have been so unconsciously internalized through historical tradition, that we are not consciously aware of any alternatives. As Bob Emiliani writes:

> the chance to fail [at Lean Management] does not occur because Lean management is not even considered by executives as an alternative to Classical Management … The tradition of Western business thinking and practices is informed by economic liberalism, hierarchical management control, and conventional leadership routines[7].

Flow efficiency often makes no business sense, as our Western thinking goes, because we assume it involves unprofitable practices like hiring excessive staff or buying expensive technology just to please customers, without any guarantee of increasing sales or reducing costs. And so, it is dismissed immediately as foolish: even if you exceed all your customers' expectations, it is not worth pursuing if it leads you into bankruptcy.

Resource efficiency is, to many, the only apparent option. It is the default mode. It is the status quo. It is the "way we've always done things around here". At the personal level, resource efficiency is keeping our Outlook calendars constantly full. Resource efficiency is why you are always busy! At the enterprise level, it manifests itself as high asset utilization. It is economies of scale. It is about maximizing short-term shareholder value.

The School of Mass Production

Business schools generally promote resource efficiency by teaching economies of scale[8]: On a simple level, if you buy some raw materials and a widget-making machine, and then hire a person to run it, it is basic math:

$$\text{cost per widget} = \frac{\text{cost of raw materials} + \text{cost of operating machine} + \text{cost of labor}}{\text{number of good widgets produced}}$$

The more defect-free widgets this person-plus-machine combo can produce in a given time period, the less your cost-per-widget is going to be. And lower cost-per-widget means higher profits, all other things being equal. Hence idle labor and/or idle machines are generally considered "bad" from a business point of view. This is resource-efficient thinking: you should be utilizing your labor and technological resources *to the fullest extent possible* or you are not making as much money as you could be. Busy equals profit.

Lest you think this only applies to physical widgets, it is the same thing in an office as it is in a factory. Professional, white-collar firms feel compelled to keep their staff busy too. Let us say you are the CEO of an insurance business: you probably would not like to find yourself in a situation where one person is underwriting an insurance policy while a bunch of others are just sitting around waiting for customers to call to take out a policy. You are paying them, after all. Time is money. To be more specific: their time, and the company's money.

So, what would you do instead? You would probably make sure that everyone is working on a policy at any given moment in time. If you have 100 underwriters, you would incentivize your sales and marketing people to generate sufficient customer demand so that there are, at a bare minimum, 100 policies waiting to be underwritten, 8 hours a day, 5 days a week, 52 weeks a year—just to make sure everyone has something to do while they are at work. Regardless of whether the customers actually want or need these policies that are being sold to them, if everyone always has something to do, your cost-per-policy goes down. Resource efficiency, driven by the simple math of profit maximization in the mass production of industrial widgets, has become the dominant operational management model for *all* industries, including service industries.

The Negative Consequences of Resource Efficiency

One of the necessary conditions of being a highly resource-efficient company is that it must *always* have a surplus of work waiting to be completed. As a financially responsible (and resource-efficient) CEO, you adjust your underwriter staffing levels to be constantly *below* the level actually capable of handling all the incoming orders, so that there is *always* a backlog of unstarted or partially completed policies waiting to be worked on (and typically, even during slower periods, the backlog is not at all small in office work). You might also adjust your Sales division's staffing levels (and their corresponding targets and incentives) to generate a rate of incoming orders that is constantly *above* the level your underwriters can handle, since the desired outcome is the same: a never-ending supply (or "pipeline", in sales jargon) of revenue-producing work. Similarly, when you call your dentist or auto mechanic, you usually must make an appointment. They are not just sitting around waiting for you to call. They have a queue of customers ahead of you. They too want to be fully utilized … at *their* convenience, not yours.

In larger companies, this system of perpetual queues and high resource utilization propagates throughout all groups, divisions, departments, and teams. Unlike most factory work, office workers are shared resources, working in multiple value streams for multiple customers. If they are not backlogged in one area, they are almost certainly backlogged in another. This happens perhaps most of all in highly specialized knowledge work, where multiple handoffs between internal experts are often necessary before a product or service reaches an external customer. For example, in a typical commercial lending business, Sales, Credit Underwriting, Legal, Corporate and Social Responsibility, Risk Management, a Signing Authority (typically a senior manager), Treasury, Loans Administration, Customer Service, and Settlements all might have to process some aspect of a loan agreement from the time the customer expresses an interest in obtaining debt financing to the time funds are disbursed. There is no linear conveyor system visibly and tangibly connecting these areas and, since the work is invisible, electronic, and instantly transferred to multiple parties at once, there is rarely any coordination between any of them regarding timing, volume, urgency, complexity, or staffing levels. Separate functional areas of the corporation act much like entirely separate businesses, with their own unique set of customers, priorities, and turnaround times. Internal customers end up waiting in a queue for an answer from another internal team, but since the other internal team is also fully utilized … well, you get the picture. It all adds up to it taking a long, long time to get anything out the door to an external customer, even though everyone is working hard and feels very busy.

A Catch-22 emerges from pursuing too much resource efficiency. Lowering your cost-per-widget by having a constant queue of surplus work in every team seemingly helps manage costs, but it is not the best way to serve customers. Your customers will end up waiting a long time to get their widget from your resource-efficient company. If they wait long enough, they will complain (requiring more time demanded from your customer service staff) or—worse—silently leave you for a competitor who can serve them faster (and they may even be willing to pay a higher price for faster service).

As a CEO of a traditionally managed, resource-efficient business, you might start to notice (eventually) that customer complaints are up, or the employee departure rate (voluntary turnover) is increasing, or your company is losing market share. So, what do you do? You hold a "retreat" at a five-star resort with your senior staff, where you collectively decide that "things have to change". Then you go back to doing what you understand best: you proclaim to all employees that the company must become more efficient!

Doubling Down

Standardize the task. Manage the performance. Control the process. In an earnest effort to comply with your commandment to become more "efficient", your managers double-down on the resource efficiency and try to generally impose more control over the chaos while also making everyone work faster and longer (often, and unfortunately, in the name of "Lean"!). With the best of intentions, they inadvertently create more queues, more backlog, higher costs (from having to hire more staff), and higher resentment and attrition (from longer hours worked). Yet customer wait times stay the same or might even be getting worse. As everything slides further and further behind schedule, senior managers may well decide that they have to form committees, commission many reports, and then hold lots of meetings to re-scope, restructure, reorganize, re-plan, reprioritize, reschedule, and re-budget everything to address the current backlog, the high attrition rate, and the complaining customers. They likely use these meetings to determine which customers count as "priority" customers (putting your lower-priority customers at greater risk of being poached by competitors). These meetings (and all the associated emails, of course) are taking precious time away from people who could be otherwise focused on doing the value-adding work that really matters to customers.

As if that were not enough, your managers may well decide that expensive and complicated "workflow management" software is needed, to allow all employees to see where everything is in the queue at all times of night and day (available on every device!), and to help differentiate the "priority" customers from "non-priority" customers. Numerous projects are launched to design (or purchase), configure, and then implement and troubleshoot such software, all of which creates, in the short-term, more work, more meetings (for status reports), and more costs to your company. Your IT department hires consultants to provide expert advice; project managers to manage all the projects; business systems analysts and architects and engineers and coders and testers to do the development; and change managers to handle all the problems with implementation and training. Now with an expensive project plan in place, as CEO, you put on a happy face in an effort to boost the morale of the troops: "Don't worry", you say, "it'll all be okay in another 18 months once we've implemented this new software".

As a result of the new software project, HR is suddenly really busy with recruitment and additions to payroll. Purchasing has to create more purchase orders. Payables now has to handle more invoices, and accountants have to accrue more expenses in the ledger. Facilities has to find and lease more floor space, and then reconfigure more desks to accommodate the additional IT staff. Leaders are busy reviewing contracts and approving invoices of the consultants, project managers, and developers. The IT help desk is handling more calls because—who knew? —the newly implemented software is glitchy and slow, has poor reporting capabilities, and is hard for most staff to navigate. Sales spends more time placating existing "non-priority" customers than it does cultivating new ones. Everyone is really busy, but no one's actually generating much revenue from customers. Software implementation projects, although almost always sold on the promise of "efficiencies", can often beget more work than they save if one is not careful[9].

If the efficiency proclamations and workflow software projects do not work fast enough to improve customer retention and growth, as CEO, you are probably going to be fired. Your own turnover then causes more recruitment efforts, more delayed decisions … and even more upset customers. Beleaguered leaders are expected to put on a happy face for their exasperated staff, "Don't worry, once we have a new CEO in place, I'm sure the new direction will be to tackle all these problems affecting our customers. For now, this is a good time to practice what you learned in your Positive Attitude Training course!".

And, after nine more months, the dust settles on the latest re-org and everyone's corporate memory has seemingly been erased. A new level of chaos, frustration, and burnout has become the new normal. The new CEO is three months into his reign and is now ready to tackle the most pressing problem facing the corporation: the company is—who knew?—losing market share because of long customer wait times and poor customer service. As a person who prides himself on making snappy decisions under pressure, he determines the company needs to become … more efficient! He calls a meeting with his CIO and head of HR: he figures he is either going to have to hire more people or purchase new software.

The paradox of resource efficiency is that *too much emphasis on resource efficiency creates additional work to do.* And the additional work grows exponentially. This is why big companies are places where nearly everyone feels they are constantly overworked and frantically busy, yet it still takes a disproportionately long time to deliver products and services to even the most important of customers. (And often smaller, nimbler companies are just waiting to eat up the dissatisfied customers of their larger competitors). Yes, *over-focusing* on utilizing resources—the very thing our business sense tells us is vital to profitability—can paradoxically end up losing us customers and money.

This is the most counterintuitive concept of Lean, and therefore the most difficult—and important—concept to grasp: working harder and faster—that is, being very busy by multitasking and doing too much work at once—creates *less*, not more, capacity. And this concept applies at the organizational, team, and individual levels.

Let us be perfectly clear: salaries and capital equipment *are* expensive, and you cannot have them idly sitting around for too long or it *will* be bad for your business. So, pursuing resource efficiency in moderation is, in and of itself, not at all a bad thing. The point is that, too often, in the absence of any other model of management apart from the traditional, Industrial Age one, we *over-focus* on resource efficiency. By over-focusing on the utilization of resources (and the maximization of profit) at the expense of flow efficiency and customer value, businesses lose sight of the *process* by which they are creating and delivering value to their customers. Consequently, they begin to lose customers (sometimes so slowly that the losses are nearly imperceptible at first, especially to executives who receive lagging information long, long after the damage is done), and then slowly slide into a downward spiral where they are repeatedly earning a return on invested capital below shareholder expectations.

The well-known Harvard business professor Clayton Christiansen has illustrated how US Steel, the large integrated steel company, did not encounter its financial (and labor) difficulties suddenly, but instead experienced them gradually, almost imperceptibly. US Steel lost its "lowest value" market segments one at a time, over decades, to more agile and competitive "mini-mills" that were able to serve customers in this "lower tier" segment better, faster, and cheaper[10]. From a purely financial perspective, the company was not making the "wrong" decisions—each time it produced less-than-desirable shareholder results, it deliberately and rationally chose to deprioritize its lowest profitability customer segments so that it could focus more on its higher profitability customer segments. The small "mini-mills", who were not even considered to be competitors, captured the low-profit customers segments one by one until US Steel had so few customers left that it was removed from the S&P 500 index. This is not a one-off case in only one industry, but a pattern Christensen has observed repeatedly.

Busy Does Not Mean Productive

Just as corporations can be overly resource efficient, so too can individuals. In fact, many of us are quite addicted to being busy all the time (do not believe me? Try to sit idle, with no distractions, for only five consecutive minutes and notice how comfortable you feel). Most of us, let's face it, would prefer to be at least somewhat busy than idle. This is not a bad thing. In fact, it means that managers do not need to worry nearly as much as they do that people will "slack off" at work if left unsupervised. The problem is that we easily confuse activity (like task completion) with value creation[11]; we confuse being *busy* all the time (resource efficiency) with being *productive* (flow efficiency). And we are addicted to being busy because it gives us the gratifying—if transient—feeling that we are being productive.

As with all addictions, there is a dark side. Being chronically busy leads to stress. And stress, we all know, diminishes our personal well-being, both physical and emotional. Employees are too frequently stuck with the dismal choice of having to work longer hours or disappointing their customers—and we all know which choice will enhance one's likelihood of rising up the corporate ladder.

We often keep ourselves so busy—and traditional management systems generally encourage and reward such behavior—that we hardly ever pause to consider, from the customer's perspective, *what* we should be busy with, or *when*. We do not devote much (if any) time to, say, working with colleagues in other functional areas to develop a commonly agreed upon system of rules governing what the most important thing to work on is, and when to work on it, and for approximately how long. Leaders, not wanting to micro-manage, cater to their employees' desire for autonomy, and leave them alone. But they then fall into the equally pernicious trap of "macro-managing", remaining so laissez-faire (*they're professionals—they'll figure it out!*) that they leave the daily work prioritization completely up to individual choice. As a result, companies have the same number of prioritization systems as they have employees.

Just as traffic on the highway is the consequence of individual drivers all trying to minimize their commute time, there are systemic consequences to well-intentioned but uncoordinated individual choices across an enterprise: delays for customers! Everyone then has *two* jobs: their own work (driving their car) *and* the work of trying to expedite the work (honking their horn) that is sitting idle in the queues of other departments (following up on requests, lobbying authorizers to "sign off", calling meetings to "get on the same page", etc.).

At the enterprise level, having too many large projects on the go means that executives are chronically busy too. Their attention is scattered, and they cannot focus on the few really important priorities that matter most to the progress of the company. This amounts to confusion and stress and long hours for themselves and all those who report to them. The cost of such stress throughout the enterprise is enormous. Creative thinking—the foundation of innovation and problem solving—has been shown to decline when people are under stress[12]. Further, individuals who are stressed and chronically busy take more sick leave, make poorer decisions, and make more mistakes. How does the stress caused by the overfocus on resource efficiency affect the performance of your company?

Flow-ver Dose

So, do we fix the problems with traditional management systems simply by going overboard on flow efficiency? If only it were so easy! Just as an overfocus on resource efficiency does not typically optimize customer satisfaction or employee engagement, an overfocus on flow efficiency does not typically optimize financial results. Modig and Ahlstrom cite the example of a luxury hotel as a type of business that might work well by having high flow efficiency and relatively low resource efficiency. Five-star hotels need to have a lot of staff on hand to respond to customer requests rapidly. Since hotel guests' needs vary widely, and their timing is unpredictable, there are going to be times where staff is underutilized. This is okay. It is a necessary part of the business model. Luxury hotels accept that there will be staff waiting around—or at least engaged in less productive tasks—until a guest requests a room-service meal of duck breast cooked *sous-vide* (with a cherry brandy *purée*, of course), while simultaneously receiving a Malaysian-style foot massage at four in the morning. This is why luxury hotels are expensive—they have to absorb a lot of underutilization of staff and facilities. If they need to be more price competitive, they will likely need to give up some flow efficiency. A city's fire, police, and ambulance services are other examples of highly flow-efficient operations. They are flow efficient for the same reason as luxury hotels are: they need to be able to respond rapidly even when demand is high. And this is (in part) why your municipal taxes are perhaps higher than you would like them to be. There is a *cost* to excessive flow efficiency.

Escaping the Trade-Off

Given that resource efficiency has been with us for at least 150 years, most businesses have an *excess* of resource efficiency. They are really *good* at resource efficiency. And they are highly deficient in flow efficiency. While most businesses will say they are "customer focused", very few have ever given any serious thought to embracing flow efficiency as its *dominant* operational strategy. This is evidenced by the fact that most businesses do not have a system in place to establish and maintain flow efficiencies in their operations. As a result, most companies, in most situations, would benefit from dramatically *increasing* their flow efficiency. The precisely right mix of *both* types of efficiency depends on a company's unique business situation, its strategy, and the industry in which it operates. Nevertheless, one thing is certain: in the long run, success means increasing both.

Yes, but how? Breaking free of the resource/flow-efficiency tension is called Lean. Lean helps align the work employees do to the value customers receive. Another way of saying it is that Lean guides companies to design its work systems in such a way that they maximize the value customers receive for their money. With fanatically customer-focused work systems in place, customers come to *love* your company and want to do business with you again and again (ROI!), while employees are better "utilized" because they spend more time being "busy" with only productive value-adding activities for the customer. Consequently, employees are not just "utilized" (i.e. made busy with many tasks and activities that add no value to customers), but feel engaged, productive, and fulfilled at work. If Lean is implemented respectfully, employees are not pushed to "be Lean" but are intrinsically motivated to contribute creatively and meaningfully at work every day. When the work system is designed to maximize customer value, not resource utilization, most of the internal heroics, fire-fighting, and workarounds disappear, and staff are happier because they no longer have to sit through endless meetings or read hundreds of emails to manage an overwhelming number of daily problems.

Lean, then, should be understood not as a set of tools used to control people, processes, and costs, but as a company's deliberate and systematic efforts to increase the flow of value to its customers. Further, it is vital to recognize the two *additional* benefits to Lean beyond customer satisfaction and business growth. Costs are the obvious one: as non-value-adding activities are made unnecessary in the day-to-day work, and flow increases, and operational costs go down (as opposed to economies of scale approach which, paradoxically, causes costs to go up).

The other, perhaps not as obvious, benefit is the development of, and respect for, people. What distinguishes Lean leaders from more traditional ones is that they genuinely care about engaging, motivating, and growing their employees. Increased flow efficiency relieves employees of many of the stresses and frustrations that come with working in a traditionally managed, frantically busy (resource-efficient) workplace. So Lean leaders create a common goal around increasing flow efficiency, but it is employees and frontline managers who must do most of the hard work of establishing flow. In this respect, Lean gives employees a chance to develop their creativity, analytical thinking, and collaboration with others in the effort to establish, maintain, and continuously improve flow efficiencies ... for their own benefit, as well as the benefit of customers and the company. In short, pursuing greater flow resolves your "busyness" problem. Flow does not mean you are idle or producing low quality work. You are busy, but busy with what matters most to the customer—and this allows you to find greater joy, meaning, and purpose in your work.

Three Main Takeaways

1. The way we think about efficiency is called "resource efficiency" and is based on economies of scale, a concept that comes from the mass production of physical goods and seeks to lower the per unit cost of production. This way of thinking about efficiency does not take into account what customers want beyond a good price.
2. Resource efficiency is deeply embedded in our thinking and management routines. It is the cause of our chronic busyness and lack of productivity because it actually creates more work for us to do. We have trouble seeing the causes of this additional work.
3. Lean offers a far more customer-centric approach to management that does not think in terms of trade-offs between low cost and high quality, or customer satisfaction and employee engagement.

Notes

1. Modig, Niklas and Par Ahlstrom. 2015. *This is Lean: Resolving the Efficiency Paradox.* Stockholm: Rheologica Publishing.
2. This model of trade-offs comes directly from classical supply-and-demand economics. Michael E. Porter, a Harvard economist, turned this trade-off thinking into one of the cornerstones of the business school (and management consulting) strategic planning curriculum with his "five forces" model of competition: Porter, Michael. 1979. How Competitive Forces Shape Strategy. *Harvard Business Review,* March, 1979: https://hbr.org/1979/03/how-competitive-forces-shape-strategy (accessed May 20, 2019). For a good critique of the five forces model, see Denning, Stephen. 2018. *The Age of Agile.* New York: Amacon. pp. 221–235.
3. The term Agile—as a set of software development practices—was born from the Agile Manifesto that was published in 2001: http://agilemanifesto.org (accessed May 20, 2019).
4. The so-called "Gilded Age" in the United States dates from approximately 1870 to 1900. It was certainly only "gilded" for the relatively few wealthy business owners who profited from this period of rapid industrialization in American society. Industrialists and financiers such as Cornelius Vanderbilt, Andrew Carnegie, J.P. Morgan, Leland Stanford, and John D. Rockefeller became prominent names during this era.
5. Sloan, Alfred P. 1964. *My Years with General Motors.* Garden City, NY: Doubleday, 1990.
6. According to *The Economist*, since 2008, the USA has seen about 30,000 M&A deals a year, worth 3% of GDP: Management Theory is becoming a compendium of dead ideas. *The Economist,* December 17, 2016: www.economist.com/business/2016/12/17/management-theory-is-becoming-a-compendium-of-dead-ideas (accessed May 20, 2019).
7. Emiliani, Bob. 2018. Supplement to the book *The Triumph of Classical Management Over Lean Management,* p. 6: https://bobemiliani.com/wp-content/uploads/2018/07/Supplement_TCMv1.3.pdf (accessed September 12, 2018).
8. Perhaps you remember Microeconomics 101, where you had to determine optimal production quantities and price based on the intersection of the average total cost and the marginal cost curves? That is basically how to optimize resource efficiency!
9. Jim Womack tells a funny story of a logistics company that was boasting how its latest expensive software could track exactly where they lost packages. Womack responded, "Why do you keep losing packages?". Womack, James. 2013. *Gemba Walks* (2nd Edition). Cambridge, MA: Len Enterprise Institute., p. 31.

10. Christensen, Clayton M. 2016. *The Innovator's Dilemma: When New Technologies Cause Great Firms To Fail*. Boston, MA: Harvard Business Review Press.
11. Taiichi Ohno said, "Everyone confuses motion with work" (from Macomber, H. and C. Davey. 2017. *The Pocket Sensei*, Vol I. Campton: Pemi River Media, p. 129). In a sedentary office context, it makes more sense to say, "Everyone confuses being busy with work".
12. Amabile, T. and S. Kramer. 2012. What Doesn't Motivate Creativity Can Kill It. *Harvard Business Review*, April 2012: https://hbr.org/2012/04/balancing-the-four-factors-tha-1 (accessed November 20, 2018).

Chapter 3

Changing the System

Ask ten people what their definition of Lean is, and you will get at least ten different answers.

Lean thinkers generally agree that there are some common qualities to the culture at Lean companies, such as:

- Trust and respect for people
- A strong sense of shared purpose and mission
- A relentless customer focus
- Exceptional quality standards
- Development and engagement of employees
- Personal self-discipline and responsibility
- Rigorous problem solving and continuous daily improvement
- Teamwork and collaboration

This list, however true it might be, is not very helpful. I can describe how a great meal tastes, but this will not likely help to turn you into a great chef. The fact that these are all desirable attributes of a company's culture is, after all, fairly self-evident (even if how you get there is not). Ask your average leader in your average, traditionally managed, resource-efficient firm if these attributes are valued in their company and they are not likely to disagree. In fact, a lot of traditionally managed companies have a high degree of some of these characteristics, suggesting that while they may all be necessary to achieving a higher level of Lean greatness, they are not entirely sufficient to distinguish between Lean and traditionally managed companies. Further, it is hard to know which of these attributes is a cause and which is an effect: e.g. is there good teamwork and collaboration because there is a great deal of trust and respect for all people, or is it the other way around? (It is probably circular).

Other thinkers or institutions define Lean as having to do with the classic eight wastes of Inventory, Scrap/Rework, Waiting, Intellect, Motion, Transportation, Overproduction, and Overprocessing. For example, the Lean Enterprise Institute (LEI) defines Lean this way:

> The core idea is to maximize customer value while minimizing waste. Simply, lean means creating more value for customers with fewer resources[1].

While this definition is not necessarily wrong, the traditional Lean manufacturing practice of focusing first and foremost on waste is not a particularly helpful framework for improving office work.

To confuse matters even more, the Shingo Institute lists ten principles of Enterprise Excellence[2]. Jeffrey Liker defines 14 principles found at Toyota[3]. Womack and Jones named five in their landmark book *Lean Thinking*[4]. The great W. Edwards Deming postulated 14 points for management (and 7 deadly diseases too!). Everyone seems to have a diagram of a house or a pyramid. Who is right? They all are! These are all great thinkers and institutions. Their principles contain much wisdom. Yet, one can best understand and define Lean in an office context by starting with two simple principles[5]:

1. Respect for People.
2. The Flow of Value to the Customer.

Yes, there are many other attributes, values and/or principles that characterize the behavior found at Lean companies, but these two are, in my experience, the most vital to distinguishing Lean companies from all others. In fact, I would venture to say that it would be hard to find a company that exhibited a high degree of both these two principles that was *not* a Lean company.

In the previous Chapter I described how Modig and Ahlstrom define Lean as *an operational strategy that prioritizes flow efficiency over resource efficiency, ultimately resolving the tension between the two to achieve a higher degree of both*[6]. I define Lean much the same way as they do, but feel that Respect for People needs to be integrated into it. Thus, I define it as follows: *Lean is an operational strategy that prioritizes respect for people and the flow of value to the customer.* It may seem strange not to see shareholder value included in either definition, since this is the typically considered the foundation and purpose of all business, yet that is what makes Lean so radically different from conventional management theory. Lean conceptualizes profitability as an *outcome* of flowing value to the customer. Profitability is as important to Lean companies as it is to any other, but it is not the purpose for why a specific company exists.

Respect for People

The first of these principles, Respect for People, is the mindset that creates the climate necessary for Lean to thrive. It provides the soil in which Lean can grow. It usually implies a much greater respect for frontline employees, the creators of all customer value, than is typical at most companies. Without Respect for People, especially respect toward employees on the part of management, Lean cannot take root. As W. Edwards Deming famously exhorted, every leader must "drive out fear"[7]. Before any sort of Lean transformation can take place, employees must first feel reasonably safe to point out problems, to question and understand their work through direct observation and data collection, and to try out new ideas ("experiments") with the aim of improvement (and the distinct possibility of failure), all without fear of retribution. If this first principle of Respect for People is not present through the everyday actions (not just words) of management, no amount of improvement efforts will ever be sustained.

That said, I devote most of this book to the second principle: the Flow of Value to Customers. This does not mean I do not consider respect or people important. On the contrary, I feel that the "people" aspect of work is exceptionally important. But the notion of respecting people—and related concepts like servant leadership, interpersonal communication, team dynamics, and so on—has been written about extensively, whereas the principle of flow is barely understood outside of Lean manufacturing. Ask your average leader in your average, traditionally managed firm if flow efficiency is a highly valued principle in their company and they are likely to say, "what's flow efficiency?" And, even if you explain in plainer terms that it means striving for excellence in "delivery" or "fulfillment" of customer value, they would probably say something like, "It's not really core to our strategy. It is not a key part of our culture either. It's just more of an operational thing". Flow is underserved by the current literature on contemporary business management.

Information Does Not Create Behavior

There is another reason why there is not much value in writing at length about the Respect for People principle: it is personal. Respect toward others comes largely from within: it is a personally held belief. And expecting other people to change their ways of thinking and behaving by simply giving them information (such as in a book like this) is largely futile. When it comes to people's personally held beliefs, one cannot realistically expect new information to go in and for new behavior to come out.

Stanford professor and business writer Jeffrey Pfeffer has written incisively about organizational culture, and how over the last 40 years or so the "leadership industry", as he calls it, has produced a titanic raft of books, videos, conferences, speeches, blogs, consultants, "thought leaders", and so on, all basically telling leaders that they should inspire more trust, act authentically, tell the truth, be humble and modest, and acquire more empathy and emotional intelligence[8]. Do not misunderstand: these are all great attributes to have. The intention of the leadership industry is, for the most part, good. Unfortunately, Pfeffer concludes, the leadership industry is not very effective. It has not changed leadership for the better—most employees in America are still dissatisfied and disengaged with their work, and many mistrust or dislike their leaders. Meanwhile, most leaders do not demonstrate many of these positive characteristics, despite the abundance of resources available to them. Moreover, leaders, especially CEOs of large, publicly-owned companies, get fired increasingly often for poor results or bad (sometimes criminal) behavior. If I tell you to "respect people" I am only going to add yet another well-intentioned and totally ineffective book to the pile that Pfeffer describes.

Information does not create behavior. This is a sobering and depressing truth. It calls into question the effectiveness most of our well-intentioned corporate training programs—including our Lean training programs—leave alone our system of higher education. We make assumptions in corporate settings *all the time* that, if we just give people the right information (e.g. the motivational poster on the wall, the insightful HBR article, the 27-page standard operating procedure, the 3-day conference, the latest best-selling book, the 4 hour workshop, or the 20 minute video), their thinking and behavior will change. We assume they will willingly absorb the new information, integrate it into their existing mental models, change their thinking, and then change their behavior forever after. If only it were that easy (see Figure 3.1).

Figure 3.1   Our Flawed Assumptions about Changing Behavior.

Thinking of Organizations as Systems

One of the ways to see how this is a faulty assumption is to see our organizations as complex socio-technical systems or networks rather than functional hierarchies. This is a fancy way of saying that people and technology interact as a whole system, and this whole system produces an output or result. (Note: I use the word "technology" here in the broadest sense of the word, so that it includes all the tools, information, and formal processes we use to get our jobs done each day). In a system, the parts alone cannot produce what the whole does, because the interactions between the parts matter. If we took all the tens of thousands of bits of information (e.g. words) that comprise a complex document—say, a corporate merger agreement—and laid them out randomly on the floor in front of us, would we then have an agreement that makes sense and is agreeable to all parties? Obviously, the interrelationship of all the words (parts) is important to produce the desired result. Meaning in written language depends on a shared understanding of the semantics, syntax, grammar, and context governing the choice and sequence of words. In other words, it is a system! If we want to change the results that our work system is producing—for instance, if we want to create better merger agreements—we have to first consider what changes we can make to the parts, how these changed parts will affect the subsequent interactions with all the other, unchanged parts in the system, and then ultimately how the whole system's outputs might be different as a result.

This may sound overly complicated, but this sort of systemic thinking helps us avoid the common mistake of using overly simplistic cause-and-effect thinking, only to get sub-optimal results. We believe that we need only change one part of the work system (e.g. provide a training course; fire the underperforming employee; update the Cro-Magnon-era IT system) and this will bring us the systemic results we want. But if we try to replace the engine of our Fiat with the engine of a Ford Mustang and expect it to go faster … all we have got is a more powerful engine that will not work with the rest of the Fiat-designed parts of our car. It is the existing system, including all of the interdependencies between the parts, that produces the result. Changing one part of a system in isolation rarely produces the desired results.

Changing Thinking and Behavior

So why am I going on about systems theory like this? Because systems thinking is key to changing other people's thinking and behavior. We simply cannot change other people's thinking and behavior directly. (Yes, we can coerce behavior out of people in the short-term with carrots and sticks, but we all know how effective that is). We can only change our *own* thinking and behavior (and, even then, it is often hard to do). But we can *create conditions* where other people will be more likely to behave differently than they do currently, and in so doing start to think differently. Creating the right conditions means making changes to aspects of the system—the *impersonal* aspects of the system that aim to change people's beliefs.

As an example, if you want to change the way people drive, do not ask people to change their individual driving habits (i.e. their thinking and behavior while behind the wheel). You are not likely to have much success. Focus instead on changing other, less personal aspects of the traffic system.

I only have to look at traffic dynamics in my neighborhood for an example. I live near a street that drivers, frustrated by the gridlock on the main roads, have started to use as an alternative route to bypass traffic congestion. When this started to happen frequently, the residents living along this street, not liking these frustrated drivers speeding past their front porches, understandably wanted to change this behavior.

First, the residents of the street tried to change the behavior of the speeders directly through appealing to their emotional beliefs and logical reasoning with the bluntest of all weapons: information. They put up well-meaning signs (provided free by the city) on their lawns, that said something to the effect of "Slow Down! Think of the Children!" against a stylized backdrop of silhouetted children playing. Did anyone slow down from this information? Nope. Then the city put up, at the residents' further urging, electronic displays that told each passing driver how fast they were going (it flashed red if you were going above the limit). Did this information slow down drivers? Not many, I suspect. (There were no consequences other than seeing the flashing red numbers and having to live with whatever sense of guilt that might induce). Then, eventually, the city put in permanent speed bumps on the streets. Did this slow down drivers? You bet! (You can damage the underside of your car if you go too fast over them).

What happened here is that the lawn signs and the flashing speedometer were external bits of information, being introduced into a pre-existing system (the traffic system) with the intention of changing people's thinking and behavior within that system. The drivers acting in this system had strong pre-existing personal beliefs that did not respond much (or at all) to the introduction of this new external information. But when an important but *impersonal* element of the system (the physical roadway) was changed, the incentives for drivers to speed were diminished in a significant way. The cost of potentially damaging one's car was now meaningful enough to outweigh some of the benefits of getting home as fast as possible, and driver behavior changed. (Note this method is both less coercive and less expensive than hiring more police officers to constantly tag speeders along the road).

This might seem like a bit of a paradox. To get an outcome that is seemingly all about caring for people (and, moreover, children), we have to change the system in an *impersonal* way. To improve the outcomes of child safety in the neighborhood, the residents (and their elected city officials) found an effective countermeasure by changing aspects of the traffic system that had nothing to do with trying to change drivers' mindsets with information. Yes, I too wish that all drivers would slow down out their deep-felt concern for the safety of all children in the neighborhood, rather than caring about the material cost of their car. But since, practically speaking, that is not likely to happen, at least not with most drivers, I am okay with drivers doing the right thing for the wrong reasons.

Systems Drive Behavior

One of the great insights of the Shingo Model of Enterprise Excellence is that *systems drive behaviors*[9]. Individual beliefs and mindsets also drive behavior, of course, but systems are much more dominant in social, organizational behavior. Just as the traffic system influences driver behavior more than individual driving habits (mercifully, even the most aggressive drivers tend to stop at red lights most of the time), your company's current socio-technical systems influence the behavior (and the resulting corporate culture) in your office much more so than any one individual's beliefs and values. If we want to create different behaviors, we are going to have the best chance at being successful by changing the management systems (the technical system) governing the work, not the people and their interactions (the social system). Management systems may sound mysterious but they are simply how the daily work gets prioritized, distributed, sequenced, scheduled, staffed, standardized, measured, communicated, recognized, and rewarded. Lean tends to focus on changing these management systems because it is simply more practical and effective.

Behavior Drives Thinking

Just as systems drive behavior, behavior drives thinking. If we change the management systems, in its technical aspects, we end up changing the social system indirectly. In other words, we end up changing behavior: if the conditions are conducive to people acting (and interacting) differently, they often do! And this, in turn, changes their thinking, which only reinforces their new behavior. If you start running, eventually you start to think of yourself as a runner. But if you try to think of yourself as a runner, with all the hope and good intention of motivating yourself to become a runner, you are not as likely to become a runner. A common Lean saying is, "It's easier to act your way to a new way of thinking than to think your way to a new way of acting[10]" (see Figure 3.2).

You have heard (and will, no doubt, continue to hear) many amazing, inspirational people telling you that doing something worthwhile but difficult is simply a matter of "mindset" or "attitude" or "self-discipline" or "willpower" or "choice". It may seem logical on the surface, but our mind often tricks us by making sense of things *in hindsight*. We mix up cause and effect. Once you've scaled Everest, you then try to recall (somewhat unreliably) what you believe you were thinking while you were climbing; you remember that you were determined to persevere in the face of challenges; and then you infer causality. You conclude that perseverance is the single most important attribute you and everyone must have in order to summit the highest of mountains (or accomplish analogously lofty goals). You might

Figure 3.2 How People's Mindsets and Beliefs Really Change.

even write a best-selling book about it and start giving inspirational TED talks or keynote addresses at international conferences.

So now I am going to burst your bubble (and my apologies to all extreme mountain climbers): you had already started your ascent before you started persevering. What were you thinking *before* you first started climbing Everest? Or first started training for it? What were you thinking when you climbed your first serious mountain? It was probably not "I'm going to persevere my way up that mountain!".

Your thoughts were probably something quite mundane like, "Geez, I don't really know anything about mountain climbing, and I don't really feel like it … but my friends want to go mountaineering next weekend and they'll think I'm a big disappointment if I don't go … it might be nice to see them … and I don't really have any other plans". And then you talked yourself into it, and then you did it, and then you discovered, to your surprise, that you liked it … quite a lot—or, at least, enough to pursue it further. And you developed a mindset of perseverance along the way, as a result of climbing increasingly challenging peaks. Despite what your best-selling leadership book claims is the cause and effect relationship, climbing the highest of mountains may well be the key to developing perseverance, not the other way around. Getting started with most things in life is often a matter of just doing it, of just taking that first little step. The mind tends to follow, not lead.

COGNITIVE DISSONANCE

In the field of psychology, the well-known theory of cognitive dissonance states that we tend to change our beliefs to be more consistent with our actions when they are in conflict. If I don't believe I possess the attribute of perseverance, but then find myself behaving in a way (such as scaling Everest) that might be reasonably described by most people as perseverant, I will adjust my beliefs about myself so that they are more consistent with my actions (since I cannot undo my actions at this point). Thus, I will come to believe, through climbing Everest, that I am perseverant. This change in belief reduces the discomfort—or "dissonance"—that results from doing one thing (climbing Everest) and thinking another (I am not perseverant). The action thus causes the belief. Stated another way: our behavior drives our thinking.

But we then have another moment of cognitive dissonance: the notion that behavior can cause (or create) new thinking and beliefs goes against our pre-existing mental schema that tells us that thinking and beliefs always cause behavior (we like to believe we are rational and free-willed people, after all, and we *do* act consistently with our beliefs most of the time). To reduce this dissonance, our minds fall prey to a fallacy of believing that *the thinking or belief must have preceded and caused the action in the first place*, e.g. I must have believed that I am very perseverant, or I would not have attempted to scale Everest in the first place.

If you were to ask the formerly speeding drivers in my neighborhood why they continue to drive on the same road now that it has speed bumps that slow them down, they would likely say, "There are a lot of children playing in this neighborhood, so I'm glad that there are speed bumps in place".

Focus on Flow

So how does any of this help you get started with Lean, or help your organization become more so? For one, stop worrying about intangible, abstract things like acquiring the right Lean mindsets or toolkits. This is like displaying signs on your lawn or putting up a flashing speedometer to get people to stop speeding: well-intentioned, but futile. If we know that systems drive behavior, and individual mindsets and beliefs are near-impossible to change directly, then it makes much more practical sense to focus on the second principle of Lean: the Flow of Value to the Customer. This is because focusing on flow is about changing the system, not the people and their personally held beliefs. As such, it is a far more effective way to get more done while being less busy. And so, I devote the entire second section of the book to this.

Change the system, and the behavior of the people working in the system (including yourself) will change. The Lean mindsets, including greater respect for one's self and others, will develop naturally over time, as the new behaviors become habitual. (Of course, it is helpful to have a few people— ideally leaders—who already have the Lean mindsets and behaviors so that they can help reinforce the new behaviors in those who are trying to turn them into habits). So, ask yourself what practical—and yet impersonal—little steps you can take to design your management systems to promote better Flow of Value to the Customer.

What about Waste?

A focus on flow brings us back, curiously, to waste. Striving for flow will, quite simply, expose waste; and removing the waste (via root cause problem

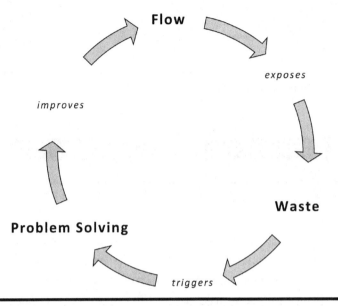

Figure 3.3   The Relationship between Flow, Waste, and Problem Solving.

solving) will then increase flow. Do not worry too much hunting for the seven (or eight) types of waste—if you pursue flow efficiency, waste will find you. No hunting required (see Figure 3.3).

In an office, if not everywhere, the greatest source of waste is really just the waste of *time*. Why? Because time is the one thing money cannot buy. You can always hire more employees or buy the latest technology (as can all your competitors) but you can never buy more time. Orest Fiume, author, and former CFO of Wiremold, explains:

> The thing about time is that it is the only resource that you can't buy more of … time is finite … 24 hours in a day with no possibility of increasing that. The only way we can "get" more time is to eliminate nonvalue-adding activities that consume some of our 24 hours. This accomplishes two things. It compresses the lead time for satisfying customer demand and frees up time (capacity) for more value-adding activities needed for increasing demand (growth)[11].

The Waste We Cannot See

Consider where waste happens most in office work. With the exception of waiting (where the work—not employees, nor equipment—is waiting around with no one working on it), the other classical types of Lean waste happen

Figure 3.4   A Simple Process Map.

Figure 3.5   A More Realistic Process Map.

almost exclusively in the "touch time"—the fingers-on-keyboard/eyes-on-monitor time when we're actively working on something. This thinking can be seen in the way we create our process maps. Take, for instance, the way we might typically depict a simple three-step process (see Figure 3.4).

The rework, overproduction, and overprocessing happen *within* the boxes that contain the tasks. Most frontline workers performing the tasks can already see a lot of this waste. They usually do not have to take any special Lean courses to see it. It is often evident to them and, if they have no means to remove it, they also find it very frustrating. Meanwhile, the arrows *between* the boxes are small and insignificant, and we hardly even notice them. Yet from the point of view of elapsed time, our maps should look much more like Figure 3.5.

So where should we be focusing our attention? The vast majority of the total elapsed time (aka lead time), from the time a product or service is requested by the customer to the time it is delivered to the same customer, is *idle* time where the work (the product or service) sits around incomplete (as "Work in Process", or "WIP") with no one working on it. The actual touch time is almost insignificant in comparison.

WAITING VERSUS INVENTORY

You could theoretically call the waste of idle work "inventory" instead of "waiting". Certainly, in Lean manufacturing, idle work-in-progress, raw materials, or finished goods are definitely inventory, and excess inventory ties up a lot of cash for a company. Increasing inventory turns and thereby improving the cash portion of working capital is often one of the main motivations for a manufacturer to adopt Lean in the first place. In office work, it costs almost nothing (at least not directly) to store billions of electrons on servers, so the term "inventory" is misleading. Unfortunately, the term "waiting" is also misleading because, as a form of Lean manufacturing waste, it refers to the waste of workers or equipment being underutilized (resource inefficiency), not the work itself being idle. It is probably best to think about idle work as simply being the waste of a *customer's* time.

The most frequent type of waste in an office—and by a huge margin—occurs not when we *are* working on a unit of work, but when we are *not* working on it. When you, your team, or even your company chooses to work on one thing, you are basically choosing *not* to work on all the other things (unstarted or WIP) that you could have chosen to work on instead. The work not chosen sits idle on servers, out of sight and out of mind, and the amount of time that it sits waiting is the opportunity cost of your choosing not to work on it. If everyone in the value stream is not using the same criteria for making choices about what to work on when, the opportunity cost goes up astronomically.

Lean helps us reduce the opportunity cost of our work by first prioritizing the work across the entire value stream (aligning value stream-level business goals to the tactical choice-making found in the daily work of every team), and then focusing our attention on the so-called "white spaces" *between* the tasks to complete all of the work faster (and the highest priority fastest of all). This does not mean that you should disregard waste like rework or overprocessing within your own process (i.e. within the boxes), especially if you can eliminate entire steps within a process through cross-training, automation, or simply ceasing to do an activity that has no value to anyone. Rework (quality issues) is especially pernicious because it adds steps to a value stream—and with each added step comes more white space before and after it. Nonetheless, the spaces in between the boxes are where most of the opportunities lie to stop being "busy" and start getting things done.

So instead of focusing on waste elimination, focus first on flow enhancement. Reduce the size of the big arrows in Figure 3.5. Focus on reducing the waiting time in the value stream. Then, afterward, you can think of additional ways to save time, such as eliminating rework, overprocessing, and overproduction by capturing the genius of the frontline employees' ideas. Time is the only waste you really have to worry about.

As you gain back time, you increase capacity. Gaining capacity can help a company absorb additional growth without a proportionate growth in salary expenses (and people to manage), and this appeals, for obvious reasons, to profit-oriented managers and shareholders. But what is often overlooked is

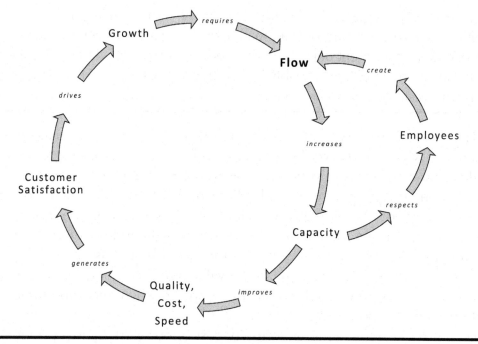

Figure 3.6   How Flow Respects Employees and Drives Growth.

that gained capacity can (and should) also relieve employees of being over-burdened. Designing the work so that it flows faster to customers is a way of *respecting people*, because it relieves frontline employees from the frustrations of having to use workarounds and heroics just to get their work done[12]. Pursuing flow is not a trade-off with the Respect for People principle. They are complementary (see Figure 3.6). While most of this book is about Flow, in fact, the two principles can never truly be separated from one another. There can be no true Flow without Respect for People, and—as we will see in future chapters—there cannot truly be Respect for People without Flow. Respect for People must be designed into the system of work itself.

Three Main Takeaways

1. Information does not change behavior; systems change behaviors. Focus on changing and improving the management systems that govern the Flow of Value to the Customer.
2. Flow exposes waste—primarily delays, or the waste of time. Focus on eliminating idle work waiting in the white spaces between the process

steps of a value stream. This is where the most opportunity to improve performance lies.

3. Increasing the Flow of Value to the Customer is a form of respecting employees because it relieves them of overburden and creates more capacity for them to do their best work.

Notes

1. Lean Enterprise Institute. What is Lean?: www.lean.org/WhatsLean/ (accessed May 20, 2019).
2. The Shingo Institute. The Shingo Model: https://shingo.org/model (accessed May 20, 2019).
3. Liker, Jeffrey. 2004. *The Toyota Way.* New York: McGraw-Hill.
4. Womack James P. and Daniel T. Jones. 1996. *Lean Thinking: Banish Waste And Create Wealth In Your Corporation.* New York: Simon and Schuster.
5. These two principles are deliberately similar to the two values—Respect for People and Continuous Improvement—listed in a 2001 internal Toyota publication called *The Toyota Way.* See Modig, Niklas and Par Ahlstrom. 2015. *This is Lean: Resolving the Efficiency Paradox.* Stockholm: Rheologica Publishing, p. 80.
6. Modig, Niklas and Par Ahlstrom. 2015. *This is Lean: Resolving the Efficiency Paradox.* Stockholm: Rheologica Publishing.
7. The W. Edwards Deming Institute. Dr. Deming's 14 Points for Management. https://deming.org/explore/fourteen-points (accessed May 11, 2018).
8. Pfeffer, Jeffrey. 2015. *Leadership BS.* New York: HarperCollins.
9. The Shingo Institute. The Shingo Model: https://shingo.org/model (accessed May 20, 2019).
10. It is hard to determine who originally said this, but it is used often by John Shook, as he does here: Lean Enterprise Institute. 2011. *Lean Enterprise Institute CEO John Shook Wins Sloan Management Review Award For Best Article On Change And Organizational Development*: www.lean.org/WhoWeAre/LEINewsStory.cfm?NewsArticleId=178 (accessed May 20, 2019).
11. As quoted by Ballé, Michael. 2018. Is Kanban Relevant To Office Work? *The Lean Post,* March 19, 2018: www.lean.org/balle/DisplayObject.cfm?o=3612 (accessed May 20, 2019).
12. This can be explained as the connection between unevenness (*mura* in Japanese), or the absence of flow; and overburden (*muri*), a form of *Dis*respect for People. Reducing unevenness reduces overburden, all other things being equal, and so flow is a method for respecting employees. But since employees play a big role in identifying and reducing unevenness, Respect for People is an input to, as well as an output of, flow.

DESIGNING FOR FLOW II

Chapter 4

Understanding Flow

Carlos is planning to go to Florida soon to attend a three-day conference on the latest practices in his area of expertise: derivatives and foreign exchange risk management. He hopes to learn the current trends in the field, find inspiration from some expert speakers, and have an enjoyable time networking and socializing with his industry peers and colleagues. He has already paid in advance for some of the bigger ticket aspects of his trip, such as the conference fees and airfare, which amounted to around $3,500. He paid for these on his personal credit card, with the understanding between him and his boss that he will be reimbursed for all reasonable expenses associated with his attending the conference. Finding the reimbursement process a little tedious, and having more pressing work to do, he decided to put off filing the reimbursement at the time he paid the $3,500, choosing to wait until he had concluded the trip and incurred all the associated conference expenses. That way, he reasoned, he would only have to do one submission and receive his reimbursement in one lump sum.

Carlos had put the upfront conference expenses out of his mind until his credit card statement appeared last week. He noticed that the amount due on his credit card was surprisingly higher than usual. Then he remembered the conference. Not only were the airfare and conference fees on his credit card balance, but to make things worse, he had had an unexpected car repair recently. He grew anxious. He did not have the funds in his account to cover the full amount of the credit card bill and his wife's birthday was coming up—he was hoping to buy her a nice gift. But the credit card balance was due in two days! He knew he was not due for another paycheck until next week, after the credit card due date, so suddenly he felt a sense of urgency to recover the $3,500 he had put towards the conference. He fished around his email for a while, trying to locate the conference receipts, and then set about the tedious task of filing a submission in APS—the company's **A**ccounting and **P**ayables **S**ystem.

Once he submitted it, he felt deflated. He suspected that all the invoices from the Project X consultants were consuming Accounts Payable's time these days. The number of consulting invoices received by AP had probably tripled in the last three months. Maybe, just maybe, he thought, if he were to send AP a desperate-sounding email, they might be able to expedite his claim.

Carlos' story shows the downside of allowing work (in this case, submitting a reimbursement claim) to sit idle. He thought that "batching" his expenses together would be more efficient than paying them as soon as he incurred them. But he discovered, unfortunately, that the high interest fees that might result by not paying off his credit card bill in full were offsetting the time savings of only submitting one claim in the system.

Carlos' story is not just a lesson in avoiding procrastination. There is another, equally important element to the story: how fast his company can reimburse him. And this element has a lot to do with limiting work-in-process too. If Carlos can get his reimbursement in two days or fewer, he will still be able to pay off his credit card bill in full and avoid any interest payments.

Understanding Flow

To teach the basic concept behind flow I usually draw a simple diagram on a whiteboard to illustrate the concept. Let us say you have three tasks to do. Each takes an hour to complete. You start all three at once (more or less) and divide your time evenly between all three so that you have finished about a third of each one every hour. By the end of the third hour, you will have completed all three tasks. You complete them all in a *batch* (even though they are for three different customers) at approximately the same time. This multitasking approach is what I call Mode 1 in Figure 4.1.

Now imagine the exact same amount of work: three tasks, one hour each, three hours of total work. But this time, instead of starting all three tasks at once, you only start one single task and work on it for an entire hour with your undivided attention until you complete it in full. Then,

Figure 4.1   Two Different Ways to Organize the Completion of Three Tasks.

without delay, you start in on Task 2 in the same way, and finally Task 3. One completed task *flows* after the other in sequential order. At the end of the third hour, you have completed all three tasks, just like in the first scenario. This is Mode 2 in Figure 4.1.

What is the difference between scenarios? Your most precious resource: time. In Mode 2, where you process one task at a time, you have completed Task 1 after only one hour. That is only *a third* of the time it took you to complete the same task in Mode 1. Note I am not talking about the total time it took you to work on it, which is from your perspective, but the *elapsed* time between when you started the task and when you completed it, which is from the customer's perspective. In Mode 1, three hours elapse before the full completion of Task 1. Similarly, you complete Task 2 in *two-thirds* of the time it took you in Mode 1. Task 3 is completed in the same amount of time in both modes: no more, no less.

In Mode 2, you have done *exactly the same amount of work* as in Mode 1, and have worked at *exactly the same pace*, but you completed *two out of three of your tasks faster*, with no additional delay for the third task. This is the miracle of good process design: you are being more productive without working any harder or faster, with no additional labor or technology, and with no compromise in the quality of your work! Mode 1 is what Lean refers to as "batch and queue", whereas Mode 2 is known as "flow".

Sure, at the end of the day, you have produced three tasks in three hours and your *average* productivity rate is one task per hour in both scenarios. If you are a hands-off, laissez-faire manager and you see from the productivity report you receive for the previous day's work that your employees are averaging one task per hour as planned, would you care how they are completing those tasks? Probably not. But you should, because, with a simple change to the design of the work, two-out-of-three of your customers could be experiencing faster lead times. In simple mathematical terms, if you take the average time-to-complete each task (instead of the more conventional average tasks-per-hour approach), you see that Mode 1 averages three hours

**Table 4.1 The Average Time to
Complete Each Task (in Minutes)**

Task	Mode 1	Mode 2
1	60	180
2	120	180
3	180	180
Average	**120**	**180**

and Mode 2 averages only two hours—Mode 2 is, on average, a third faster than Mode 1, as you can see in Table 4.1.

It may seem like a small detail, but measuring in *time-per-unit of work* rather than *units of work-per-period of time* can make a world of difference in terms of how we see the work flow. Make sure time is the numerator and one unit of work is the denominator when you calculate productivity.

Still skeptical? Think of it this way: if you were the one working on these three tasks and your boss decided to come around after two and a half hours to check-in on your progress, which work mode would you prefer to be working in? "Done" sounds a lot better than "still working on it".

This concept of designing the work for better flow applies to all work, small and large, and is equally applicable at the individual, team, and enterprise levels. Instead of this scenario being three small hours, these could just as easily be three large, strategic projects that you had to complete over the course of a calendar year. It is the end of April. You have already finished one project in Mode 2—your productivity (projects fully completed as a percentage of the full year target) is 33%. In Mode 1, you have started three projects (and all are at 33% completion) but have finished none. Yes, you have accomplished things. Yes, you are working hard. But from your clients' point of view your productivity is 0%. At the end of August, it is the same thing: you have now fully completed two projects in Mode 2, and in Mode 1... still nothing, although they are all approximately 66% done. By October, in Mode 1, you are seriously stressed out because you have scarcely got two months to go in the year and, while progress is being made (all three are now about 80% done), nothing—*nada, niente*—has been delivered in full to the clients yet. It is getting harder and harder to tell your clients that it is "almost" done.

Inwardly you are not feeling confident that any of them are going to make it by year's end. There are so many dependencies and unanticipated issues, as there are with all large projects. Unfortunately, you are dealing with three of them concurrently, so you have three times the dependencies and issues than if you were dealing with only one project. To deal with all the issues, you start holding more frequent status meetings with the project teams to discuss how to address the blockers, issues, risks, delays, and escalations. You hire a program manager to help you oversee the three project managers. You get your program manager to make sure the project managers update their data in the project tracking software more diligently, so that everyone has visibility to the most up-to-date info on the progress of the projects at any given point in time. You start to prioritize in your mind which projects can slip into January and which cannot, just in case. You spend a lot of time preparing presentations to the steering committee, explaining what is holding the projects back, what risks and issues you have identified, which you have mitigated, and what parts of the original scopes you are recommending to omit from Phase 1 (previously there were no phases to your projects, but now, "phase" has become the politically acceptable word to use when talking about delays or downsizing the original scopes). And, oh yes, you now have a *new* task to add to your growing to-do list: asking for more money for Phase 2! Because these extra meetings, staff hiring, software purchases, decisions, and presentations are eating up a lot of your and others' time, you are becoming even more stressed out than usual because there is even less time to devote to actually working on the project.

Much less of this happens in Mode 2[1]. Worst case in Mode 2 is that Project 3 carries over into the new year, but since you have already completed and delivered to your clients two out of three projects planned for this year (with some of the inevitable slippage in both Projects 1 and 2), Project 3's late delivery is not as dire as if all three were late. You also have the advantage of being able to focus all your undivided attention on it, so you feel more confident it will be delivered on time. Conversely, the multi-tasking Mode 1 *creates additional work* to address all of these "secondary needs"[2]. The delays caused by working in Mode 1 create *a need* for status updates, progress reports, tracking systems, program managers, sponsor sign-offs, and a plethora of meetings to re-scope, re-prioritize, re-assign, re-budget, and rethink all three projects simultaneously. These activities are time-consuming, tedious, and now absolutely necessary—but also *non-value-adding* from your customer's point of view. Amazingly, it is nothing more than *the sequence of the work* that has created all this additional, time-consuming work. And choosing to organize your work in Mode 2 would have meant mostly—or even completely—avoiding it.

Table 4.2 The High Cost of Context Switching[3]

Number of Simultaneous Projects	Percent of Time Available per Project	Loss to Context Switching
1	100%	0%
2	40%	20%
3	20%	40%
4	10%	60%
5	5%	75%

From an employee's point of view, Mode 1 and Mode 2 *appear* to involve the same amount of actual work time, even though we know the total elapsed time is better for the customer in Mode 2. Yet, in reality, Mode 2 is also *less* work for the employee (and therefore even faster for the customer), because it avoids much of the non-value adding work needed to address the secondary needs that Mode 1 creates. Simply speaking, Mode 2 increases organizational capacity and productivity.

Back in 1991, the computer scientist and consultant Gerald Weinberg studied the effects of context switching on productivity in software development projects, and produced the data found in Table 4.2.

The more you try to do at once (aka Mode 1) the more time you lose to context switching. When you try to do even two things at once, you lose 20% of your productivity. Since 1991, psychologists have produced an abundance of incontrovertible evidence on the high cost of multitasking or "context switching"[4]. Most of the research on the negative effects of multitasking, such as that of Weinberg's, focuses on *individual* productivity, but it applies equally to team and enterprise productivity as well. At its most mature, Lean is about reducing *organizational* multitasking.

Handoffs

"But *my* work is not like that!", you are no doubt thinking. It is true, you probably do not know exactly how long a project is going to take before you start it (even though management may be asking for a precise time-line), and your work certainly cannot be broken down and packaged into three neat and tidy projects that all take the same exact amount of time and effort. Even worse, you depend on the timely inputs of so many other internal teams, not to mention your external customers and suppliers, to get your stuff done. What are you supposed to do when Project 1 is waiting on an outside customer's response? Nothing? Really? When you have not even started Project 2 or 3 yet? How are you supposed to explain to your boss and the clients of Projects 2 and 3 that you have not even started their projects yet, even though you have *nothing* to do right now? And what about those last minute "emergency" requests from Senior Executives? Or those unanticipated requests for members of your team to participate in high-visibility projects in other functional areas?

You are absolutely right: real work is not nearly as predictable or as easy as this simplistic illustration (see Figure 4.1) would suggest. However, the benefits that you get from *pursuing* flow—that is, striving to focus on and complete as few units of work at a time as possible, to create an uninterrupted flow of value to the customer—are still just as applicable to even the most variable and customized of knowledge work. Flowing your work, rather than batching it together and then multitasking between everything that you have in progress at once, will *always* (yes, always) enable you to finish it faster.

One of the big challenges to obtaining better flow is handoffs. When the completed work depends on others, whether external or internal to the firm, you have to hand it off to them and then wait an indeterminate amount of time for them to either: (1) get it back to you; or (2) hand it off to the next process step in the value stream. In Figure 4.1, we imagined three tasks, each performed by one single person. The work to complete the tasks can take two paths: the multitasking path (Mode 1), which ends up being slower for two out of three customers, or the sequential, "flowing" path (Mode 2), which ends up being faster for two out of three customers. In Figure 4.2, we again have three tasks, but now each task requires a different functional specialization to complete it, and so has been split into three separate subtasks. In a lending process, for instance, it could be the underwriting of credit, the authorization of risk, and the legal documentation of the loan agreement that are the three subtasks required. All of the underwriting for all three financing deals is completed by an underwriter and then handed off to the authorizer, who will review and authorize the deals (perhaps after asking for some clarification and revision), and then each deal is handed off yet again to the Legal team to complete the documentation subtask.

As before, we have two ways of organizing the work: Mode 1 or Mode 2. In Mode 1, each person switches tasks, working a little on Deal 1, then Deal 2, then Deal 3, jumping back and forth between each as additional

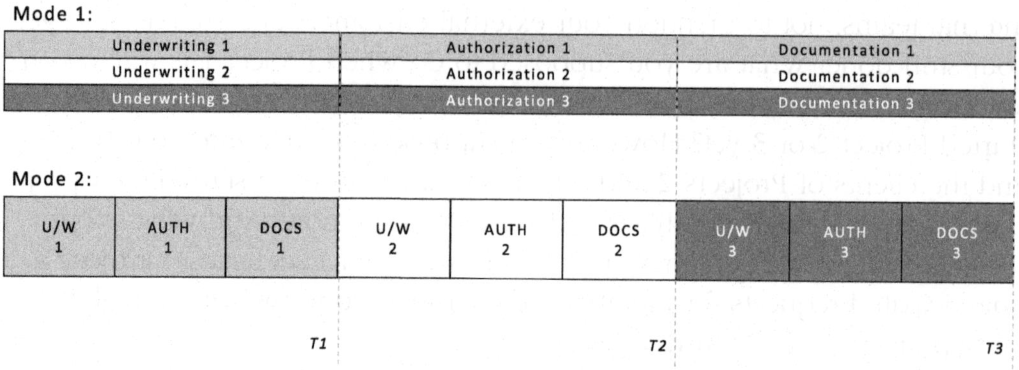

Mode 1:

Underwriting 1	Authorization 1	Documentation 1
Underwriting 2	Authorization 2	Documentation 2
Underwriting 3	Authorization 3	Documentation 3

Mode 2:

U/W 1	AUTH 1	DOCS 1	U/W 2	AUTH 2	DOCS 2	U/W 3	AUTH 3	DOCS 3

T1   *T2*   *T3*

Figure 4.2 Two Modes of Working When the Work Requires Multiple Team Handoffs.

information comes in, until they eventually finish all the deals at approximately the same time and pass them along to the next step, in a batch. Note that it does not *feel* like we are handing work off in a batch because all the work is not finished precisely at the same time—there could be a number of days in between completing the separate subtasks. But if we drew out the timeline of Mode 1 it would look roughly like the top of Figure 4.2, where all of the underwriting for all three deals is handed off for authorization at approximately the same time.

In Mode 2, each of the three respective groups coordinates and organizes the work so that they all work on one and the same deal together. The work must be done in sequence, and so they create a logical sequence of handoffs between them. In both modes, we do not know how long exactly each component will take in each functional area, since this is a complex deal with many variables that could dilate or contract the time it takes to complete each stage. So, the time is indicated only with the variables T1, T2, and T3.

Just like in Figure 4.1, Mode 2 delivers the same amount of work output as Mode 1 but does so faster for two out of three customers. The trick to making Mode 2 work in cases where work is handed off between different functional areas is to build such strong *connections* between the process steps (the subtasks) that the work moves along *as if the same person were completing it.* This means establishing strong cross-functional, collaborative work management systems to handle the prioritization, scheduling, and coordination across all teams involved. If you are a football quarterback and you handoff the ball, you need to have a running back who is ready and able to receive the handoff and run with it immediately—same thing in business! With IT systems most of the problems happen in the interfaces between applications. Good handoffs are the secret sauce of good workflow.

In practice, of course, this will not be so smooth. It is hard to demand that your external customers get back to you with the additional information you have asked for within a certain timeframe, for instance. They are the customer, after all, and they will get back to you when it suits them, not you. The distribution of work within and between teams (and within and between firms too) is always uneven, but pursuing flow will nonetheless always enable the work to be completed faster than if it is done through random multitasking (which is our default mode, typically lacking any coordination across functional teams). Yes, your handoffs will never be perfectly timed. Yes, you will probably always have to do some multitasking. Yes, your type of work may never flow between process steps as smoothly as widgets on a well-designed assembly line. But this is all irrelevant. Unless you are competing against other widget producers, all you need is to have your work flow better than that of your competitors. And the first step to doing that is to flow your work tomorrow better than you do today.

So How Do I Create Flow?

One of the first things one needs to do to establish flow in an office is to *make the work visible*. Draw it out on a whiteboard or large piece of butcher paper hung on the wall. It does not have to be complicated or pretty. To help us visualize flow in an office-work context, let us return to the simple case of Carlos, where he is hoping to receive reimbursement for his conference expenses in two days or fewer. Figure 4.3 depicts the simple, multi-step expense reimbursement value stream for Carlos' company. Four different people in two different functional groups (Carlos and his boss work in Risk

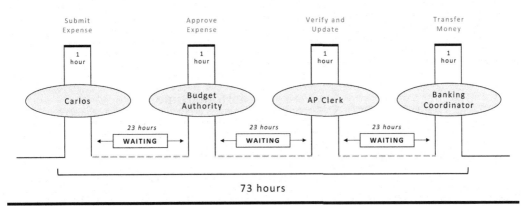

Figure 4.3 The Flow Efficiency of a Simple Four-Step Reimbursement Process Is Only 5.5% (4 out of 73 Hours).

Management; the Accounts Payable Clerk and Banking Coordinator work in Finance and Accounting) perform four separate tasks (or sub-processes, if you prefer).

The sequential steps are:

1. Employee (e.g. Carlos) submits expense in system and uploads the scans of the supporting documents (receipts, etc.).
2. The appropriate budget authority (Carlos' boss) approves the amount for the expenses in the Accounting and Payables System (APS).
3. An Accounts Payable clerk verifies that all info has been entered correctly into the system, and that the supporting documentation matches.
4. The Banking Coordinator updates the banking system to transfer funds into the employee's bank account.

Let's say each task takes an hour to complete, and the entire "touch time"[5], if we added up only the time when it is being *actively worked on* by someone, in total, is exactly four hours—one hour for each of the four process steps[6].

Unfortunately for Carlos, it takes over *three days* (73 hours) from the time he starts entering the details of his expenses in the payment system until the money transfers into his bank account (in Lean lingo, the total elapsed time is usually referred to as the "lead time", and it is the only time-based measure the customer—Carlos, in this case—truly cares about). The work sits around with no one working on it for 95% of the time that it has been "in process", which is a bit of a misnomer, since no one is actually "processing" the work when it is just sitting idle. The diagram indicates this as the waiting time. When all process stakeholders actually see the lead time because it is now visible in a value stream map or similar diagram, they are much more motivated to improve it. You cannot improve what you cannot see.

A second step to achieving flow is to simply measure it. The measure of flow efficiency is the percentage by which touch time makes up the total lead time (elapsed time from start to finish):

$$\text{Flow Efficiency} = \frac{\text{total touch time}}{\text{total touch time} + \text{total wait time}}$$

In this example, from a flow efficiency perspective, the four hours of "value-adding" touch time in the entire end-to-end process represents only 5% of the total 73-hour lead time (see Figure 4.3). If 5% seems like a small percentage to you, typically the percentage is much, much *less*—often only a fraction of a percent. It is quite common in office workplaces to find work involving two hours of touch time that is completed and delivered to a customer in two months (yes, months!). You can try it yourself: pick any process in your office at random and measure the time it takes (the "lead time") for one unit of work to flow end-to-end, beginning and ending with a customer (internal or external). Then compare it to the total "touch time". I am willing to bet the touch time will be less than 1% of the total elapsed time[7].

You do not have to measure every process step of every unit of work down to the second. If measuring the time within and between process steps is impractical (you are likely to hear "it depends!" a lot), try to get an approximate range from those performing the work and use the average. The point is to appreciate just how small the ratio of touch time to wait time really is—and then strive to increase it.

The third step is to generate a sense of caring about customers. All stakeholders have to want to improve the flow efficiency of the entire value stream and not just their own piece of it. Leadership plays a big role in communicating the importance of the end customer across all functional areas in a value stream. The shared purpose of the end customer enables better collaboration between different functional areas.

Focus on Wait Time

Most Lean programs, unfortunately, focus only on reducing touch time. There is a tendency for both teachers and students of Lean to focus on the classic seven wastes, the non-value adding aspects of doing the work itself, rather than the white spaces in between it. This is a natural human tendency—we all want to make the work we are doing *right now* better, faster, and easier ... for ourselves. The waiting time feels like it is out of our control and, additionally, we do not really care much about the work we are currently *not* doing. Or, at least, we do not care until we can see it.

In a factory line setting this focus on touch time makes more sense. You want to standardize the quality and timing of the work at each process step so that the line can continue to move consistently forward at an even pace, producing defect-free widgets on a reliable and predictable schedule. So long as nothing causes the line to stop moving, the physical movement (transportation) from one station to another of the work in progress occupies the white spaces, and it is often facilitated by an automated conveyance device of some sort. This movement is visible, predictable, and measurable in a factory. The inventory sitting between stations is visible too. For these reasons, measuring and controlling the waiting time between process steps is easier in manufacturing than it is in environments where all conveyance of "material" is electronic.

In offices, in-process work sits idle, hidden in computers, far longer than most factory work ever does. Out of sight, out of mind. As a result, wait time makes up much of the total lead time in office processes. Therefore, if we want to improve flow, it is simply more logical to start by trying to shrink the wait time. Conversely, we might be able to automate or otherwise improve the touch time to a small fraction of what it currently is. But if wait time accounts for 95% or more of the total time it takes to deliver the product or service to the customer, will the customer really notice?

Compress the Value Stream

The best way to reduce lead time is not by removing waste from inside the process steps, but by *compressing* the value stream, so that there is less waiting time *in between* the value-adding process steps. 100% flow efficiency is the theoretical point of maximum flow efficiency[8], when the touch time and lead time are the same and the unit of work is never idle. In the ideal state, someone (or a machine) is constantly working on a unit of work from start to finish, until it is completed and delivered to the customer. In our example of Carlos, this means that, if there were no reimbursement claims ahead of his in the queue, he would be reimbursed in a mere *four hours* from when he began to submit his expense claim, 69 hours *less* than the original 73, or about a *20-fold improvement* in flow efficiency (see Figure 4.4).

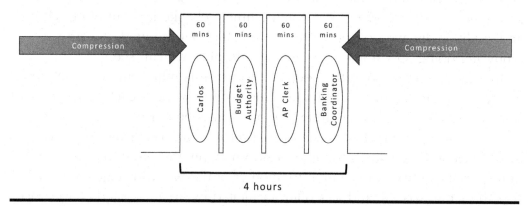

Figure 4.4 Compressing the Value Stream to Achieve Better Flow Efficiency.

Flow Creates Capacity

The biggest objection I find with flow is that people say,

> Ok, I see how this is better for customers, but I don't see how it is going to relieve our capacity problems. Three hours of work is three hours of work, any way you slice it. We're so busy with work that we don't have time to reorganize the way we sequence and prioritize work between teams.

They do not see how their busyness—their capacity problem—is also caused by the sequencing and prioritization of their work.

The fact is, how you slice up the work *does* matter to the capacity of employees. As I mentioned above, multitasking, batching, and prolonging lead time create secondary needs. These secondary needs take up way more time than you would think. And because they become necessary to do, we call them "work" instead of "waste". We do a lot of so-called "necessary" work in our day-to-day jobs that would not have been necessary had an earlier, upstream process done something differently (and better). For instance, if you wait too long to answer your email, or do not set the right expectations for when the sender will get a reply, you get more email in the form of follow-up emails, reminding you of the first email request. Now you have more email to read. Reading your email now takes up more time than it would have had you responded earlier. The net result is that you now have less time to do other tasks. So, you delay other tasks in favor of reading your email and then you end up with even more email asking you about the status of the other tasks you have delayed so that you have time to read your email. It is a vicious circle—secondary needs disguise themselves as work, and thus they are very hard to see. Working in Mode 2 breaks this vicious circle and increases your personal capacity. In other words, Mode 2 saves both you and your customer time! When an entire enterprise works this way, then the entire enterprise gains more capacity and delivers to customers faster.

I do not expect you to believe me until you try it. So try it. Run an experiment on your personal workflow: do not start any new tasks before finishing (completely!) everything that you are *currently* working on (this includes items where you are waiting on information from others). If you have not started working on something, do not start it! Focus on what is already in progress and see what you can do to get it finished. If something is "on fire", let it burn (unless, of course, human safety is at risk, or it would be absolute career suicide). Most people are amazed at how much more they can accomplish when they focus on one thing at a time, eliminate interruptions, compress their lead times, and deliver faster to their customers. I have a friend who implemented this technique and got personal productivity gains in the realm of 40%: i.e. it now takes him 24 hours where it used to take 40 hours to do the same amount of work (and he has not told his boss yet). If you find yourself unable to completely finish a task, ask yourself, "what would have to be true to enable me to finish this?" You will discover all sorts of opportunities to coordinate better with your upstream and downstream colleagues (your "suppliers" and "customers") on when and how you receive and hand-off information. If you have some success with personal flow improvements, try taking it to the team level: coordinate with other teams to schedule hand-offs of work so that one unit of work gets completed—with as little waiting as possible—before starting a new unit of work. Instead of starting new work on your own, see if you can help a teammate finish her work faster.

Even when we try to work on one thing at a time, what thwarts us is that we hit a gap: we are stuck waiting for information (e.g. data, evaluation, approval, confirmation, etc.) from someone else and have to choose between starting to work on something else or sitting around with nothing to do. And since we do not like having anything to do, and are addicted to being busy, we innocently start working on some other piece of work. Other work creeps into the white spaces of our work. And then the first thing we were waiting on comes back to us, so we switch back to that first thing … and so on, and so on, until we have dozens and dozens of things waiting on information from others and dozens and dozens of more things that we are supposed to be working on (and which someone else is waiting on). We "actively" work on these things by dividing our attention between all of them. We multitask. Now multiply this work system by the number of employees in your office and you get a pretty good mental picture of how a typical enterprise evolves, unintentionally and organically, into a paradoxical culture where everyone is very busy all the time, but where very little actually gets done.

STOP STARTING AND START FINISHING

We are taught from a young age that we should not "leave things to the last minute". That school science project is due in a month so you'd better get started! This is generally good advice. We should not procrastinate. But what is often not taught is how to finish tasks before starting new ones. Do not wait until the last minute, but do not treat everything you have to do as urgent either. Array everything you know you have to do: assess when it is due and estimate, generously, how long it will take if you worked on it continuously *without starting anything else.* This should then tell you what you need to start first, second, and third. Start the first task and *only* the first. Finish the first task in the time you estimated or less. Then start the second one. And so on. Repeat the assessment periodically as needed as new demands on your time are received. Do not allow yourself to start everything immediately as soon as it comes to your attention.

Carlos is hoping that a process requiring only four hours of actual "touch time" work will be completed in less than 48 hours, and he can pay his credit card bill on time. In technical terms, Carlos is hoping the flow efficiency of the reimbursement process improves from its current state of 5% to 8%. Is Carlos being so unrealistic? If Carlos were CEO, I am willing to bet the process would easily perform with 8% flow efficiency. So why not for Carlos and every customer of the process?

Three Main Takeaways

1. The time it takes to deliver completed work to a customer depends a lot on the way the work is sequenced and prioritized within and between teams. Batching or multitasking creates additional work for everyone to do and consumes more of an organization's time and capacity. To avoid this, choose, as a team, to work on as few things as possible, minimize interruptions, and complete what you start.
2. Think about the work as a horizontal value stream: make the end-to-end workflow visible; measuring the time a unit of work is being actively worked on as a percentage of the total elapsed time from start to finish; and unify all stakeholders around the common purpose of creating value for the end customer.
3. One of the keys to improving flow is to compress the process steps that make up a value stream closer together in time. This requires effective connections between process steps. Creating good connections requires making efforts to improve cross-functional prioritization, scheduling, coordination, and communication.

Notes

1. Those who are familiar with Agile methodologies for software development will recognize the iterative, sprint-based continuous-delivery approach to project completion.
2. This term of "secondary needs" is the one used by Modig and Ahlstrom. It is also very much akin to what John Seddon calls "Failure Demand"—additional work created by a failure to do something right for the customer the first time.
3. Weinberg, Gerald. *Quality Software Management*, Vol. 1. Dorset House: 1991
4. See, for instance: American Psychological Association. 2006. Multitasking: Switching costs. www.apa.org/research/action/multitask (accessed February 26, 2019).
5. Touch Time is typically called Process Time or Cycle Time (when there is only one operator) in Lean manufacturing.
6. In reality, these tasks would take only a few minutes, but it is easier, mathematically, to illustrate the concept if we deal in hours, not minutes. If we dealt in actual minutes, the lack of flow would be even more obvious and extreme, and we would be dealing with such miniscule fractions of a work day that the math would seem more complicated than it need be here. The concept is still the same.
7. A world-class ratio in a manufacturing assembly operation is above 25% according to the website iSixSigma.com: www.isixsigma.com/dictionary/process-cycle-efficiency-pce (accessed October 9, 2018). Note flow efficiency is calculated slightly differently than Process Cycle Efficiency (PCE) because the former includes the non-value-added activities within the processes themselves, so flow efficiency will generally be higher than PCE for the same task.
8. If it takes more than one working day to deliver the product or service, as is frequently the case in office work, the maximum flow efficiency becomes 33%, based on a work day of eight hours. Daily lead time is counted as 24 hours (as opposed to eight) because this is the elapsed time that the customer experiences.

Chapter 5

Busy Does Not Mean Productive

Amy has never seen the queue of unpaid invoices so big in the three years that she has been working in Accounts Payable. There are 648 of them as of 8:03 AM this morning, when she first turned on her computer. She feels a little twinge of anxiety when she thinks about the number. She knows her boss understands that the higher than normal volume is putting the team behind schedule, but she still feels a little guilty and nervous whenever they fall behind, as if it were partly her fault. She knows she should not take it personally, yet she cannot help but feel that others might think she is not working fast enough.

And, to make things worse, she feels badly for the people who have not been paid yet. She understands what it is like to have to pay the bills. Her husband is still in school, completing his Master's degree in Pharmacology, and they hope to save for a down payment on a starter home in one of the more affordable suburbs once he has graduated and has a full-time job. But for now, they are living in her drafty old one-bedroom apartment, riding the subway, and struggling to get by on her modest salary.

She does not have time to feel sorry for herself now, she reminds herself. It is now 8:10 AM, Monday morning and, in addition to all the invoices in the queue, she has got 173 unread emails to deal with. The first one is from that new Sales VP. He submitted his parking expenses three weeks ago and wants to know when he can expect to receive payment. He has sent an email every Monday morning at exactly 6:45 AM for the last three consecutive weeks asking where his payment is. The truth is she has *no idea* when he is going to get paid. She will get it to it when she gets to it. She could go look up his reimbursement request in the queue, but with the time she would spend finding it and responding to his email, she could be processing two more expense claims, bringing his (and everyone else's) claim two places closer to the front of the queue. Best to keep slogging onwards, she thinks, but then suddenly pauses in doubt: wait, this guy is a *Vice President*. It might upset him if she does not respond right away. As she begins to search for his claim, she cannot help asking herself why this VP needs his $50 in parking expenses reimbursed so urgently ... she figures he probably makes four times her salary and lives in a big house in Riverglen ... jeesh, if only she had *his* problems! Anyhow, she had better expedite his claim and respond to him, she decides. It is not good to have a VP annoyed with you. It could get back to her boss and make her look bad.

After ten minutes of searching, she finds his claim (missing the correct accounting code, she notes). She has to politely ask him to go back into APS and update his claim with account code 478-645 (she would do it herself, but due to system restrictions aimed at reducing the risk of fraud, she cannot). While it was his fault—or, more likely, his executive assistant's fault—for omitting the account code, she still feels terrible that he is hearing this news after three weeks. He is probably going to be annoyed, she thinks, and she cannot even tell him when he can expect payment! *Your expense claim is of the utmost importance to us and we endeavor to process all claims as fast as we possibly can. We expect to process your claim by* [insert expected completion date here] ... "the end of this week" she writes bashfully into the email template she has been instructed to use for all communication of this sort. The truth is she is just guessing. She has no idea how long it will really take; "the end of this week" is being very optimistic.

She knows that once he resubmits the claim, it will go straight to the very back of the queue again. Nothing she can do about that—it is just the way APS is designed. When she once suggested a change to IT, they matter-of-factly told her that it would have to be prioritized by the Financial Application Enhancement Steering Committee, and the FAESC has already lined up enough work to keep the IT shop busy for the next three and a half years, by which time APS will probably be up for replacement. So, she and her colleagues just gave up on suggesting any further enhancements to APS, even though they have plenty of daily frustrations with it. She puts a sticky note up on her computer, alongside dozens of others, with the VP's claim number on it. She has to remind herself to go back into the queue periodically and check if the accounting code has been updated so she can then expedite it. If she does not check, it will take at least another three weeks from the time he updates the account code for him to get reimbursed.

The next email she sees is from some desperate-sounding guy named Carlos, whom she has never heard of before, from Risk Management. He has written in all caps (somewhat rudely, she feels, if she is being perfectly honest with herself): IF YOU COULD PLEASE PLEASE PLEASE PROCESS MY REIMBURSEMENT SO THAT I CAN HAVE IT BY THIS WEDNESDAY … *yah, right*, she thinks, as she stops reading the email. *You and the 647 others all want their claims by this Wednesday. You will get it when you get it.* She has already been working overtime for the last few weeks because of the backlog. Her boss has been saying that they are not going to be able to hire any additional staff anytime soon, so it does not seem like the situation is going to improve… but still, she is not going to stay one-minute past 6 PM tonight. At least, not for anyone who is not a VP, she decides. While she does not exactly know who Carlos is, she knows for sure he is not a VP. She is beginning to feel resentful that she has to work ten-hour days quite often. It is not like she gets paid overtime wages or earns such a large salary that long hours should be expected. She remembers her friend Beth recently got a job at the aerospace firm down the street. She wonders if they are hiring and resolves to text Beth over her lunch break.

No one would say that Amy is lazy or idle in this scenario. But is she being productive? This depends on how you define and measure productivity. She is not waiting around with nothing to do, yet the expense claims are. There is an important distinction between what people do and how work flows. As we saw in Chapter 2, the difference between a focus on flow (of the work) and a focus on utilization (of the employees) is a fundamental difference between Lean and traditional management thinking.

The traditional, industrial way to measure productivity is on an individual worker basis: e.g. how many widgets-per-hour each person can produce per time period. This rests on the assumption that people will naturally slack off if not monitored and supervised closely. Productivity numbers, in this mindset, are often used as a way to reward or punish individual workers. This happens just as much in non-industrial settings. In professional office environments, performance evaluation is often done—at least in part—using measures of individual productivity (e.g. how many deals you closed; the increase in the size of the assets you personally managed; how many new customers you signed, etc.)

Lean thinking, in contrast, mostly takes humans out of the productivity equation. Lean takes a more holistic approach because it understands productivity as the combined output of people, processes, technology, and information working together as a system to produce results for customers. The output of the system depends on many interdependent parts, not just the individual doing the work. So, it is impossible to isolate the precise cause of low productivity and point a finger at a specific person unless we know exactly how much the related processes, technology, and information are contributing to the problem. This systemic way of thinking about work is both more humanistic—it respects employees more by blaming them less—*and* more customer focused, because it focuses on improving the output of the entire system, not its component parts.

Lean productivity is simply measured as the number of (error-free) units of work completed and *delivered to the customer* within a given time period. It is about giving the customer exactly what she wants, when she wants it, in the right quantity, at a price she is willing to pay. In other words, it is purely a measure of *value*, from the customer's point of view. Lean measures productivity as a measure of the company's delivery of value to the customer, not individual worker performance.

Of course, individuals *do* play an important role in value streams, so people's performance cannot be completely ignored. Most companies understandably want to manage costs, so they might measure how many employees it takes to have a value stream perform at a level that the customer expects. But by and large, Lean assumes that, when given the ability to perform a good job, most people, most of the time, will do so. And what is more, they will feel proud of their work! So when you see the word "waiting" in a value stream map such as the one in Figure 4.3 in the previous chapter, it is important to note that it refers to the *work* waiting, not the people. The people, as we have seen in the likes of Amy, are not slacking off—they are working as fast as they can within the constraints of the current system. Look around your workplace. People (including you!) are, in all likelihood, very busy. Are most of the employees really shirkers who need to be supervised all the time? If not, why do we need to measure their individual productivity? Why not measure customer value instead?

It is Amy's value stream, as opposed to Amy herself, that is not very productive in this case.

MEASURE FROM THE CUSTOMER'S POINT OF VIEW

You are probably measuring your "capacity"—if only in your head—on the basis of how busy you are as an individual, which, as we know from Chapter 2, is a resource efficiency measure. In some offices, individuals indicate their personal capacity on their whiteboards with traffic signal colored magnets: green (I can take on work), yellow (I am fully utilized but I can handle it unassisted), and red (I am overwhelmed and need some help to complete everything on time). This system is helpful for work-sharing (which I discuss more in Chapters 8–10), at least if there is an equal or greater amount of green than red, and everyone is candid enough to admit it when they are under- or over-capacity. But measuring individual capacity like this is not great for measuring improvements in the delivery of value from the customer's perspective. Even though you know if you are having a busy day or not, you probably do not know if the customer is experiencing faster or slower lead times. When you are "green", you will not likely remain so for very long because there is almost always more work to do. This is the nature of our resource efficient offices. If you improve your work flow, you will never know if the customer experiences a difference or not—all you know is that you are constantly busy.

So, measure capacity in terms of "widgets" produced (by the value stream) in a given time period. If your HR team can fill seven vacant positions per week, that is their current capacity. Try redesigning the work to compress the value stream so that work flows with less idle wait time between process steps. How many vacant positions per week is your value stream now filling? eight, nine … fourteen or more? Doubling productivity is not uncommon, once the initial kinks in the process are ironed out. Yet everyone is still working no more than a standard eight-hour day. No one's personal capacity is radically different, even though they are being twice as efficient (flow efficient!). There is also far less stress because there are fewer annoyed customers (and more happy ones); far less daunting of a backlog; and fewer people trying to expedite work informally by pulling political levers, playing titles, and calling in favors. But to get there you have to start measuring output rate (aka productivity or throughput) in terms of "widgets" (whatever they might be in your office) produced per time period, or you will never truly know the amazing levels at which your people are capable of performing.

Activity Is Often Confused for Work

We are so busy, yet nothing ever seems to get done. For a whole value stream to be productive—as opposed to just being a collection of busy individuals—we must learn to see and think differently. This means seeing and thinking about the work in terms of flow.

How do we see flow? First, it means thinking of work as a system that is greater than the proverbial sum of its isolated parts. The system certainly includes people and technology (as parts of the system), but it does not, despite appearances, depend on solitary heroes or superstars, nor does it depend on one killer app. It is the systemic connections and interactions between the people, technology, and information that matter.

Second, it means thinking about work from the perspective of how *a single unit of work* travels from request to fulfillment. It does not matter what the work is: it could be reimbursing an expense for $3,500, performing a kidney transplant, assembling a dishwasher, or creating a multi-national agreement to curb nuclear arms proliferation. The unit of work is, in these cases, the $3,500, the new kidney, the dishwashing machine, and the document. Work is not an activity (e.g. updating the IT system), nor is it a person (e.g. Amy), nor is it an intangible outcome like "world peace". Your work is merely the system that creates whatever unit of work that is valued by your customer. So how efficient is the system at keeping that unit of work constantly moving forward without interruptions and delays?

Lastly, we have to think about the *time* it takes the system to deliver one unit of value to one customer. It may sound overly simplistic to focus on time, but, remember, time is the mother of all wastes. We cannot increase the quality of the product (or design new ones) without our smartest employees having sufficient time to make quality improvements and design new products. We cannot improve the price that the customer has to pay without shrinking the time the company spends creating it (in knowledge work, people's time is the single largest expense). And, most obviously, we cannot increase the speed of delivery without condensing time.

Thinking in terms of time is very counterintuitive. It means thinking about what is *not* there more than what *is* there. It means asking ourselves the "what if?" questions about things we cannot see: "If the information were made available earlier, how would this improve the process?" or "What would it take to make it unnecessary to perform this activity (or hold this meeting) in the first place?" It is very hard to see beyond the people and technology right in front of them to the larger systems of work. In offices we cannot see the work itself. We cannot see the parts (information) or the conveyance mechanism (Wi-Fi)—even the majority of the tools and machinery (software and servers) of "production" are completely hidden from view.

As humans, we are hard-wired to be people-centric in our thinking. This is generally a great thing. We are social animals and we think about people constantly: those we love, those who might do us harm—and that person in the elevator whose face looked very familiar but whose name you could not remember and so you avoided eye contact. But when it comes to improving our work, our instinctive overfocus on blaming and rewarding people (that is, overfocusing on managing individual employee performance) can actually prevent us from seeing the larger system that produces the value for those *other* people, the ones we are actually trying to serve: our customers!

WHAT YOU SEE IS ALL THERE IS

The flow of work is obscured from our view because it lies beneath the frenzy of the people and the technology we use every day. We do not see the flow simply because we cannot see the processes and systems governing our work as easily as we can the work right in front of us, and the people and software on whom we rely to get it done. Yet the larger work systems and processes are certainly there, creating our unproductive chaos. As W. Edwards Deming is purported to have said, "The system is perfectly designed to give you the results you get[1]." And a typical office work system is perfectly designed to give you work sitting idle for long periods of time, with missing critical inputs, and with no reliable estimate of completion.

Why do we not see processes and systems as easily? One reason is that we tend to give outsized importance in our brains to what we can immediately see, hear, and feel. Cognitive psychologists call this "WYSIATI": What You See Is All There Is[2]. It basically describes our brain's tendency to focus nearly all of its attention on what is visibly happening right in front of us, right now, and on the information that is most easily available and accessible to us (e.g. our digital newsfeed, what we already know, or what the first result in our Google search tells us). The consequence of our cognitive laziness is that the immediate and proximate crowds out and obscures from our attention what is happening elsewhere in place and time, and discourages us from contemplating what is not happening at all, even though the occurrence (or non-occurrence) of these other, less mentally accessible events are often of much greater importance to our making well-informed decisions. In other words, we tend to focus on the problems we see and the solutions that first jump to mind, and not on the problems (and the solutions) we do not see, or at least that would take some time and mental effort to uncover. For instance, we tend to be quick to blame people ("lack of accountability") or technology ("the systems don't 'talk' to one another") without considering how our larger but *invisible* work systems and processes are affecting the outcomes we are getting. We do this even when we acknowledge that the quality of our decision-making would benefit from taking the time to think about them.

Similarly, we tend to see effort rather than output. Someone who is very productive might be seen as too "relaxed" or "lazy" because he is not nearly as stressed out as the others, who are half as productive but way busier. We tend to recognize and reward effort over output because it is easy to see.

Bruce Hamilton, President of the consulting firm GBMP, once said: "so much of business is based on 'easy-to-see, easy-to-do[3]'". Lean challenges us to work on the hard-to-see work, and gives us the confidence to do the hard-to-do work. No company is sustainably successful by taking the "easy-to-see, easy-to-do" short-cuts.

This is our intuitive, employee-centric way of thinking about our invisible office processes: first, Bob in Department X does this; then Jane in Department Y does that; then Ralph in Department Z does this; and so on. We look at *who* (or, at a minimum, which functional role) is doing *what* activity, and we might even diagram it in a "flowchart" such as Figure 5.1.

These diagrams are inappropriately named *flow*charts because they measure only the *who* and the *what* of a process. They are really only *activity sequence* charts. They do not really merit the word "flow" in their name because they do not measure time (both in the sense of when to initiate the work, and how long it should last), especially all the time in between the boxes when no one is doing anything to a given unit of work. The waiting time, which, as noted in Chapter 3, is usually the largest source of waste in any office process, is represented only by little arrows in the proverbial "white-spaces". Without our having even an approximate idea how long any unit of work typically sits idle, conventional flowcharts do not tell us what really needs to be improved.

If we do add in time measures, we often believe it is only the touch time *inside* the boxes that matters most—e.g. the 60 minutes it takes to complete each task in our Carlos example. Yet, as we have seen, touch time almost always represents *a very small portion* (e.g. < 5%) of the overall lead time. While these sorts of conventional flowcharts do have some genuine value in identifying customers, establishing roles, responsibilities, and the sequence

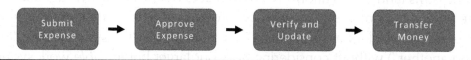

Figure 5.1 Conventional "Flowchart" of the Reimbursement Process.

of tasks that are required to bring a product or service from request to fulfillment—and so are a very good first step—they cannot stop there or they will omit the vast majority (e.g. 95%) of the total elapsed time. Yet elapsed time is a big part of what the customer truly cares about.

People Are Not the Problem

Amy's work scenario is typical of most office work. Nearly everyone is working in multiple processes concurrently, chronically fire-fighting the most urgent issues, and expediting work stuck in long queues. This becomes our reality when our business culture values resource efficiency more than flow efficiency. The fact that we are caught in the frenzy of the immediate work means that we overfocus on the people doing the work, and unintentionally blind ourselves to the larger processes and systems that govern work's flow and people's performance. This blindness to the deeper causes of our work problems means that we are unintentionally sub-optimizing the value we are trying so hard to deliver to our customers when we try to "fix" people instead of processes.

What if we thought that Amy was the real problem? If only we could get a better "Amy", we could process expense claims faster and the time to process expense claims would be shorter, or so we believe. Let us pretend that we can justifiably fire Amy, and we hire a "superstar" to replace her—we can call her Jane. Jane, having twice Amy's experience and education, is the best AP clerk money can possibly hire. We utilized a lot of resources in hiring superstar Jane: not only her higher salary (and Amy's severance), but the search, the interviews, selection, onboarding, and training took a lot of time and effort. It appears that we got our money's worth, however: after 3 months on the job, Jane finds a way to reduce the time she spends on her part of the process by 50%, so that it only takes her 30 minutes compared to the previous 60 minutes (Amy's time). The question is: does this make Carlos receive his reimbursement any faster? (see Figure 5.2).

Even though 30 minutes of work has been removed from AP's process, the flow efficiency in Figure 5.2 (identical to Figure 4.3, minus the 30-minute savings) would now be 3.5 hours/73 hours … still 5%! Even though Jane has saved time in her specific process, the customer does not experience any time savings.

But this scenario does not represent reality, you protest. In reality, we have at least 47 different things to do in a day, and not just one block of work that lasts only 60 minutes. AP, for instance, does not just work on employee reimbursements, but lots of *other* tasks too, like processing invoices, reconciling bank accounts, setting up new vendor information in APS, and so on. No one is making the same type of widget over and over again. Typically, in any professional office, in any department, workers participate in multiple value streams and have to respond to multiple sources of customer demand (whether internal or external) on a daily, if not hourly, basis. This is perhaps most noticeable when a team is a "shared" resource—e.g. IT, HR, Accounting, Risk Management, Audit, Purchasing, and so on—all have to support many or all of the functional groups within an enterprise. The customer-facing teams also have a number of different customers with different individual needs to deal with at the same time.

Figure 5.3 takes our simple example and adds in two more tasks for each functional area. Each of the four roles now has three tasks to complete in

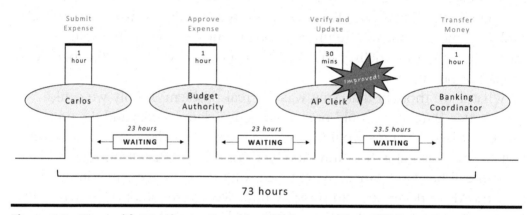

Figure 5.2 Even with 30 Minutes Saved in AP's Process, Flow Efficiency Remains at 5%.

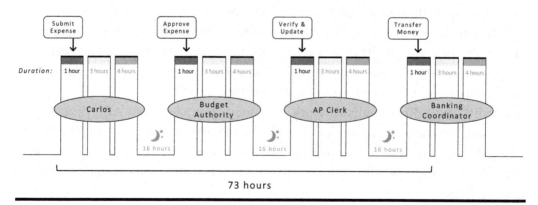

Figure 5.3 The Process Flow of a Simple Four-Step Reimbursement Process (Indicated by the Arrows), Mixed in with Two Other Tasks.

their eight-hour day. Task 1 is related to employee reimbursements, but the other two tasks are not.

Figure 5.3 is identical to the scenario depicted in Figure 5.2, except now each employee in the process is spending eight hours a day working on three separate tasks, rather than one hour a day working on just one, so Figure 5.3 approximates an eight-hour workday slightly more. (Everyone knows you do more than three things in a day, but for the sake of illustration, I am limiting it to just three. Also, Amy's been re-hired, so the AP task takes one hour again.) Because of the functional specialization/expertise required to bring each task to full completion, just like in the Figure 5.2 scenario, each of the tasks takes four different people to complete it.

What is different in Figure 5.3 is that all four of the employees could quite possibly *feel* they are being much more "productive" than in the Figure 5.2 scenario. Now they are working a full eight-hour workday, so they *are* legitimately being more *resource* efficient. They are working as hard as they can, and do not feel like they have any spare time to devote to improving their process now. They are *busy*, without a doubt, and might easily be misled to believe that their process' flow efficiency is now much higher than it was in Figure 5.2[4].

In reality, just like in the "hire a superstar" solution, the flow efficiency of any individual value stream is no better when we work more hours. It is still 5%; from Carlos' point of view, Task 1 is no faster than before. Task 1 takes *exactly* the same amount of time (73 hours) to be completed as in the previous scenario. Just because we are busier does *not* mean we are actually any faster or better at delivering value to the end customer. Carlos is not getting his $3,500 any sooner. Busy does not mean productive! Busy is not the same as getting things done. Our busyness is the grand illusion of work that keeps us from actually seeing the whole value stream and making real, meaningful improvements that are felt by the end customer.

So, what can we do to shift from being "busy" to being "productive"? How do we stop multitasking, shift from Mode 1 to Mode 2, and compress our value streams? There is no specific and detailed recipe that anyone can give you, because ultimately the frontline employees and their immediate managers doing the work have to set up a system that works for them and their customers in their specific business contexts. Fortunately, however, there are two helpful guiding concepts—what I like to call the design principles for flow—that ensure you can make changes that are actually significant improvements for your customers and for your business: establishing Continuity and achieving Balance.

Three Main Takeaways

1. Work is produced by a system of people, information, and technology that is held together by a collection of processes (formal and informal). In Lean language, we call such a system a value stream.
2. The productivity of the system is dependent on flow. We see flow by thinking about all the elements of the system interacting together; seeing the system from the perspective of the unit of work; and focusing on the time it takes for the unit of work to flow through the system.
3. Working on multiple value streams during the course of the day will make us feel busier. And this gives us the illusion of productivity. But when we use facts and data to measure the flow efficiency of the work, we can see that being busy does not amount to being more productive from the customer's point of view.

Notes

1. The W. Edwards Deming Institute. It is questionable that Deming said this and it is more likely to have been one of his associates: http://quotes.deming.org/authors/W._Edwards_Deming/quote/10141 (accessed May 20, 2019).
2. See Kahneman, Daniel. 2011. *Thinking, Fast and Slow*. Doubleday Canada.
3. He said this at a workshop at the 2015 Shingo Conference in Provo, Utah.
4. 24 hours out of 73 is 33%. So this is about six times the flow efficiency of 5.5%.

Chapter 6

Design Principle I: Continuity

You and a friend go into a diner and you each both order the same thing: a cheeseburger, fries, and a drink. Ten minutes later, the waiter brings you your cheeseburgers, but not your fries, nor your drinks, then goes away quickly before you can get his attention. Ten minutes later, he brings you and your friend your fries, but not your drinks, then disappears again before you can remind him of the drinks. (He is running around frantically trying to serve so many tables at once that you cannot get his attention). Other tables around you, even those who ordered after you did, are getting parts of their meals before yours, which annoys you even more. Eventually, another ten minutes later, your drinks finally arrive. Your half-eaten cheeseburgers and fries have gone cold. No matter how good the food might have tasted, would this be a good dining experience? Of course not!

So, spend a few seconds thinking about how, if you were the restaurant's manager, you would go about fixing it. You might start by having some simple organizing system for your order tickets whereby an entire table's order is grouped together, and then sub-grouped by each person at that table. This organizing system would have to be commonly understood by both the kitchen, so that all the food preparation can be timed to be ready at approximately the same time; *and* by the wait staff, so the right food can be brought to the right people at the right table, in a reasonably short time, all at the same time. This might be as simple as printing one complete order chit per table, and then arranging them in the kitchen visibly in sequence by the time of ordering, in a first-in, first-out basis (such a FIFO ticket system is, in fact, what most restaurants use). Perhaps color coding them would also help. Whatever the best solution for your restaurant, you first need to understand what the customer values: not only tasty food and good value-for-money, but good service too. A basic expectation of good restaurant service is that all the components of all the meals for the same table—and for the same course—are brought to the table at the same time. Then you need to create a system to ensure this can happen, repeatedly, and predictably for every customer without fail, regardless of who the waiter, manager, or cook happens to be (employee turnover is high in restaurants, and people work different shifts[1]). The content of the work will change (not everyone orders the same thing) but the basic delivery mechanism (aka "the process") should not. In Lean language, you have to design flow into the process.

Contrary to popular belief, Lean is as much of a *creative* discipline as an analytical one, and successful Lean practitioners have at least as much in common with industrial designers as they do with industrial engineers. Designers are quite comfortable with collaboration, experimenting with new and sometimes unconventional ideas, creating prototypes, taking risks and failing (in controlled ways), and being—gasp—*creative*. Despite the stereotype of creative types being unconstrained by any rules or conventions, good designers are actually very rigorous in adhering to design principles that they define with their colleagues and clients at the beginning of a project[2]. This guides them toward doing their best and most effective work. As we look at how to create flow in your office, it is important to think in terms of similar design principles.

The first design principle to creating flow in your daily work is that of establishing **continuity**. By continuity, what I mean is what Jim Womack calls the *compression* of the value stream[3] (see Chapter 4), or what Modig and Ahlstrom have called the *densification* of value-adding activities[4]. The unit of value, whatever it is in your work context, should in its ideal state move from customer request to fulfillment with as little delay or interruption as possible. While in manufacturing this often involves compressing physical distances—from changing the layouts of plants, so that the machinery of adjacent process steps is closer together, to even locating supplier firms closer to the assembly facility—but co-location of office workers working in the same value stream is not necessary. Co-location of office workers *can* be very beneficial, but it is often not practical, since many people work in multiple value streams every day and may be separated in different offices across different geographies. It is more feasible in full-time project work where there is a dedicated team. In typical office work, continuity is better thought of in terms of compressing *time*, not physical space (ultimately, it is all about time in manufacturing too—just the means are different). Since the electronic conveyance of information largely renders transportation waste irrelevant in offices, continuity is about eliminating the waiting time between the "touch time" or "value-adding" activities. It is about eliminating the queues in between the boxes on the process maps. It is, in other words, about improving flow efficiency.

In the case of the diner previously, the unit of value is actually one table's worth of orders, and the restaurant needs to compress the time between the different production processes—making the cheeseburgers, the fries, and the drinks—for all the meals for all the customers at the same table. In other words, the restaurant needs to think in terms of *one table at a time* rather than trying to serve all the tables at once. Thus value (the whole table's orders) flows to the customer quickly rather than separate elements of the table's orders arriving haphazardly across a longer time span.

DO NOT COMPRESS REWORK

What about quality? Yes, there is a risk, of course, that one might try to condense all the tasks related to producing one unit of value, without examining what the quality of the work is. If the task is purely rework—that is, undoing and redoing the work of someone else because it does not meet your (or your customer's) requirements—then it is only delaying the flow efficiency of the whole value stream. You can try to do rework faster by compressing the rework activities together in time, but that would be merely doing the wrong thing faster. Fortunately, rework is a quite obvious form of waste in offices, and almost everyone doing rework will recognize it as something to be eliminated.

Let us return to Carlos' story. Recall that four teams are involved in processing Carlos' expense reimbursement claim, and each team is dividing its time between three different tasks within their work day.

In Figure 6.1, we see the *exact same tasks* as we did in Figure 5.3 from the last chapter, but now sequenced and coordinated so that all of the Task 1 (Reimbursement) sub-tasks are compressed together in a *continuous* sequence, as are all of the sub-tasks for Tasks 2 and 3. All four steps required to complete each task are now grouped together so that each task as a whole is completed in the fastest possible time. It is much the same as if the tasks were different tables at a restaurant, and each of the subtasks were the meals for each person at each table.

Adopting a flow efficient (Mode 2) way of working, and assuming all three tasks were requested at roughly the same time, the lead time for

Task 1 is now only four hours, for Task 2 is 16 hours (12 hours to perform + 4 hours wait time in queue, since it is behind Task 1); and for Task 3 is 32 hours (16 hours to perform + 16 hours wait time in queue, since it is behind Tasks 1 and 2). This is the miraculous nature of flow efficiency at work: we have taken a process (Task 1) that previously took 73 hours to complete and reduced it to 4 hours—that is a 95% improvement! Similarly, we have reduced Task 2's lead time to 16 hours from 76 hours, a 79% improvement; and Task 3's lead time to 32 hours from 80, a 60% improvement (see Figure 6.2).

No new technology. No additional labor or effort. All the extra efficiency is gained by simply organizing the sequence by which the tasks are performed! Note that the duration of the tasks is *exactly* the same as in the scenario in Figure 6.1. No one is working any harder or faster than before, but every task is being delivered to the customer much sooner, and the process is now capable of producing a whole lot more value for *all* customers in far less time. In other words, the productivity of the process has increased (making management and shareholders happier), while the workers are more focused and less stressed (making employees happier), and the lead time has also been reduced (making customers happier). Win–win–win.

What has happened in the compressed scenario (see Figure 6.1) is that the process has been re-designed to squeeze out the interruptions and

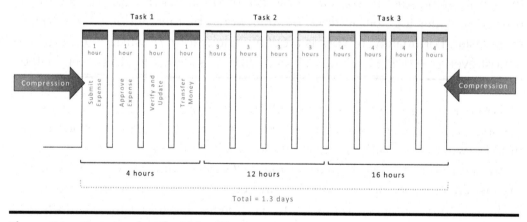

Figure 6.1 Compressing the Value Stream.

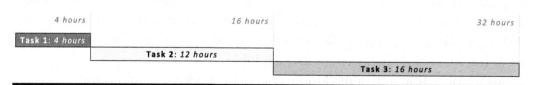

Figure 6.2 Flow of Work in Continuous Time, after Compression.

delays that typically insert themselves in between the touch time. In essence, the movement of the work, from one functional area to another is *continuous*: it never sits in backlogs or queues but is continuously being worked on. When it is handed off to another person in another functional team, that person is ready and able to start work on it right away, just as a relay sprinter takes the baton from the previous runner while already running at full speed. When absolutely all the waiting is eliminated, the touch time and the lead time are the same, and flow efficiency is at 100%. When Task 1's flow efficiency is at 100%, it only takes four hours to reimburse Carlos and he can pay his credit card bill on time.

If only it were so easy. As you have likely guessed by now, there are a couple of challenges in achieving this utopian scenario. First, people do not usually work around-the-clock shift work in offices. While professionals do often work long hours, it is very uncommon for four people to be expected to work 32 hours straight without going home. If you tried to introduce shift work to overcome this, you would likely not have many volunteers, or you would have to give employees large salary increases to get them to work night shifts. It is not usually viable in markets where labor is expensive.

Second, the scenario in Figure 6.1 presumes that every subtask of Task 1 takes exactly one hour (and exactly three hours each for Task 2; and four hours each for Task 3). Yet we all know that work is never like this—it is often highly variable in its duration. Some instances of our work take more time, and some less, and we rarely know ahead of time how long a task will take. Even with something relatively straightforward like an employee reimbursement, a complex claim (say a long, multi-destination business trip that involves many receipts and a few different currencies) might take hours, and a simple one (a local taxi ride) might take minutes to process. Additionally, every individual has a different style and speed of working.

When we try to make this reimbursement process flow better in the context of these real-life constraints, things naturally get a little more complicated. For instance, how do you schedule employees and tasks to maximize flow when the work has to be done sequentially, one step after the other? For instance, since the Budget Authority cannot start her part of Task 1 until Carlos has finished his part, the Budget Authority has to wait an hour on Carlos before she can start her work. So, she has the choice of either doing nothing or working on unrelated work for an hour.

Imagine you are the manager of all four processes, and you are trying to schedule all three tasks in our example. It is harder than it looks: each has four sub-tasks and they all have to be done in sequential order, one after the other, by four different people—which is fairly typical of a lot of professional work, since skillsets are highly specialized, and handoffs are necessary. Everyone works an eight-hour day, from 8 AM to 5 PM, with an hour's break for lunch, which they all take between 12 and 1 PM—fairly normal in many work environments. You are trying to maximize this "flow efficiency" thing you have been reading about, so you direct them to work on Tasks 1, 2, and 3 *in that order*, and to start their respective parts of each task as soon as the previous person has handed it to them. Having been told that it is inefficient to multitask, you instruct them to *not work on anything else* except for Tasks 1, 2, or 3. You are highly skeptical, but you know that Lean involves experimenting with new ways of working, so you decide to give it a try. You take a deep breath and you start to track the completion of the work on an hour-by-hour basis. Your tracking of Day 1 looks like Figure 6.3.

You reflect back on your day. Well, Task 1 worked out fine. Carlos started submitting the claim at 8 AM sharp. By 9 AM, your other three employees had been sitting around for 60 minutes doing nothing, but this did not worry you too much… at that early point in the day. The Budget Authority worked on her part of Task 1 from 9 to 10 AM; the AP Clerk, from 10 to 11 AM; and finally, the Banking Coordinator from 11 AM to 12 noon. The money went out the door by noon; reimbursement was paid to Carlos; task done in four hours. So far, so good … for Task 1.

But then it all went downhill. Carlos, being a diligent worker, started on his part of Task 2, which took him three hours, as soon as he had finished his previous work on Task 1, just as he was instructed. The Budget Authority could not start work on her part of Task 2 until Carlos' part was completed, and so this did not happen until 1 PM, after the lunch break. The Budget Authority sat around doing nothing for most of the morning. The AP Clerk could not start his part of Task 2 until the Budget Authority's part had been

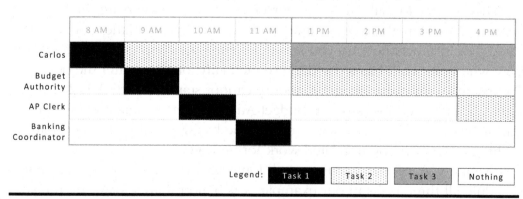

Figure 6.3 Your First Attempt at Establishing Flow.

completed, and by then it was 4 PM and almost time to go home, so he started—but did not complete—his work on Task 2. For that reason, the Banking Coordinator could not do any work on Task 2 that day. These latter two, both the AP Clerk and the Banking Coordinator, did not do much work at all. Meanwhile, Carlos started task three right away at 1 PM, but, given that it took him four hours to complete it, the Budget Authority could not start her part on the same working day. Only Task 1 was fully completed during one complete day's work.

This is a *terrible* system, you are thinking. 32 hours of paid work and the only thing they accomplished was Task 1. Besides Carlos, your people were barely working. And, outside of Task 1, work was not "flowing" at all. You conclude that Lean and flow efficiency are a bunch of baloney that the consultants made up, and that it simply does not—*cannot*—apply to your work, which (as your employees have been saying all along) is very different than an assembly line. "We've got hundreds of things to do every day … and we pay people good money to work on these things! We can't have people sitting around doing nothing!" screams your common sense. "We'll never get anything done. We'll go out of business!" it adds. At the very least, you believe people should be able to stay busy on *other work* while they wait. You quickly put together a productivity scorecard for Day 1 to prove your point (see Table 6.1).

53% productivity! That means people are working only half the time they are in the office. You cease this Lean experiment right away and decide to revert back to business as usual tomorrow, where each functional area works on their own work in their own way, and they are never sitting around with nothing to do. All the employees seem relieved about your decision. They never believed this Lean thing could apply to their kind of work.

For the next day, you reconfirm to them that Tasks 1, 2, and 3 are the top priority items, but now they are allowed to finish their work on their own

Table 6.1 Scorecard for Day 1

Employee	Hours Worked	Hours Paid	%
Carlos	8	8	100
Budget Authority	6	8	75
AP Clerk	2	8	25
Banking Coordinator	1	8	13
Average			*53*

schedule, according to their best judgment of how to manage their time. And, in between working on Tasks 1, 2 and 3, they can use their time "productively" by working on other, lower priority tasks.

You are curious about how work will flow under normal, "business as usual" conditions, so you continue to track it (see Figure 6.4).

To your surprise, the completion rate of Tasks 1, 2, and 3 is even *worse* when teams are left to their own devices. While they are now working on a lot of *other* things, you are somewhat shocked at how little is actually getting done on the key Tasks 1, 2 and 3. But they are so much busier now! You are confused. You jot down your scorecard like you did last time (see Table 6.2).

They are working 100% of the time, so why … and then you realize your mistake. "I am measuring resource efficiency, not flow efficiency!" you say to yourself, whacking your forehead with your palm. You are now wondering if you should not have let them continue the flow experiment for a day or two longer. In any case, you decide to continue to let them work for the next few days in their "normal" way, without any of your managerial intervention into their work scheduling, until all the tasks are completed.

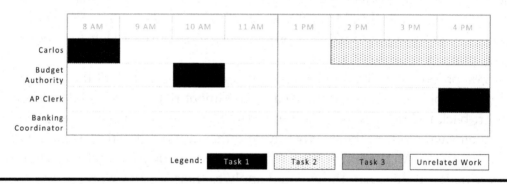

Figure 6.4   When Teams Are Left to Schedule Their Work on Their Own: Day 1.

Table 6.2   Your Productivity Scorecard for Day 2 in "Business As Usual" Mode

Employee	Hours Worked	Hours Paid	%
Carlos	8	8	100
Budget Authority	8	8	100
AP Clerk	8	8	100
Banking Coordinator	8	8	100
Average			**100**

After three days, only Task 1 is done. You call an emergency meeting between all four areas at 9 AM on Day 4. You are frustrated and impatient, raising your voice, "Nothing's getting done around here! Customers are upset. Why is it taking so long to get Tasks 2 and 3 done?"

After listening to 60 minutes of melodrama that include stories of saving the day, delayed reports from the data intel center, people calling in sick, senior executives making unexpected and urgent requests, people blaming each other for not pulling their weight, and the server being down for an entire afternoon, you decide that there is nothing you can do about all these issues right now. The most practical course of action is to focus on just getting the remainder of the two outstanding tasks done as quickly as possible.

"So where are we at with Task 2 right now?"

"Almost done", chimes in the chipper AP clerk. "I'll have it done today".

"Ok, great, but when will it be sent to the customer?" you ask, turning to the Banking Coordinator.

"If I get it before 2 PM, it'll go out today. Otherwise first thing tomorrow. Bank cut off is 5 PM, as usual".

"Let's make sure it gets done today", you respond to both of them. "Now, what's happening with Task 3?"

"Just finished it!" says the Budget Authority.

"So, who's got it now?"

"AP" adds the Budget Authority, a little too eagerly.

You turn to the AP Clerk: "So when do you expect to complete your part of Task 3?"

"As soon as I finish Task 2", says the AP clerk, trying to sound as serious as possible.

"Look, both Tasks 2 and 3 are for really important customers", you explain. "We can't let them down. We have to focus and deliver this work as fast as possible! Do you all understand?"

"I completed all my stuff on Tuesday", offers Carlos quickly.

"And I finished up all of my work just now", adds the Budget Authority, smugly.

The AP Clerk and the Banking Coordinator are quietly looking down at their shoes.

"I'm trusting all four of you to get everything done by the end of today! And do not forget that Task 3 is a little more complex and will take a bit more time than Task 2. Don't leave it until the last minute".

The AP Clerk, remembering that you said that Task 3 was a little more complex, thinks that he had better get started as early as possible on the bigger of the two tasks. He dives into Task 3 right after the meeting. A couple of hours later, struck by a sudden panic, he remembers that he needs to get Task 2 to the Banking Coordinator before 2 PM. Unfortunately, it is already 2:05 PM, so he scrambles frantically to finish up Task 2 as fast as he can and sends it over to the Banking Coordinator around 2:40 PM.

The Banking Coordinator realizes it is late but does her best to rush Task 2 toward the 5 PM banking deadline. Unfortunately, it takes her the two and a half hours of work to complete her updates, so the money does not make the cut. She was willing to stay late to get it done, but the bank has strict cut off times. It is going to have to go out in tomorrow's run. Nothing she can do about it.

You, as their collective manager, continue to track their progress. Eventually, everything is completed by 2 PM on day 5. Five days! You cannot believe how long this work took to complete. You finish your tracking diagram (see Figure 6.5) and do a calculation of the lead time and flow efficiency (see Table 6.3).

Thirty-two hours of work spread out across four people … technically, they could have done it in a day … you shake your head. And only 16%

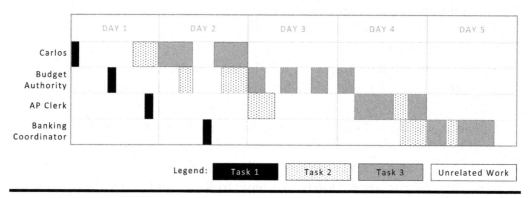

Figure 6.5 Work Completion When Everyone Gets to Make Their Own Schedule.

Table 6.3 Everyone Gets to Make Their Own Schedule

Task	Start (day and hour)		Finish (day and hour)		Touch Time (hours)	Lead Time (hours)	Flow Efficiency (TT ÷ LT)
Task 1	Day 1	0800	Day 2	1200	4	28	14%
Task 2	Day 1	1400	Day 5	1000	12	92	13%
Task 3	Day 2	0900	Day 5	1400	16	77	21%
Average					**11**	**66**	**16%**

flow efficiency. Everyone was working as hard as they could, and they were certainly busy every hour of the day ... they were even really stressed out and focused on getting it all done after the status meeting ... but, you keep thinking, there must be a better way to get the most important work done sooner.

Out of curiosity, you start to diagram what would have happened had you allowed the "flow" scenario to continue past Day 1. As it turns out, they could have completed everything in only two and a half days! (see Figure 6.6; Table 6.4).

Your calculations make you think, wow, maybe this flow thing is not as terrible as you thought ... the average lead time is nearly cut in half, and the average flow efficiency—at 31%—is nearly twice as good as it was before. Impressive.

And this notion of designing the work for flow instead of for resource efficiency gets you thinking a little more ... what would happen if you

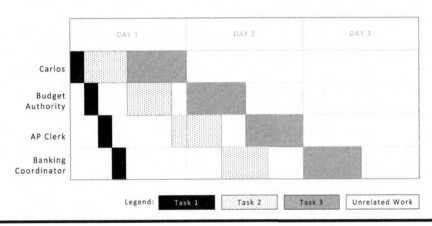

Figure 6.6   Flow Sequence Where One Task Is Started As Soon As Received.

Table 6.4   Improved Flow

Task	Start (day and hour)		Finish (day and hour)		Touch Time (hours)	Lead Time (hours)	Flow Efficiency (TT ÷ LT)
Task 1	Day 1	0800	Day 2	1200	4	4	100%
Task 2	Day 1	0900	Day 2	1400	12	29	41%
Task 3	Day 1	1300	Day 3	1200	16	71	23%
Average					**11**	**35**	**31%**

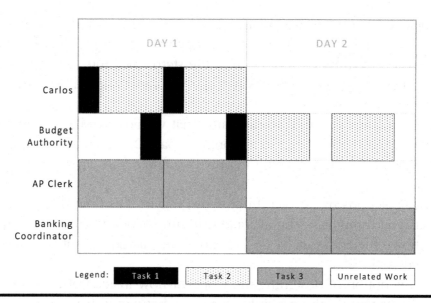

Figure 6.7   Flow Sequence After Cross-Training and Re-Allocation of Tasks.

cross-trained certain people on certain tasks, and this allowed the work to be scheduled more flexibly? Even though they are expert-specialists, there are some aspects of the work that can, with adequate training, be shared, if everyone is really honest with themselves and willing to learn new skills. So you get Carlos and the Budget Authority to learn how to do some more of the other subtasks associated with Tasks 1 and 2. "Don't worry at all about Task 3", you tell Carlos and the Budget Authority, "Just focus on learning all the parts of Tasks 1 and 2". Meanwhile, the AP Clerk and Banking Coordinator are no longer worried about Tasks 1 and 2, because you have asked them to focus all their attention on learning how to do all four parts of only Task 3. It takes everyone a few months to cross-train, but eventually, your new schedule looks like Figure 6.7.

Now the lead time for Tasks 2 and 3 is only two days—when previously it would have taken them four or five days (recall Figure 6.5). The lead time for Task 1 is still one day but has been extended to eight hours to accommodate the completion of the sub-tasks of Task 2 in three-hour uninterrupted blocks. The customer finds an eight-hour (same day) lead time perfectly acceptable for Task 1 and does not need it to be four hours (i.e. Carlos can still pay his credit card bill on time). Your scorecard now looks like Table 6.5.

The actual flow efficiency in the cross-training has gone down for Task 1, stayed roughly the same for Task 2, but has gone up dramatically for Task 3. Because Task 3 takes the longest, the increase in its flow has boosted overall

Table 6.5 Improved Flow with Cross-Training and Re-Allocation of Tasks

Task	Start (day and hour)		Finish (day and hour)		Touch Time (hours)	Lead Time (hours)	Flow Efficiency (TT ÷ LT)
Task 1	Day 1	0800	Day 1	1700	4	9	44%
Task 2	Day 1	0900	Day 2	1600	12	31	39%
Task 3	Day 2	0800	Day 2	1700	16	33	48%
Average					**11**	**24**	**44%**

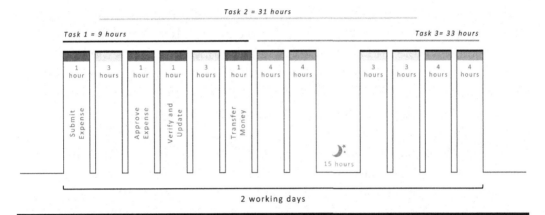

Figure 6.8 Realistically Improved Flow of Tasks after Cross-Training of staff.

average flow efficiency to 44%, nearly three times the 16% that we started with. The average lead time is only 24 hours for all three tasks, compared to 66 hours when no schedules were in place.

Unlike Figures 6.1 and 6.2, where we had ideal (but purely theoretical) flow, we now have a realistically scheduled process that looks something like Figure 6.8.

This process could be improved even further, no doubt, by staggering shift start times, cross-training even more, doing some of the sub-tasks simultaneously (if feasible), removing waste within the tasks themselves, and/or reducing the variability in the duration of tasks.

THE FREEDOM OF TYRANNY

One compelling example of this kind of rigorous scheduling for the purposes of creating continuity is the system in place at Menlo Innovations, a small but well-known software company based out of Ann Arbor, Michigan. At Menlo, every piece of work related to any given project is written down on a "story card" which describes a functional client need/desire for the software they are creating. Each card is estimated for duration, and then each week is planned to be the sum of the highest priority cards (as determined by the customer) that add up to *no more than 40 hours a week* (actually 32, because they devote 8 hours every week on every project to the standard work of time estimation, reviewing progress and consulting with the client, and holding brief stand up meetings). Once the 32 hours (*billable* hours, I should add) of work have been determined, the cards are transferred to that week's Work Authorization Board by the project manager and assigned to specific developers (it should be noted that these "story cards" are just manually written cue cards, and the tracking board is a corkboard on the wall—for a high-tech software company, the tools and systems they have devised are deliberately low-tech because they are more visible and adaptable). A simple string runs across the Work Authorization Board indicating the dividing line of the present day between tomorrow and yesterday. If a card is above the string (time moves top to bottom on their board) but does not have a green "passed testing" sticker, it immediately becomes visible to the team and a quick, collaborative, blame-free discussion is initiated on how to get back on track. There is amazing teamwork around the board, with no managerial intervention or exhortations.

Everyone at Menlo knows what they and their colleagues are working on at any given point in time, and what they will work on next once they have finished. On Monday morning, there is no ambiguity on what the developers are going to work on for the next five days. While they have the professional autonomy of deciding *how* they will develop their code to meet the needs of the customer, they have no choice over the *what* and *when* of their work. Their scheduling system does not exist, as some might assume, because there is a culture of micro-managing, authoritarian leaders imposing this discipline on the teams. On the contrary, it is because the teams themselves understand, respect, and appreciate the value of "Freedom Through Tyranny", as Menlo CEO Richard Sheridan likes calls it, tongue-in-cheek[5]. The team can always weigh in with opinions about any of the selections and even request changes if desired, all done within the spirit of teamwork. Also, if estimates turn out to be less than what is actually needed, there is no punishment or cajoling regarding a missed estimate.

The culture of (self-imposed) discipline and accountability is so strong at Menlo that it seems slightly "tyrannical" to those who are used to having a laissez-faire boss and the "autonomy" or "freedom" of being able to choose what they work on from moment to moment. But Menlonians paradoxically enjoy far greater freedom because they limit their amount of work-in-progress (no multitasking) and have only one prioritization system (coordinated focus).

They hardly ever work overtime and enjoy a great work/life balance. They create very high-quality software quickly while only working 40-hour weeks, because they are laser-focused on the value-creating work that has been prioritized and scheduled by one singular, authoritative source: their customer. They have very little need for extended meetings and other superfluous work created by the need to deal with all the uncoordinated busyness that is typical of most modern office environments.

What is interesting about Menlo is that they have "pull ahead" cards, so that if they finish their allocated work for the week early, they can get started on the next highest priority piece of work ahead of schedule. Even at the project level, they arrange contracts with some clients who will, in exchange for lower fees, accept a more unpredictable pace of delivery. When there are dips in demand between projects (as there inevitably are in such work), Menlonians are kept utilized by working on these "back burner" projects. When demand increases, they have flexible staffing[6] and rapid hiring techniques that allow them to respond faster than any bureaucratic, large company. While Menlo first focuses on maximizing customer value (flow efficiency), it secondarily focuses on the utilization of personnel (resource efficiency). It is an advanced example of a knowledge-work company that has successfully broken free of the trade-off mentality and has managed to increase *both* kinds of efficiency.

The key to these efficiency gains is largely a matter of scheduling *what* work will be done *when*. This is different than telling people exactly *how* the work should be done. Most knowledge workers are smart people who can do their work with a high degree of competence and autonomy, and they do not benefit from others telling them how to do their job. But a bunch of smart people who are allowed to work on whatever they want, whenever they want, will create pronounced flow inefficiencies for every value stream they touch. This is not because they are evil, but because they simply have multiple, competing demands on their time and uneven workloads. Without any coordination, the system is only as good as the sum of its scattered parts. And such lack of coordination creates longer lead times for customers, more capacity constraints for employees, and less productivity for the company. Lose–lose–lose.

Typically office work is never scheduled hour by hour. The mere idea of it strikes most people as overly rigid. As stringent as the above style of scheduling and sequencing of tasks may seem at first, the capacity gains and lead time reductions are too good to not give it a try (see Sidebar).

You might start with taking one task completed by two separate teams, A and B, and simply have Team A work on its respective part in the morning and Team B in the afternoon.

As you try, remember that the goal is not to achieve perfect flow with your processes. The goal is to move in the direction of *better* flow by creating a flexible and commonly shared system for coordinating and sequencing the work across the value stream to minimize interruptions. Strive to compress the time *between* tasks belonging to the same unit of value (the complete product or service being delivered to the customer) to achieve more continuity of related tasks. As you experiment with establishing and improving your system, the flow of work will get better and better, and it will get to a point where it becomes largely self-regulating. As teams learn what works and—more importantly—what does not work, they can adjust their workflow with little or no managerial intervention. Without having to invest in additional labor or technology, and without anyone working harder or faster, the benefits of flow can be truly astonishing.

Three Main Takeaways

1. The principle of continuity states that compressing the time between various process steps related to one unit of customer value will create more flow than multitasking one's way through many process steps for separately related units of value.
2. Compressing process steps is technically challenging because of the constraints of work hours, specialized skillsets, competing priorities, and variation in the complexity and duration of the work.
3. Compressing the process steps is psychologically challenging because it goes against our conventional resource-efficient ways of thinking that being busy with any work is more important than coordinating the timing of the prioritized work. Professional knowledge workers are not accustomed to having their work rigorously scheduled and will typically resist it at first. Despite these challenges, the benefits for customers, employees and shareholders makes it worth it.

Notes

1. Even in very high-end restaurants, where perhaps the chef is considered an artist, there have to be rigorous systems. In reality, the celebrated head chef is not cooking the food for every diner. High-profile chefs create unique recipes and then set up a system of "production" for a team of far less famous chefs to replicate them reliably and consistently. The systems in high-end restaurants have to be even more precisely managed and executed than in average restaurants because customer expectations are even higher. It is incorrect to think that creative professions cannot benefit from using Lean systems to govern work processes.
2. See, for instance, Brown, Tim. 2009. Some design principles. IDEO blog, November 29, 2009: https://designthinking.ideo.com/?p=409 (accessed July 2, 2018).
3. Womack, James P. Jim Womack on where lean has failed and why not to give up. *Planet Lean*, August 29, 2017: http://planet-lean.com/jim-womack-on-where-lean-has-failed-and-why-not-to-give-up (accessed July 2, 2018).
4. Modig, Niklas and Par Ahlstrom. 2015. *This is Lean: Resolving the Efficiency Paradox*. Stockholm: Rheologica Publishing. p.27.
5. Sheridan, Richard. 2013. *Joy, Inc*. New York: Penguin Group. p.80.
6. Menlo, who's labor force draws largely on graduates from regional Universities, including the very local University of Michigan, has a list of "on call" people who are willing to work on a periodic, "as needed" basis. As you might imagine, these are often former full time Menlo employees who have chosen to pursue other careers or lifestyles, but who are have the flexibility to work occasionally. When project demand is high, Menlo calls the names on their list to see who might be available. They also offer different choices to full-time employees. Employees can choose, as their regular hours, a 32-, 36-, or 40-hour work week. Some of those who do not work the full 40 hours may choose to periodically work extra hours (up to 40) if there is a demand. There is never any obligation, however. It is entirely up to the employee.

Chapter 7

An Accounting Story

In 2017 an accounting team was trying to improve their month-end process. The month-end process is stressful for most accounting teams because there is a lot of work to do with tight deadlines. In this case, the team had five days to complete month-end, and when I first met them, they were often working overtime to get it done within that window.

Six people plus a manager made up the team. Each person had his or her specific tasks that they had become quite good at, as individual experts. I watched them do their work for about an hour each and asked them the same question: "How do you know what to work on next?". They all told me more or less the same answer: first they did a task, such as Analysis A, and then they would go on to do Process B … except (and there was *always* an exception) … the only problem was that if person X in their team had not finished Task Y, they could not start Process B, so they would start Task C instead, which had no dependencies on Task Y. In other words, the sequence for the whole month-end process was highly variable. They knew what they each had to do as individuals, and in what sequence, and they did it as soon as they were able. Like most employees, they worked hard and kept busy. But they worked as individual islands, doing their own work without knowing what their teammates (each on their separate island) were working on much of the time. The mindset was, "You do your work and leave me alone so I can concentrate on doing mine. If we all get our own stuff done as quickly as possible, month-end will get done as fast as possible". Yet the customer—in this case, the Corporate Controller—cared most about the quality of the monthly financial statements and the analysis of significant variances. In other words, she cared about the collective output of the team, not their individual efforts.

Part of the manager's job was to ensure the team completed all the required tasks on time. The team knew which tasks to do each month from a spreadsheet list that the internal audit department required them to keep. The manager used it as a checklist to make sure the team did not miss critical tasks, so it doubled as a quality standard. He also reviewed their work for errors[1]. He spent most of his time fighting fires, however. Problems would come up: e.g. the data-mart was down and they could not extract their needed reports; the numbers from Team X elsewhere in the company were late; or, the numbers from Team Y were on time, but were rife with errors and would not reconcile with the general ledger, so they would have to embark on a lengthy detective search to find the source of the mismatch. It was never quite the same thing two months in a row. They had seemingly unique problems every month.

Before they could start to solve problems, which were often caused by upstream teams or unreliable data warehouses that they could not fix themselves, I knew that they needed to see their own process as a whole and redesign it so that the work would flow better. Being sensitive to the fact that they were busy and under tight deadlines, I did not want to ask them to do much additional work, so the first thing I did was to encourage them to simply make their work visible. I taught them how a basic kanban board (see Sidebar) could work[2].

WHAT IS KANBAN?

Kanban is a Japanese word simply meaning "signboard" or "billboard". In Lean manufacturing, they are typically physical cards that signal information from downstream processes to upstream processes. The signals work in two basic "make or move" ways: (1) to initiate production of a certain part or product (in a specific lot size); and/or (2) to replenish a store of materials to be used in production, much like in a supermarket where if a product falls below a certain quantity on the shelf, this acts as a signal to restock the product so that there is never a shortage. Both modes of kanban usage have the purpose of minimizing the overproduction of inventory and preventing bottlenecks and overburden on workers. In practice, the kanban system in a large manufacturing operation can become quite complicated, with every part number having its own unique card system. The cards can manage the sequence and timing of the production of multiple products in different lot sizes, in response to the pace of customer consumption (demand). They convey information between production process steps, between internal material stores and the production line, and between a firm and its external suppliers.

In office and knowledge work environments, the cards are usually sticky notes posted to a whiteboard—aka a kanban board. It is a tool that helps visualize work, prioritize new demand, and limit work in process (WIP). The purpose is to focus employees on only the few most critical tasks, prevent multitasking, improve flow, respond quickly to problems, and minimize over-burden. It has become especially popular as a process management tool in software development and is usually, in conjunction with Scrum and other methods, associated with Agile.

At first, they did not understand why they had to do this, and there was some resistance. They did not understand why they had to track their tasks visibly, on hand-written, low-tech post-it notes, when all of them could rely on their existing electronic checklist. It seemed like duplication to them. When people are used to working as individual islands, rather than as a collective team, they do not see the need to see their work holistically in (almost) real-time—something which an electronic spreadsheet simply cannot do unless it is displayed on a large monitor that is always on and visible to everyone. I explained the benefit of having a collective, holistic view, but they did not really buy it. I also explained how the sequencing of work—i.e. condensing it—could improve how fast they were able to complete it, but they were just skeptical and puzzled. To them, an apple plus an orange equals an apple and an orange. If you change the sequence of the equation to become an orange plus an apple, you still have an apple and an orange!

I did not try to convince them that an apple and an orange can be different than an orange and an apple, depending on which fruit you need first. Verbal explanation really does not really convince anyone of anything. We all learn nearly everything we know how to do by first seeing it done by others, and then doing it ourselves (repeatedly) with increasing competence until we achieve a desired level of mastery. Knowing that everyone is a visual, hands-on learner, I knew that words would not make them "buy-in" to it. Only experiencing it would make them believe it[3].

I was able to convince them to give the kanban board a try for a short time, and promised them that if it did not work for them, they could go back to their old system ("100% satisfaction or your money back!", I joked). I was not asking them to take on more work (other than the minor bother of tracking their work with sticky notes on a board). I was not asking them to work any faster or harder, and they already felt confident that they could meet their five-day target. The worst that could happen in this case is that things would stay the same. Fortunately, the manager was supportive, and I could tell that one or two of the staff intuited that there could be some merit in this low-tech visualization of the team's work that I was proposing. I recruited these more enthusiastic team members to carry out the first assignment: build the board. This way the doubters did not have to make any effort other than to go along with what their colleagues asked of them, while the cautious optimists on the team were actively taking part in the creation of their own visual management system. People do not mind change; they mind *being* changed[4]. You must involve people in changes that affect them.

They set up their kanban board with sticky notes for all the month-end tasks on the left-hand side. Since they had five working days to complete the month-end "event", they categorized their tasks by day and used different "swim lanes" and distinctly colored stickies for each day. This was all of their own design—I never told them how to design their board other than that they had to have, at a minimum, three columns representing their task status, something akin to "to do", "doing", and "done". They had never before broken down their work day by day, and the exercise was eye-opening to them because they began to understand the dependencies between the tasks. You can see a lot just by making it visible, as Yogi Berra might say[5]. They also started to question the order—e.g. they had always done Task A on Day 4, but now that they could see it sitting there on the board, they realized there was no reason they could not do it on, say, Day 2. They split up larger, multi-day tasks into Task X (Day 1), and Task X (Day 2), and so on.

The system was effective because it was simple. As they started a task, they would take it from the left-hand column of "Ready" and place it in the middle "In Progress" section. They put their initials on it so anyone could see who was working on it. The rule was that they could not work on more than one thing at once—they had to finish their task/sticky note and put it in the "Done" column before they could withdraw another task/sticky note from the "Ready" pile. This created greater focus and productivity (recall Mode 2 from Chapter 5) by limiting their work in process. They also tracked the time they took to complete it—with no expectation of what the "right" duration should be. The timing was simply for them to learn about the duration of the tasks. Importantly, the manager did not evaluate how quickly or slowly everyone worked. After completing a task, they simply noted the duration, moved it to the "Done" column and then selected the next task from the "Ready" pile for that day. By the end of Day 5, all the stickies would be in the right-hand "Done" column (see Figures 7.1 and 7.2).

The first month they did this, as I expected, things did not flow super-smoothly. I just kept telling them that, in the words of Tracey and Ernie

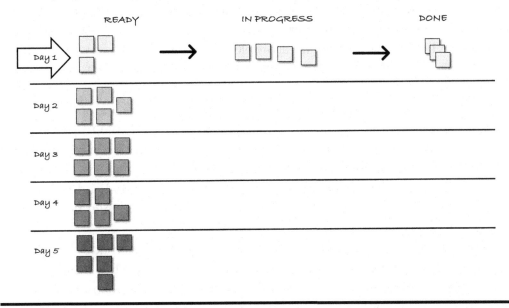

Figure 7.1 An Illustration of the Team's Month-End Kanban Board, On Day 1.

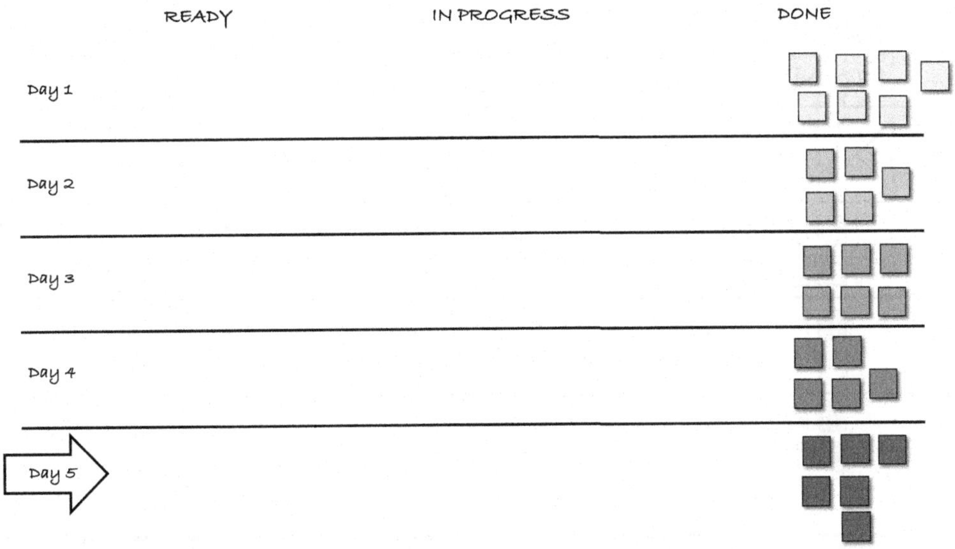

Figure 7.2 An Illustration of the Team's Month-End Kanban Board, On Day 5.

Richardson, "problems were their friends[6]". If you are a Lean coach or leader, it is important to tell teams to expect problems and to embrace them as a *good* thing. If you do not admit you have problems with your work, you cannot improve anything—so you need to embrace seeing problems in the flow of work as the first step towards improving the work. It is a common misperception that Lean tools like kanban boards, fishbone diagrams, or standard work will fix things. Tools do not fix anything: *they help you see problems*. Seeing problems may not always feel like progress, but it is. When you can no longer plausibly deny a problem's existence, the only reasonable thing left to do is fix it. In many corporate cultures, it takes a lot of courage to see problems clearly.

The team made many "friends" that first month, and we learned a lot. What the team members realized is that they were not all able to pull the very next task from the "Ready" pile. Sometimes it would be Day 1, but they were only capable of doing work that corresponded to Day 4, because that work was their area of specialization and expertise. They realized that their work—collectively, as a team—was out of sync with the optimal flow of the process. It was discontinuous (see Figure 7.3).

Exposure of these problems in their month-end process made the whole team, even the sceptics, understand the utility of the tool. They were starting to see problems they did not realize they had. The team manager's demeanor, very fortunately, was one of being very calm, kind and

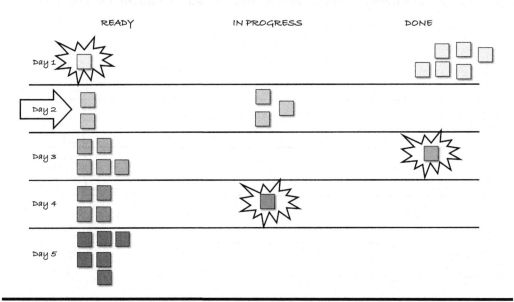

Figure 7.3 Problems Became Visible When the Team Realized That People Were Sequencing Work According to Their Skillsets, and Not According to Optimal Flow.

understanding, and this was vital in creating a climate free of blame and fear. So instead of getting defensive, the team saw these newly found problems as a challenge and an opportunity.

They came to realize that there were no real downsides to the use of the kanban board and so agreed to continue to use it for a few months more. They were still able to complete month-end on time as they had in the past, although still with occasional overtime, so nothing got *worse* through their use of the board. And there were some immediate benefits. For instance, the team, the manager, and anyone else who happened to be walking by, including the VP of Finance and Accounting, could see at a glance if the team was presently ahead or behind in their five-day schedule based on the placement of the colored sticky notes relative to the current day. This meant the team could address the problems causing them to fall behind in the process earlier and get support from management if required. There was also no need to provide interim status reports up the chain of command anymore, saving them some time to focus more on their work.

The team huddled briefly in stand-up meetings every morning in front of the board to address any issues that had come up and, if they had fallen behind, what they would do to get back on track to meet their deadline. I asked them to note what issues came up, but I did not ask them to start any in-depth, root-cause problem-solving right away. Instead, I encouraged them to make what quick fixes they could and to do what they would normally do to get back on track. We could then collect the issues over the course of a few months to determine their frequency and see the emerging patterns.

One of the issues that came up was the need for cross-training. This was no surprise. The manager of the team already knew, as most frontline leaders know, that he needed to cross-train his team more. It was just that he and his team, like most leaders and their teams, never seemed to have the time. He needed all his people to be working at full-steam all the time just to keep up with deadlines. This left little time for teaching or learning. As anyone who has cross-trained team members has experienced, it is time-consuming: it takes work time away from the trainer, who must teach, and work time away from the trainee, who must learn. It is time very well invested, but it is still time away from doing the pressing, value-adding, deadline-driven work for the customer. (The same thing happens when onboarding a new employee—which is partly why turnover is so costly to productivity). The kanban board acted as a catalyst to actually doing the cross-training. It provided the team more of a compelling direction and purpose for it. The whole team could now see that they were not completing some tasks as soon as they could be, so they focused their cross-training efforts on the most vital ones first.

CROSS-TRAINING IN KNOWLEDGE WORK

A lot of "knowledge work" involves knowledge that can be taught and shared from one smart individual to the next. Many people like to be specialized experts who hoard knowledge—it makes them feel smart and valued, perhaps even "indispensable"—so they will try to convince you that their work *cannot* be shared. But do not give in to this. Much of their work (not all of it, but much of it) *can* be shared. Few companies can guarantee permanent, lifetime employment to their employees in exchange for sharing knowledge, but they can explain to the knowledge hoarders how cross-training will benefit their own professional development (learning new skills), will increase the flow of value to the customer, and will reduce the capacity burden placed on them (after all, since they have all the knowledge, they are in high demand!).

Additionally, leaders have to stop recognizing individuals for simply being smart and hardworking in their narrow specializations. Being smart and hard-working is commendable, but leaders have to instead think, above all, about how the system as a whole (in which the employees are only one element) is designed to serve the customer. They can improve customer experience by con-sciously rewarding and recognizing behaviors like sharing work and acquiring new skills from other colleagues as a way to reduce lead times, that is, the total elapsed time as experienced by the customer. One simple activity leaders can initiate is to set up mentoring relationships between more senior staff and more junior staff, with clear timelines and objectives for the transfer of knowledge and gradual mastery of new skills. These relationships can be formal—i.e. they meet at regular intervals to discuss a certain topic or issue—or more informal, such as when they are given a joint project to work on together. Developing people through cross-training *always* pays off for customers and employees.

As expected, it took some time. While they were all professional accoun-tants, they all did not know the specifics of each task being performed by each member of the team. The manager set up a reasonably-paced schedule of who would train who on which tasks every month. Additionally, they would update their documented procedures as they trained people.

The use of the kanban system and the improved sequencing of tasks gradually freed up a bit more time each month to carry out more cross-training. Because of the added time required for cross-training, however, it was still taking about 225 person hours to complete month-end (6 people working 7.5 hours/day × 5 days). They were completing month-end on time, with only modest amounts of overtime, but they had not yet realized any big gains in flow efficiency.

After six months of cross-training, the team was ready to go "live" with allowing everyone on the team to grab (in the correct sequence, of course) any task they were capable of doing without immediate support from a colleague who was more experienced at that task. Not everyone knew how to do everything, but there was now enough breadth of knowledge for all team members to select from a much wider variety of tasks. Month-end took about 150 person hours that month, a 33% improvement. The system had become more flexible and agile, able to match the sequential demand of work with their supply of ability and knowledge, and it saved them 75 person hours per month, without anyone working longer or harder than before.

Further improvements, based on implementing some countermeasures to recurring issues, drove the number down even further to about 125 person hours on average, where it eventually leveled off and has, for the time being, stabilized. This is equal to just over three people working 7.5 hours/day over 5 days. Instead of electing to do month-end faster, the team redeployed their three "extra" team members to work on important projects for five days a month, like preparing for compliance with new accounting standards that were coming into effect the following year. They achieved a 44% improvement in month-end efficiency without investing in any additional technology other than a whiteboard and some sticky notes. They also expanded the skillsets of every team member.

Three Main Takeaways

1. Make your work visible in a way that allows you to see, on a daily basis, if you are ahead or behind in accomplishing your team's most important tasks.
2. Involve as many people as possible from the team in the creation of new work systems. Their creativity will amaze you.
3. Cross-train people wherever possible. Have a plan. A flexible staffing model allows for more agility in responding to variations in customer demands.

Notes

1. Although double-checking the numbers might seem like wastefully "inspecting-in quality", as Dr. W. Edwards Deming might say, reproachfully, it is really an important and necessary quality control to have two sets of eyes look at the numbers. There is a low threshold for error when it comes to reporting substantial amounts of money because errors are costly. By the same logic, airlines require two pilots to fly a commercial airplane.
2. My favorite book on kanban for knowledge work is Benson, Jim and Tonianne DeMaria Barry. 2011. *Personal Kanban: Mapping Work, Navigating Life.* Seattle, WA: Modus Cooperandi Press.
3. The existence of individual "learning styles" is, I believe, a myth. It *seems* like there are learning styles because we tend to learn some subjects better through different modalities, e.g. we of tend to learn about the forms of music best through our ears. In fact, we all learn the same subjects best through the same channels—the subject matter dictates the best channel, not the individual's preference. When it comes to most elements of business, it is all visual and hands-on ("kinesthetic"). For further discussion, see, for instance: Guterl, Sophie. 2013. Is Teaching to a Student's "Learning Style" a Bogus Idea? *Scientific American*, September 20, 2013: www.scientificamerican.com/article/is-teaching-to-a-students-learning-style-a-bogus-idea/ (accessed May 21, 2019).
4. Scholtes, Peter R. 1998. *The Leaders Handbook: Making Things Happen, Getting Things Done.* New York: McGraw-Hill, p. 227.
5. Yogi Berra actually said, "You can observe a lot by just watching". BrainyQuote.com. 2018. Yogi Berra Quotes: https://www.brainyquote.com/quotes/yogi_berra_125285 (accessed October 13, 2018).
6. From one of the many Tracey and Ernie Richardson workshops I was lucky to attend.

Chapter 8

Design Principle II: Balance

As mentioned in Chapter 5, there are two fundamental principles of value stream design to achieve better flow: continuity and balance. Continuity, as we have seen, means that the time delays between process steps in a value stream are compressed, so that work, once initiated, does not sit idle and half-finished, waiting for someone to work on it. The second design principle, balance, means that the rate of completing work needs to be evenly distributed across all the steps.

Bucket Brigades

Balance and continuity are complementary and mutually reinforcing concepts. A way to visualize it is to think of the bucket brigade method for putting out fires (which actually existed up to 1850 or so, after which horse-drawn, hand-pumped fire engines replaced them nearly everywhere). In the bucket brigade system, the fastest way to get the most water to the fire is to have everyone pass the bucket to the next person in line in unison, at the same tempo. You pass a bucket of water then turn back to the other side and receive the next bucket. For the buckets to flow optimally, people need to be close enough to one another to pass a bucket between themselves. This is the continuity part. Visibility of the upstream and downstream people in the line helps to ensure continuity. You can see when the person upstream from you is ready to pass you the bucket and you can see when the person downstream from you is ready to receive the bucket, and both of these things are visual signals to perform a fairly standardized action (passing or receiving).

But another crucial element of a well-functioning bucket brigade is that the time to "process" one unit of work (that is, receive and pass a full bucket) for any given person in the line should be roughly equal in duration to all the others—in other words, it has to be *balanced*. Everyone should take approximately the same time to receive and pass along a bucket, or you can easily imagine how inefficient the line will get. Everyone along the line must basically act in pairs, with one person receiving and the other passing a bucket, and then alternating roles, at the same time—together, as one team, in concert—*continuously*, without interruption, as if it were one single person doing the work. If even one person in the whole brigade were to go faster or slower than the common tempo, he would create imbalance. If someone gets the bright idea that because he has two hands he can be twice as "efficient" by waiting until he has two buckets to pass, and therefore puts his first bucket aside (where it sits idle for a moment) and waits for a second bucket before passing, with the best of intentions, both at once (in a batch), he creates imbalance and lack of flow for the entire fire-fighting system. Imbalance impedes the buckets flowing to the fire as fast as they can.

Good value stream flow in a workplace is like a well-functioning bucket brigade. It is an uninterrupted human chain of value-adding activities. Contrary to our common intuition, where faster is always considered better, the design of any value stream should seek to maximize the balance and continuity of the entire system end-to-end over trying to maximize the speed of any individual process step in isolation. In that way the value stream will perform faster but the individuals working within the value stream do not have to rush. No one believes this until they try it and see the results, but balance and continuity are far more influential at freeing up human resources and delivering value faster to the customer than increasing the speed at which any single individual within it works.

Think of driving along a highway at rush hour: every individual driver wants to go as fast as she can, yet collectively no one is moving very fast because the system is discontinuous and unbalanced. The cars do not maintain an even distance between the cars in front and behind them (continuity), and there is no effective way to get everyone collectively to drive at the same constant speed (balance). Everyone wants to drive 60 mph (97 kmh) but ends up going 10 mph (16 kmh). If everyone maintained a constant 30 mph (48 kmh), everyone would get to where they were going three times faster than if they were allowed to choose to drive at whatever speed they like. As with any complex adaptive system, optimizing the whole yields far greater benefits than optimizing the parts in isolation.

Bob the Bottleneck

Why is balance so important? Mostly because it avoids what happens when there is imbalance: a bottleneck. Consider a simple, four-step value stream like that in Figure 8.1. Imagine that the customer requests five "widgets" a week (that is, five separate customers each want a policy, report, quote, booking, disbursement, contract, credit rating—or whatever it is your company does—per week). To meet this customer demand, a different functional department performs each of the four steps, such as Sales, Operations, Quality Control, and Customer Service. It does not really matter what the four departments are, just that they have different reporting lines in the vertical organizational structure. The only person that belongs to the same org chart as all four of them is the CEO, and they all have different bosses who assess their performance independently.

Now look at their capacity—that is, their *potential* "production" rate (the average rate at which they could complete their work). Importantly, their capacity is what they are capable of, not what they are actually doing. Joe is capable of producing four widgets/week and, because the customer is asking for five, he lacks capacity. One widget gets stuck at the bottleneck of Joe. Although he might say that he is "overworked", he is really saying that the customer demands on his time are greater than his current capacity to handle them all. Jen is underutilized and can handle easily the four widgets that Joe gives her. She has capacity to spare. Bob—who's manager considers him a laggard—is only capable of processing three widgets/week and so, similar to Joe, is overburdened because he receives four

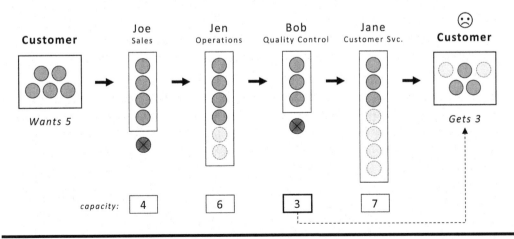

Figure 8.1   A Four-Process Value Stream Capable of Producing Three Widgets/Week.

widgets/week from Jen. One more widget is stuck at the bottleneck of Bob. Meanwhile Jane—the "superstar"—can handle seven widgets/week but processes only three, since that is what she gets from Bob. While each widget is quite different and unique, and therefore varies in the amount of time it spends in each process step, the stated rate of production in each step is the *average* rate.

There are two basic rules of bottlenecks that can be noted in this example:

1. Bottlenecks will form wherever the rate of production/completion of work in any given process step is *slower* than the step immediately *prior* to it (indicated by the dark widgets left behind in Figure 8.1—note these are also the steps where people are working at full capacity).
2. The end-customer receives value at the rate corresponding to the *slowest* rate of production of all the steps in the entire value stream. In Figure 8.1 this is three widgets/week, or Bob's rate, since his process is the slowest.

The flip-side of the first rule is that process steps that have a *faster* processing rate than the previous step will be *under*-utilized (their actual output will be below their potential capacity), because they are downstream from a bottleneck. In this example, Bob's process is a bottleneck because Jen's process produces at a faster rate than his does. Bob has a backlog to deal with. Joe's process, too, is a bottleneck. Jen and Jane, in contrast, are under-utilized because they have the potential capacity to produce at a faster rate, but are receiving work at the rate of the process step immediately upstream to each of them, respectively. Jen receives work at the rate Joe passes it to her; similarly, Jane receives work at the rate Bob passes it to her. With their spare capacity, they will, of course, turn their attention to other work in other value streams in order to stay busy.

The second rule of bottlenecks tells us that the customer receives their widgets at a rate of only three/week (on average) because Bob's process, producing at a rate of three/week, is the *slowest* of the entire value stream. If the customers' weekly demand is greater than three—as is the case here, where there are five customers/week—some customers are either not receiving their widgets on time, or, much more likely, employees are working overtime (effectively adding capacity to the process) to keep up with demand.

Invisible Bottlenecks

The problem with offices is that you cannot typically see where the bottlenecks are. In part this is because office work is electronic and therefore queues of work are largely invisible. But there are other factors, like the fact that overtime for salaried workers is not typically accounted for very precisely in offices. Everyone will say they are "busy" (and they are!), and working overtime (some more regularly than others), but it is likely irregular, and no one can tell you specifically how many hours/week on average. "I'm overworked" could mean a 50-hour week or a 60-hour week. No one typically times their work in an office. In a factory, in contrast, where there are wage workers, the payroll accountants can usually tell you exactly how many hours were worked (and how much in wages the plant paid) in overtime hours last pay period. I am not suggesting that office workers should punch-in and punch-out with time cards—I am saying that when there is evidence of overtime being worked (in significant amounts and/or for a significantly long period of time) in an office, it should be investigated as a potential bottleneck because it is both bad for morale *and* customers. As we have seen, if we counteract resource efficiency with flow efficiency, we often find we can serve customers better with *less* effort, not more.

OVERTIME AS PROFESSIONAL VIRTUE

I once questioned an executive about why his staff was constantly working overtime and he was genuinely puzzled by my question. He replied, somewhat defensively, "Ken, these people are *professionals*. They don't just go home at five o'clock". As I discussed in Chapter 1, people like to boast about being busy and working long hours in many professional settings. It is part of the corporate culture in certain industries (like investment banking), and more generally part of the work culture in countries like Korea and Japan.

Employees are not bad people for working overtime. While some work long hours only to get to the next rung of their career ladder (where they will likely work even longer hours, but for more pay), most employees work overtime for benevolent reasons: they want to serve their customers, feel like they are contributing as much as their peers, and meet their commitments. This customer dedication is admirable in the short-term but can become problematic if it decreases morale and increases voluntary leaves. Unfortunately, overtime for professional, salaried workers in corporate America has become such a cultural norm that it is tacitly expected. Yet there is plenty of evidence that it is not good for business or for individual mental and physical health to have lots of overtime as a "normal" part of the job on a sustained basis[1].

Companies cannot dictate what people do outside of work (nor should they), but they do have a large influence on how much non-work time employees get. Requiring employees to spend less time at work can be thought of as a long-term investment in their well-being. It is like having management say to them, "I don't want you to wake up one day in middle age and have a deep regret that life has passed you by". That may seem odd, given that younger employees are not likely to be thinking 10 or 20 years ahead about their potential mid-life crises. And, in this day and age, they are not likely to be working for the same company during their middle-age. But is that really a good reason not to care about them?

Bottlenecks are additionally hard to see in office work because everyone, like Jen and Jane in our example, works on multiple units of work for different customers in multiple value streams. If they are underutilized in the delivery of one service or product, they will find work to do on another service or product. We love to multitask, in part, for the sake of variety. Think about it: do you perform the same singular task over and over again all day? If some office workers were visibly sitting around idle while others were toiling away ardently, it would be much easier to find bottlenecks. But we simply cannot see bottlenecks the way we might see the inventory of half-finished widgets (for one product type) piling up in a queue at a specific station on an assembly line, while other stations downstream are idle. No one is truly underutilized (or, at least, they are not idle) in an office, and nearly everyone has some sort of backlog. Thus if you were to ask Jen or Jane how their work was going, they would say that they are very busy and have no capacity, even though technically, if they were dedicated exclusively to the widget value stream in Figure 8.1, they would have spare capacity. The constant multitasking of office work obscures bottlenecks from easy view.

If you were the CEO and you could see the entire value stream like we can in Figure 8.1, what would you do? You might first thank everyone for working so hard, but then, not wanting to keep your customers waiting, you would probably assume Bob was the problem and try to figure out how to get Bob to work faster. You might send a fairly terse note to Bob's boss. Or perhaps you would send in your "Lean Team" to go do some sort of "Rapid Improvement Event" to eliminate "waste" in Bob's area. Regardless of the means, if you managed to get Bob's process capacity up to, say, four widgets/week (assuming this does not cause any other prob-lems), the customer would experience a gain in lead time by one widget/week because we have now raised the lower limit of production to four. Bob and Joe now share the honor of being the slowest process in the value stream (see Figure 8.2). And this is genuinely better than the three widgets/week that the customer was receiving before, so it really *is* a customer-felt improvement. Now the value stream is producing four widgets/week and the bottleneck has moved from Bob to Joe's process (note rule of bottle-necks #1). The problem is that the value stream is still not yet perform-ing at quite a level to satisfy customer expectations. In the context of this one product or service, Jen and Jane still have spare capacity, and the only queue (or the build-up of "inventory") is found in front of Joe, since he is still not yet at five, the rate of customer demand.

Bob's boss calls you up (remember, you are CEO) and crows, "Problem's fixed! Bob can now process four widgets a week!". As CEO, you thank Bob's boss for this pleasing news, but your healthy sense of skepticism still leaves some doubt in your mind. So, you go out to speak to some customers to ver-ify if the value stream has truly been "fixed" or not, just to be sure. The cus-tomers say, "Well, it's better than before, but it's still not quite fast enough for our needs". If you were CEO, would the improvement of Bob's process capac-ity be considered an unambiguous "win"? What would your next step be?

Usually, and for a variety of reasons (most of which are not hard to figure out), the CEO of most traditionally managed companies does not spend a lot of time looking closely at specific processes like Bob's. She leaves operations

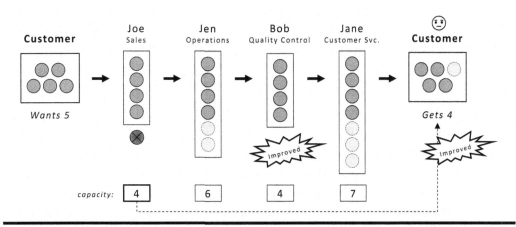

Figure 8.2 Bob's Process Capacity Has Improved from Three to Four Widgets/Week. Overall Lead Time Has Improved to This New Lowest Rate of Production: Four Widgets/Week (Joe and Bob).

to others lower down in her chain of command. If everyone takes care of their respective functional areas, as they are expected and incentivized to do, the CEO believes that the overall speed of delivery will be adequate to what the customer expects. In a simple, mechanical, cause-and-effect system, where the whole is no more than the sum of the parts, this thinking makes sense. If the executives take care of the bigger parts—setting the strategic direction of the vertical functions—and the lower-level managers take care of the smaller parts—the performance of teams and individuals within each vertical function—then the performance of the whole, the value stream that moves horizontally toward a customer, will simply take care of itself. Or so the logic goes. There is no perceived need or desire for executives to get "down in the weeds" of operations, especially when their calendars are already so overstuffed with meetings with other executives, shareholders, customers, suppliers, partners, media, government regulators, and so on.

No one in upper management typically will know that it is Bob's process that is the bottleneck for that specific product. Regrettably, even Bob's immediate boss likely does not know that Bob's process is the bottleneck. Bob's boss compares Bob's individual performance to that of Bob's peers (who perform approximately the same type of tasks) within the same team, not to the rates of production of other functional areas up and down the horizontal value stream. He believes it is not his job and not his concern to worry about what speed *other* teams do their work. After all, he is evaluated based on how fast *his* team can perform its specific tasks.

But even if Bob's boss *is* aware that Bob's process is underperforming, the cure may be worse than the disease. The method he will likely use to improve Bob's productivity is the familiar go-to strategy of "set the targets and hold 'em accountable". This sort of "Deliverology[2]" has become the primary tool of modern industrial management. Bob's boss will likely deliver a message that sounds something like, "I'm going to keep an eye on your weekly productivity numbers. The CEO is saying customers are unhappy, so I need you to be at four … or more". The unspoken subtext is, of course, "Work faster, or else…!". Unfortunately, the successful execution of the "setting targets and holding them accountable" strategy in this value stream rests on some flawed assumptions: namely, that Bob is not currently working as hard as he could be—that he has got some spare effort up his sleeve that he is withholding—and that he can improve his rate of production because it is within his uniquely individual ability to do so. And, further, what truly motivates Bob most to cough up this effort he has apparently been withholding is the fear of negative consequences (i.e. the threat of a poor performance review).

Yet chances are very high that Bob is working as hard as he possibly can. He probably wants to improve, but *does not know how*, exactly. His work is not only dependent on his current abilities, knowledge, and work ethic, but the work performance of a half-dozen other teams that supply him with information, as well as the performance of the tools (i.e. technology) he uses to do his job. Having his boss tell him he is underperforming likely just makes him feel demoralized. Even his boss knows, deep down, that Bob's lower productivity could be due to unreliable software, inadequate training, incomplete and/or inaccurate work being passed to him from Joe, a lack of clarity on the priority of work, personal issues, or a host of other reasons completely or partially beyond his individual control. Unfortunately, Bob's boss does not have time to contemplate the complexities of the situation. He is getting pressure from the big boss upstairs and needs to fix this problem quickly. Setting targets and holding individuals accountable is the only quick fix method he knows.

Bob will likely try his best to work harder, but without being able to improve his process, this just means longer hours. And even when Bob, now resentful that he is working longer hours, boosts his productivity to four widgets/week, it still means that everyone upstream from him has to also produce a minimum of four/week for Bob to meet his boss' expectations. Joe's process cannot, say, suddenly become understaffed due to an unforeseen re-org, medical leave, promotion, or vacation. Technology cannot have any unanticipated lapses or downtime. And no one can suddenly ask anyone in the value stream to work on a special, "urgent" project for a senior executive, thereby limiting the resources available to widget production. If the actual productivity of Joe's process goes below three (Bob's process' previous rate), the overall speed of delivery, from the customer's perspective, will actually get *worse*—remember, a value stream is only as fast as its *slowest* step. See Figure 8.3, where Bob's capacity has increased to four, but Joe's (for whatever reason) has now declined to three: the customer is only receiving value at the rate of three widgets/week. In short, the customer's experience is dependent on a whole lot more than just Bob meeting his numbers at any cost.

Balance

Instead of exhorting Bob to "do better and try harder to meet your numbers!" and then hoping for the best, there is a much better solution to this

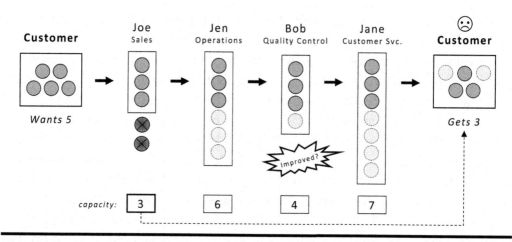

Figure 8.3   Overall Lead Time for the Customer Gets *Worse* Because, Even Though Bob Has Improved His Rate to Four, Joe's Has Declined to Three.

dilemma of randomly roaming bottlenecks, but it is not nearly as obvious: balance. That is, *balance the production rate across all the process steps in the entire value stream.* Since Jen and Jane's processes are "underutilized" (although they are very busy with other, but lesser priority, work), some of their labor could be redistributed to the slower process steps upstream from them, so that every process is producing at approximately the same rate and no one is working any harder. Jen could help out Joe and Jane could help out Bob. If every process could produce at an approximate rate of five widgets/week, there would be no additional effort required on the part of anyone, not even from Bob (and even if he is still working at his original rate of three/week), and all customers would be receiving value predictably, reliably, and at the speed and quantity they require.

What is important to note about the Figure 8.4 scenario is that Jen and Jane's processes actually have *less* capacity than they had previously, even though the value stream is now producing more for customers. How is this possible? Because, according to process bottleneck rule #2, as mentioned previously, the customer receives the product or service at the *slowest* rate in the entire value stream. According to the logic of this rule, there is absolutely no point in having Jen, Jane, or anyone else working faster than the slowest rate in the value stream. All they would be doing is creating bottlenecks. This is at the heart of a common but seemingly paradoxical saying in Lean thinking: "you've got to go slow to go fast".

Of course, this is all so easy … on paper. This simple example relies on a couple of key assumptions: shared priorities and the ability to share work. Shared priorities mean that everyone is working on the single most

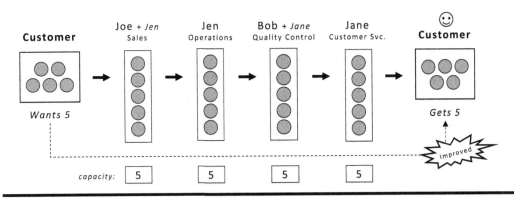

Figure 8.4 The Capacity of Each Process Step and the Actual Rates of Production Have Been *Balanced* across the Value Stream.

important piece of work at any given moment. In the example in Figure 8.4, the three different functional areas have agreed what their common priority is, and everyone is clear about this. For instance, if Jane is working on something she perceives to be more important (perhaps because her boss has suddenly told her to work on something urgent at the last minute) than the current work of Bob, she is not going to be inclined to help him out. Since leaders are typically measured by the productivity within their own area (and by different bosses, who each have their own individual urgent requests), they are not inclined to lend a hand to other areas that may be struggling simply because they fear it will jeopardize their own performance, even if they know overall customer outcomes would improve. Siloed goals and key performance indicators (KPIs), misaligned with end-customer outcomes erode the level of teamwork and collaboration required for work to flow across value streams. For a company to be truly customer-focused (instead of just saying it is), competitive mindsets like "I'll work on *my* KPIs and you worry about *your* KPIs" need to be replaced with "We will work on *our* KPIs"—where our KPIs are aligned to customer wants and needs, and fulfilled by a balanced and flexible value stream in which every team is working toward the same purpose: producing more customer value.

The second assumption is that Jen and Jane are capable of doing the work of Joe and Bob, respectively. This implies that Jen and Jane possess the skillsets needed to do at least some of the tasks that Bob and Joe normally do. As with establishing company-wide, commonly shared goals, this is easy to say, hard to do. The phenomenal benefits of Lean are not gained through quick and easy fixes. Yet with a little creativity and a lot of hard work and persistence, these hurdles to improving customer-felt performance can most often be overcome.

The third assumption here is that Jen and Jane both have spare capacity to go around. If Jen's capacity were only five instead of six widgets/week, or Jane's capacity any fewer than seven, the entire value stream would still be unable to meet customer requirements of five widgets/week. In this case, further improvements or additional capacity would have to be added to the value stream.

Nonetheless, the big benefit of balancing out workloads is that not only do customers enjoy faster lead times, but employees are also not overburdened. Asking Bob to "meet his numbers at all costs" without providing him with the skills and tools to improve, does not respect him very much. Instead, we can redesign the allocation of labor in the value stream. In a better designed value stream, no one has to work harder or longer hours, and yet customer expectations are met or exceeded. This is how achieving better flow leads to more respect for people. And when you respect people, you get better individual performance too. Take care of the design of the whole value stream, and the parts will often take care of themselves.

People and technology are easy to see, so they are easy to blame. If only you could hire better people and have better IT systems, all your problems would be solved, right? Not entirely. What is always needed, regardless of the qualifications of your people and the sophistication of your technology, is a system to integrate and coordinate the people and the tools (the IT systems) to produce more value for customers. That means thinking and acting in ways that are not always "easy-to-see, easy-to-do". (Better IT systems and human skillsets, after all, can usually be acquired simply by *buying* them. Throwing money at problems may not seem "easy" if your company cannot afford it—but it is still a solution that requires minimal creativity or thought). Achieving sustained business success is rare because good thinking is rare. Figuring out how to remove bottlenecks and balance the rates of production—at the systemic, value stream level, using both people and technology—is hard and rare. Yet the best Lean companies manage to do it. Respect for People. Flow. Easy to say, hard to do.

Three Main Takeaways

1. Not only is condensing the value stream important, it also needs to be balanced: each process step needs to have approximately equal workloads or else a bottleneck will form at the slowest step.

2. Bottlenecks are hard to see in offices because: the work is invisible—it moves around electronically; office workers generally work in many different value streams or have multiple work items in progress at once; and they do not usually record overtime hours worked.

3. Balancing a value stream is hard to do in practice because: vertical silos are reinforced through distinct priorities and "key performance indicators" in each functional area; the skillsets of one functional area are not necessarily useful for other areas; and the entire value stream, even after workload balancing, may still be below the capacity required to meet customer demand.

Notes

1. The stress that kills American workers. *The Economist.* July 21, 2018: www.economist.com/business/2018/07/21/the-stress-that-kills-american-workers (accessed May 21, 2019).

2. "Deliverology" is the title of a popular business book (and its related sequels) by Michael Barber, primarily aimed at government and public education. It basically advocates for a private-sector "meet the numbers" approach (made famous at GE during the Jack Welch years of the 1980s and 90s) to be applied to public sector institutions. For a full analysis of this method, see Seddon, John. 2014. *The Whitehall Effect.* Charmouth, UK: Triarchy Press.

Chapter 9

Creating Balance

"Yes, but how do I implement this in *my* office?" is a question I often get, often accompanied by a woeful tale about an intransigent boss or corporate culture. Aside from the principle of making the work visible, I cannot give you some easy paint-by-numbers approach. Real improvement, unfortunately, requires that you have to think about it yourself. Lean is about learning to think differently. No one can do that for you. I can, however, offer a framework that might help stimulate your thinking.

There are only three basic ingredients to the concept of balance: people, time, and work (see Figure 9.1)[1]. You can bake a lot of different cakes simply by manipulating the quantities of one or more of these ingredients. The trick

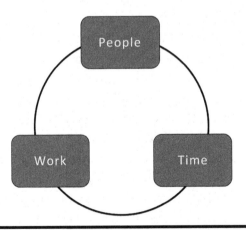

Figure 9.1   Balance Is the Constant Adjustment of Three Factors: People, Work, and Time.

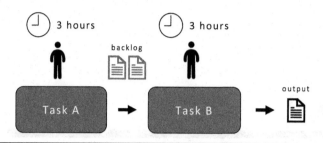

Figure 9.2   Two-Step Process Where it Takes Six Hours (Total Elapsed Time) to Produce One Unit of Output, and a Backlog of Two Units Is Stuck in Front of Task B.

is to find the best recipe for your unique workplace. Your recipe for balance will involve a lot of experimentation before you get it just right. And you will need to constantly improve upon it as conditions change over time. It is the *flexibility* of the system—its ability to identify and respond to abnormal conditions—that is just as important as its stability.

Balancing the system is important because, in any given process or value stream, some process steps take longer than others. If you think about the simple bucket brigade example from the previous chapter, some buckets might be very heavy and take longer to pass to the next person, while others might be small and light and can be passed more rapidly. In more complex work, the variation in the duration of even two tasks being performed within the same value stream can be huge, for example, the credit analysis of a solvent, established, long-time borrower may be relatively quick and easy, but the subsequent risk analysis of its overseas subsidiaries' environmental practices may be long and difficult.

As an illustration, let's say two separate teams need to complete one task each, in sequence, to produce one final output: Task A and then Task B. Task A takes one person hour and Task B takes three person hours (see Figure 9.2).

Figure 9.2 depicts a simplified model of how work is typically organized: one person, one task, regardless of how long a task takes. As a consequence of this work design, a bottleneck will naturally result between Task A and Task B over time. That is, work will electronically "pile up" in an invisible, electronic queue of WIP waiting for Task B, which has one-third the capacity of Task A. Because employees are concerned mostly about what their boss thinks and how to meet their numbers, Task A does not care that Task B is overwhelmed with work, while Task B is overworked (but very resource-efficient) and resentful of Task A.

People

When it comes to people, cross-training is the key to creating a flexible work-force and balanced flow. While highly-skilled experts cannot always switch positions (e.g. lawyers cannot become application infrastructure analysts as easily as hourly workers can be trained on different stations along an assem-bly line), there are still many ways that you can expand and develop people's skillsets in a more expert, knowledge-work environment. For instance, some-one who does company valuations in the technology sector could learn to do similar valuations of companies in the mining sector. A software developer specializing in .NET can learn C# or Python. And, as in any workplace, more senior people in the same department can (and should) convey knowledge to more junior people through coaching, mentoring, and teaching. The advan-tage of cross-training is that it helps individuals grow and develop new skills as part of their professional development, while also creating more flexibility to balance the value stream for the benefit of the customer.

The best way to mitigate and manage the sort of variation in workloads found in Figure 9.2 is to balance the "production rate" of each process step by scheduling different amounts of people devoted to different process steps. Since Task B takes three times as long as Task A, you ideally want to have three times the number of employees performing Task B as you do Task A in order to balance both tasks.

In Figure 9.3, more people are allocated to the longer task (Task B), balancing the elapsed time evenly across both tasks. As a result, we have a shorter lead time of only two hours, no backlog, and fewer total hours worked (four). Swarming people on the work is a highly effective way to condense lead time and deliver faster to customers. If you have seven projects to do and seven employees, you are much better off picking the single most important of all the seven projects and assigning all seven

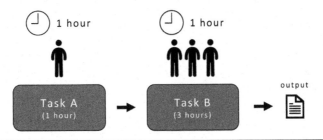

Figure 9.3   Achieving Balance through Distribution of People.

employees to that *one* project rather than choosing to allocate one project per employee, as is the natural tendency.

This method of allocating additional people to a task is, of course, not always feasible. In your current state, you may not have enough staff with the right skillsets available at the right time. That's ok. That should prompt you to ask why this is the case and undertake some problem solving to implement countermeasures (e.g. cross-training, hiring strategies) to address the situation. But it may not even be desirable. Sometimes adding people to a task will not help. In many circumstances, there are "diminishing marginal returns to labor", as economists would say. In simpler language, this means that adding more qualified people to a task decelerates its completion rate until it reaches a point where adding people actually *decreases* the completion velocity (that is, it is faster to use *fewer* people; see Figure 9.4). You can easily imagine this happening on an assembly line where there are more workers than there is space, tools, parts, etc. This is just as true in highly-skilled knowledge work, where a specialized task or job is often (but not always) best completed by a single expert worker. Does a project complete faster if there are two project managers instead of one? Would Picasso's paintings have been more valuable to art collectors had he trained a bunch of assistants to paint his paintings for him? Software developers have a name for it: Brooke's Law. This law describes the phenomenon of throwing

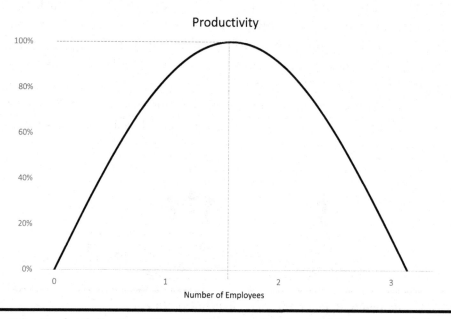

Figure 9.4 Productivity Can Often Decline As a Result of Adding More People.

headcount at a late software project, thereby causing it to complete even later. But there is no universal law of workforce planning that applies to all work situations in all industries all the time: just as trying to make a baby is usually—but not always—optimized by involving two people, it really depends on the nature of the work and the desired outcome! Companies need to experiment with different configurations of the work breakdown and the allocation of people and time to the work to find out what works best for them in their context.

EXTREME CROSS-TRAINING AT MENLO INNOVATIONS

The example of Menlo Innovations, the remarkable software company I mentioned in Chapter 7, is arguably the apex of cross-training. The company has a work system that pairs all its programmers, so that two programmers sit side by side at the same desk: one keyboard, two people. One codes, while the other watches, comments, questions. Both learn. They take turns at the keyboard and, amazingly, the pairs change *every week*. Really. As Menlo CEO Richard Sheridan has written[2], visitors to Menlo often state how amazed they are that the company can withstand such a "productivity loss" when 50% of their coders are not actively coding at any given time (note the concern over *resource* inefficiency, not flow inefficiency, on the part of the visitors). But Sheridan writes that there is no productivity loss; only productivity *gains*.

Pairing and rotation means that nobody becomes overly specialized in their knowledge of a specific coding language, so nearly anyone can work on nearly any project at nearly any time, while everyone is developing his/her skillset far more broadly than their industry peers. (The world of software development, like many other knowledge-work professions, tends to be very specialized into silos of expertise). Pairing also means that everyone has what is essentially a full-time, private tutor, so they learn fast. The extra set of eyes means most errors are detected and corrected right away, resulting in far less rework; and the extra brain helps the other get "unstuck" and come up with creative solutions faster (two brains are, after all, better than one). The social benefits are also huge: everyone can take their vacation or a sick day whenever they want (with no guilt) because they always have a backup; and they develop a familiarity, if not a deep friendship, with every single one of their colleagues. Trust, teamwork, and collaboration are just part of the Menlo culture. The design of the work elicits these behaviors.

What is really remarkable is that Menlonians (as they call themselves) focus so intensely on their work. Just by virtue of having someone sitting beside you,

you do not tend to check personal email or browse Facebook in moments of distraction. You do not check the sports scores or start texting your friends and family about trivial matters. There is no hard rule at Menlo against any of these behaviors. The intense work focus is just a natural consequence resulting from the paired working arrangement. Professional workers in more conventional working arrangements struggle to squeeze in three to four hours of "real" value-adding work into every eight-hour day because of all the meetings and interruptions (work-related or not). Menlonians do not have these problems and accomplish twice as much as their competitors in the same time frame. Cross-training at Menlo not only improves flow efficiency; it improves resource efficiency too!

Time

When it is impractical to add people to a task, an alternative way to avoid the bottleneck that appears in Figure 9.2 is to diminish the amount of *time* that the person performing Task A spends on it each day. Ideally, it should be a third of the time that is dedicated to Task B (see Figure 9.5). Even if the person working on Task A in Figure 9.5 did *nothing* for the three working hours after 2 PM, this method is an improvement on the scenario of Figure 9.2, because the lead time is now only four hours instead of six and there is no bottleneck. It is admittedly not as fast as the scenario in Figure 9.3, where the lead time is only two hours: swarming people on the work is always better than distributing the work across many people. But when adding additional people to the work starts to yield diminishing returns, which it frequently can, apportioning time to tasks is often the best compromise.

Achieving balance through the coordination of time requires having a standard work schedule. When Leaniacs like me talk about "standards",

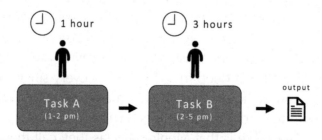

Figure 9.5 Achieving Balance through Distribution of Time.

audiences—especially professionals—usually bristle. Nobody likes being told what to do, perhaps least of all professional experts. The word "standard", like the word "process", connotes coercion, restrictions, and inflexibility: the weapons of a stultifying bureaucracy; the source of everything they perceive is *wrong* with the company. And, sadly, they are often right. Plenty of leaders, not appreciating the bottom-up, respect for the people aspect of Lean, often impose standards and processes on their people … and end up making things worse.

But standards do not have to be crippling. People often think that standards apply only to the *content* of the work: what task to do, how, in what sequence, to what specifications, and so on. In other words, lots of specific details telling the employees exactly *what* to do and *how* to go about making their widget. This makes sense in manufacturing where there is a high degree of precision required to meet the engineering quality standards. Not surprisingly, people who work in jobs that require more reliance on analysis, interpretation, and synthesis of multiple sources of information find such standards inadequate in satisfying their customers.

What many do not realize is that standards can apply to the *timing* of the work. Your work may or may not benefit from having detailed and documented standards for what to do and how to do it, but it can almost always benefit from some standardization around *when* you do it and for approximately how long. We saw this in our previous example of Carlos' reimbursement and we can see this in Figure 9.5 too.

In manufacturing, frequent line changeovers are generally understood to be costly and time-consuming—this is precisely why Lean companies work on perfecting quick changeovers. Because there are no heavy dies to changeover in an office environment, switching between tasks is (wrongly) assumed not to have a large cost. It just involves switching from one window to another on your PC. You do not even have to get out of your chair! Thus frequent "line changeovers" are expected as part of office culture. It is just the "way things are done around here". The information that triggers "production" flies between actors in the value stream as fast as light, and your priorities (and workload) are expected to change in an instant. You have a lot of different work for different value streams to manage, and you switch between them too quickly and too often. You get last-minute, urgent, unplanned requests, often from people with higher paygrades, that derail your plans for the entire day (or week, or month). The cost to frequent changeovers in an office, of course, is not in the low utilization of labor, but in the massive amounts of WIP created—and the subsequent delays in the flow of value to the customer—every time you switch priorities. No one in your office is making the same widget over and over again. The main problem then becomes a lack of synchronization, not a lack of compliance with quality standards.

This situation of discontinuity and imbalance is only exacerbated by handoffs. If you cannot do everything from marketing to accounts receivable in the same value stream, you are going to have to handoff your work at some point. So, to optimize it, coordinating *when* you do it helps it flow: the work keeps moving by minimizing delay and interruption. As we saw in the case of Carlos, when the upstream process hands-off to the next downstream process with little to no delay in between processes, value flows much faster to the end customer. If Team A works on a specific process step in Value Stream One in the morning, Team B, who receives the work and performs the next process step in Value Stream One should perform their process step in the afternoon. If Team B decides to work on its specific process step in Value Stream One "whenever they get around to it", all the work that Team A has done will sit around idle (WIP!) until Team B gets a chance to work on it. So having a common goal (customers), common priorities (which customers first), and commonly understood standard timing (aka scheduling) for the work is important to compressing the wait time and improving flow. This is, as we know, the importance of continuity. But if we schedule the right amount of time for each team to complete their work without rushing or stressing, it also creates balance and respects those doing the work. Whatever it is that you do, and however you do it, *when* you do it, and for how long, matters.

Work

The third option for establishing balance is to break down the work itself into smaller bits and then distribute them evenly across a fixed amount of people. In Figure 9.6, we subdivide task B (which takes three hours in total to complete) into three hour-long parts: B1, B2, B3. Then we re-allocate B1 to Person A, so that both persons A and B have work of equal duration (two hours each).

Note this scenario yields a lead time that is just as good as the one in Figure 9.5 (four hours) but still not as good as Figure 9.3 (two hours).

In practice, of course, achieving balance through the redistribution of work can be just as hard to achieve as redistributing people or time.

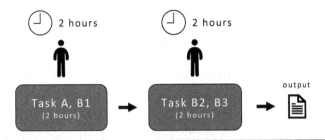

Figure 9.6   Achieving Balance through Distribution of Work.

Dividing up the work into smaller bits and then redistributing it implies people have the skills to do the work. And, as we know, in the short-run, cross-training takes time from the teacher and time from the learner. Yet increased staffing flexibility has massive payoffs in the long-run.

Additionally, like adding additional people, dividing up the work may not always be desirable. For instance, if you need to write up an analysis of, say, the effects of US steel tariffs on the global economy, it is not always wise to break up the analysis into smaller, discrete parts that can be performed by different people. The quality of the analysis comes from the fact that the author comprehends the whole situation, not just one-third of it. Further, that comprehension depends on her drawing from her reservoir of knowledge and expertise: her brain. She is an expert in the economics of the steel industry, and one cannot easily subdivide all aspects of an individual's unique expertise. When it comes to "thinking work" like analysis and report writing, having one person doing it makes sense much of the time. The additional work of coordinating and synthesizing the separate pieces together into a coherent whole again at the end might not outweigh the benefits of distributing the work. Could you break up a single gall-bladder surgery into discrete parts and share it between two or more surgeons? Practically speaking, probably not.

Despite these potential restrictions, be careful not to think that your work is so complex that all of it is unshareable. We should always challenge the "unshareability" of our work before we dismiss it as impossible. When I was a child, my mother would take me to my family doctor for a checkup and he would measure my weight, height, reflexes, blood pressure, and so on. Nowadays, a nurse or medical assistant takes these routine measures and the doctor limits his time to interpreting the results and prescribing further courses of treatment if required. Turns out some "expert" work does not need to be done by certain types of experts like medical doctors! As a result, doctors can see more patients (and bill more fees) without diminishing the quality of medical care that patients receive. Similarly, underwriters can sometimes divide up the quantitative and qualitative aspects of the credit analysis involved in a financing agreement. A team of economists could divide up their US steel tariff analysis by grouping it into different sections for different trading partner regions, either by geographic region or by trade volumes. It is a matter of trying different configurations of work, people, and time—and then measuring the outcomes. As always, small-scale experimentation, or "learning by doing" is the only way to learn which arrangement will be optimal for your work.

MAKING EXPERT KNOWLEDGE EXPLICIT

Just because knowledge work happens inside someone's head does not mean the knowledge has to be trapped in there forever. Two business school professors studied the large Indian IT company Wipro in 2011 and found that "a surprisingly large amount of knowledge work can be specified". They noted that because many knowledge workers perform a mix of both judgment-based work and more logical, algorithmic thinking, and rapidly switch between the two, they assume that *all* of their work cannot be standardized. Additionally, people assume that all their knowledge is tacit because they have trouble articulating their thinking in words. The professors found that, in reality, effective questioning can often allow a company to extract, document, and ultimately improve on the knowledge and thinking behind more repeatable processes[3].

Dealing with Variation

What if your work takes more (or less) time to complete than the time scheduled? High variability is common in office-based knowledge work. When you ask anyone how long any given task takes, they will say, "it depends" and then, if prompted, offer only a range of time. This is because our work is often *emergent*: we often do not know what we are dealing with and how long it will take until we start working on it. We must accept that this variability will always be—to some degree—part of the nature of our work. We can never eliminate variation entirely, but we can manage it better by studying two patterns: (1) the duration of the work; and (2) volume of the work (relative to staffing).

To handle variation in duration/complexity, start with the 80/20 rule. Aim to have the time scheduled for the completion of each task to accommodate about 80% of the range of time variation. You may need to collect some data over time to establish what the time range is that captures 80% of the cases. It can be 70/30 or 90/10, depending on whatever makes the most sense based on some solid data analysis.

For instance, it may take 2–5 days to draft and sign a certain type of contract approximately 80% of the time and take 6–20 days the other 20% of the time. Plan for the upper limit of the 80%. Plan to produce 80% of contracts in 5 days or fewer and 20% of them in 20 days—and then promise your customers the same. Try to determine if the case is destined for the fast or slow lane as soon as possible (i.e. upon receipt of the request) and communicate this to the customer immediately, to manage expectations. Then have dedicated staff work in each lane—either the fast or the slow one—with the ability to shift people fluidly between lanes as needed. You'll need to continuously monitor the results to ensure conditions are "normal". If you finish your work earlier than the prescribed time, the customer will typically not mind and you can: (1) help out colleagues in the other lane if they are struggling to keep up; or (2) have a reserve of important but less urgent tasks to fill in any spare gaps in your time schedule.

The second dimension to variation is to know what volume to expect. Say you get, usually, 25–30 contracts per week, but occasionally (e.g. 20% of the time) you get up to 50. Staff for the maximum of the upper limit of the normal amount (e.g. 30) and then frequently monitor the volume in the queue. If it exceeds 30 (or whatever your threshold is), then you need to have a Plan B. Similarly, if the distribution of regular duration versus long duration (complex) contracts is not 80/20, you need to have a Plan C. Perhaps, as the case necessitates, others can help out; people can work a little overtime (and take time off later); or some other work can be deprioritized and rescheduled. Every team must experiment with different countermeasures to find what works best for them to improve their flow without unduly overburdening employees. The crucial elements are:

1. Criteria: there are commonly agreed-upon criteria established for when work volume falls in the "normal" (80%) or "abnormal" (20%) range for both the slow and fast lanes.
2. Signal: there is a visual signal to indicate if the workload is currently normal or abnormal.
3. Plan: there is a plan (aka standard work) in place to respond to changing conditions.

The whole team must understand and agree upon all three of these elements. After establishing a definition, do not waste time arguing what is or is not "normal"—use data and change the definition only if the data warrants it. The signaling mechanism (usually something as low-tech as a colored flag—like a magnet on a whiteboard) tells the whole team what the current condition is. The scary sounding "standard work" is simply the plan that everyone follows in response to this signal to bring the current condition back to normal (or to maintain it at normal).

The way it works is very straightforward: the signal communicates to all the employees participating in the value stream when they need to shift to Plan B because they are in the 20% zone—where work volume and/or complexity is exceeding the capacity needed 80% of the time. Everyone knows ahead of time what Plan B requires them to do. The manager of the team should *not* have to get involved. If there are good data (updated frequently and displayed visibly), clear signals (normal/abnormal), and the whole team understands and agrees to the plan for each scenario, the team should be able to naturally adjust *without* any management intervention. Of course you should expect to go through multiple iterations of improving the plan before the manager can fully step away. This then eventually allows management to focus on more value-adding things like developing employees, working on longer-term improvement projects (e.g. information system improvements), fostering collaboration with other teams, or finding more customers.

Note that if the tasks take *less* time than the time allotted, there should *also* be a plan. For instance, this time can be used to temporarily help out other teams who might be behind, to check and respond to email, to learn something new (by, say, reading a work-related article or watching a short video), or to just take a break to relax (see Sidebar). I am not promoting laziness here: often the most creative, innovative ideas come to mind when we have a little time to think, dream, and imagine. Counterintuitive as it might seem, what one should *not* do, at least if the conditions are still "normal", is to cherry-pick some item from the queue, because it will have a negative effect on the flow of the entire system. This would be like being a waiter and starting to deliver fries to all the tables waiting for their food, without thinking about what other items need to be delivered at the same time to ensure each customer and each table get their entire meal in a coordinated fashion.

So, go out there and check on the brigade: how many buckets are in process right now? How full are they? At what pace are they moving? How long, on average, does it take to pass one? Is this normal or abnormal? Is the customer satisfied with this pace? Are some or all employees overburdened? Where is the bottleneck? How do you know? How you can redistribute people, buckets, and/or water right now to achieve better balance?

If your office is like most offices, you have little or no data on work volumes or completion rates—so gathering relevant process data (volume and time!) is where most offices need to start. My experience is that there is only a small subset of office staff who love to work with data. The data-crunching nerds that do exist are rare and valuable assets to your business: entrust them with the data gathering and analysis!

YEAH, BUT …

- *Yeah, but … #1*: how can I stick to one task at a time when I have jobs that last months or even years? Obviously large, long-duration projects (like writing a book) have to be broken down into smaller parts. Ideally, we are working on the most important and urgent part. However, priorities change over time. The longer we work on one task, the higher in urgency become the other tasks that you are not doing. At some point in time, another task will surpass the one you are currently working on in urgency. This could be something obvious like eating or sleeping. But it could be an urgent request from your boss' boss, too. It is ideal then, to break down your larger tasks into smaller parts and try to complete the smaller parts quickly without interruption. The trick is to complete smaller subtasks as quickly as possible, and that happens when there are as few interruptions and distractions as possible. Intense, deep focus gets things done faster.

    Your boss' boss probably does not appreciate this, however, and so until you can convince him otherwise, you have to be agile enough to respond to urgent requests. This is still best handled by breaking down your larger tasks into smaller ones, so that you can at least finish off a subtask (ideally even delivering some value to the customer) before switching to the more urgent task. The idea is that you do not have to start all over at the beginning after every interruption—that is just wasteful rework.

- *Yeah, but … #2*: what if you timebox your work but it takes longer than anticipated? The risk of working on one thing at a time is that it takes you forever to finish that one thing, and you never get around to starting anything else. Timeboxing—giving yourself deadlines—is a great way to avoid the real risk of work expanding to fill the time available (Parkinson's Law). Sometimes, despite best efforts, you will not meet those deadlines. This may then have a domino effect on the next process steps that are waiting for your handoff. The only way to avoid this is: (1) buffer your time estimates so that you allocate enough time for the most complex case, not the simplest; (2) get better at estimating. This takes practice; (3) communicate frequently with your downstream partners to ensure expectations are managed and allowing them to make adjustments; (4) ask for help. If you can share parts of the work to get it done faster, share it.

Agility

Striving for balance causes us to focus on designing the value stream for *flexibility*, rather than wishing people or technology were better than they are. Like walking a tightrope, balance is a dynamic state of constant adjustment. We constantly need to identify and respond to changing conditions, adjusting from Plan A to B to C and back again, sometimes multiple times a day. We also need to adjust for seasonality (are there times of year when your volumes tend to be higher than usual? If so, does everyone know what the plan is?).

Lean does not solve all your problems. Nothing will. There will always be problems in business. There are many things that, to a considerable extent, a business cannot control. These can be both external, like the unpredictable peaks and valleys of customer demand, or internal, like unforeseen staffing shortages or technology downtime. Just as we cannot do anything about the force of gravity, we *can* learn to become a better tightrope walker—and to install a safety net! A firm does not gain competitive advantage through the elimination of problems, but through its ability to respond to and handle problems (or different conditions) with more agility and effectiveness. If we build the systemic capability to move people to the work where it is most needed, or work can be subdivided and transferred to different people, the value stream becomes far more flexible and dynamic, able to absorb all sorts of external complications and internal shocks much better, and continuously deliver consistent, predictable value to its customers. Guaranteed.

Three Main Takeaways

1. Finding the optimal way to balance work in a value stream involves experimenting with different combinations of people, time, and units of work. Generally speaking, swarming people on the work is the best way to increase flow.
2. It is not always possible or desirable to add people to a task or subdivide and distribute work because there can be secondary needs that outweigh the potential gains, such as the time and effort needed to coordinate and synthesize the parts back into a whole again. You have to run experiments and study the results to see what works.
3. The purpose of seeking balance is not to solve all the world's problems but to make you, your team, and ultimately your company more agile and effective in response to the inevitable variation in business conditions. A helpful three-pronged approach is: (1) using data to distinguish normal vs. abnormal conditions; (2) using visual signals to communicate the current condition; and (3) having standard plans in place so everyone knows what to do.

Notes

1. In the longer-run, you can also implement technological automation that may shorten the average duration of tasks.
2. Sheridan, Richard. 2013. *Joy, Inc*. New York: Penguin Group.
3. Staats, Bradley, and David M. Upton. Lean Knowledge Work. *Harvard Business Review*, October 2011: https://hbr.org/2011/10/lean-knowledge-work (accessed May 22, 2019).

Chapter 10

The CapCell Experiment

A commercial insurance underwriting and credit-granting group had a capacity problem. When a higher-paying job elsewhere in the company would occasionally lure away a more experienced underwriter, client service levels suffered. Since the more senior underwriters handled a portfolio of clients on a dedicated and personalized basis, filling these vacated positions with a junior person was difficult. The new underwriter would require a lot of training on the specific wants and needs of the customers in the portfolio they were taking on. The approximate time lag between when a position became vacant and when there was an adequately trained replacement available was four weeks. Consequently, teams found themselves short-staffed every time there was turnover. As a potential solution, leadership was contemplating creating a small pool of experienced underwriters to deploy into the vacant positions more quickly.

But then the capacity pressure worsened. The company had just launched a major, multi-year IT project to upgrade and modernize its legacy insurance underwriting systems. The insurance group knew that they would, within the next year, have to dedicate some subject matter experts from their regular operations on a full-time basis to support this important project. They would not be able to replace the staff seconded to the project, but they still had to serve their existing customers on the old IT system until the new one was ready. Suddenly leadership had to find "efficiencies", and fast.

This insurance group was organized into five separate sector teams, each comprised of multiple "cells" of underwriters who had specialized knowledge in certain key areas of the economy—such as oil and gas, mining, infrastructure, agriculture, light manufacturing, telecommunications, and so on—and each team underwrote the policies for companies only in their sectors of expertise. Leadership hypothesized that it could find some spare capacity in the fluctuations of the workloads. They knew that demand for insurance coverage in any given sector varied day-to-day and, more noticeably, at various times of the year. For instance, agriculture tends to be highly seasonal, and the volume of oil and gas policies tends to fluctuate with the price of crude. That meant there were peaks and valleys of demand for each team. At any given time, some teams were extremely busy while other teams had a lighter-than-normal workload. How could they leverage the underwriters who had a bit of spare capacity to help relieve those who were overloaded?

Figure 10.1 depicts this scenario. In this diagram, the vertical bars represent the volume of work for each team. Since the staffing in each team was a fixed number, variable work volumes overloaded some teams while leaving others with spare capacity. This meant inconsistent service for customers, who would have to wait longer if their policy was with an overloaded team, and less time if they were dealing with an underutilized team. In other words, the flow of work was uneven and unbalanced.

What the Insurance leaders did to address their situation was quite remarkable. They took their original idea of creating a small pool and made it bigger. To accomplish this, they gathered some data and determined the *minimum* number of staff required in each sector team to maintain a consistent lead time (the total elapsed time from when the customer requests insurance coverage to having an active policy that meets their coverage needs). They established their target staffing levels based on the *valleys* of the fluctuating demand, not the peaks, nor even the average.

The expected lead time for customers was five working days: one work week. (Note: the specific numbers have been fabricated for the sake of

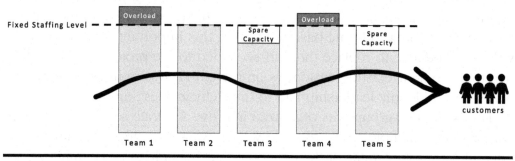

Figure 10.1 Unbalanced Employee Supply and Workload Demand Created Uneven Customer Experience.

illustration, yet the case is based on actual events). The group's analysis of the data told them that the total average weekly customer demand was 125 policies a week, and that it varied from 100 to 150. They wanted to find out the amount of staff needed to underwrite the *minimum* of 100 policies/week within the expected 5 days. In their current situation, they employed 50 people. With a bit of quick math[1], they figured out that they would need 40 people to underwrite 100 policies/week (see Figure 10.2).

Since the directors were seeking to reduce the total underwriting staff to align it with the *minimum* demand, they went to the managers of the five teams and told them that they had to give up ten staff in total, or two from each team. The managers would now have only 40 underwriters between their five teams. The managers were not overly pleased by this request. Their superiors were asking them to reduce their staff by 20%. They felt this was a big hit to their already strained capacity. *How were they possibly going to manage?* they asked themselves.

The good news, the directors continued, was that there would be a newly formed pool named the "CapCell", short for "Capacity Cell", of ten experienced underwriters who would be available to all sector teams when they were experiencing higher than usual demand. This would allow flexibility of staffing and reduce the variation in workloads that resulted when the supply of underwriters did not match and customer demand for policies in any given team[2].

The managers' first reaction was that it would never work. "We have sector expertise!", they claimed. "Each sector is different!", they protested. "You can't just ask an underwriter from the mining team to underwrite a policy in the retail sector. They are completely different industries!" Many underwriters had deep sector knowledge and were, additionally, very well acquainted with the specific needs of their biggest policy holders from their respective

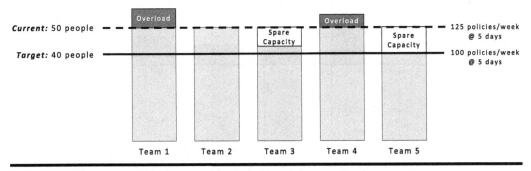

Figure 10.2 Analysis of Over- and Under-Staffing per Team, Relative to Workload, on Any Given Day, to Maintain a Constant Lead Time.

areas. Handing off this work to generic, jack-of-all-trades underwriters who did not know specific clients in specific sectors would, they felt, slow work down and provide a negative customer experience.

The directors listened to their concerns but did not give in. They told their managers that they did not expect 100% of the work to be shareable, but, nonetheless, that the managers would have to identify opportunities within their respective teams to share work with *any* underwriter, regardless of sector expertise. They would have to document and standardize the shared work to maintain the quality of service customers expected.

The managers agreed to try it. All the managers and directors would huddle briefly every morning in front of an electronic dashboard that displayed how many policies each team had in its queue. This determined which teams needed help, based on workload. Depending on each team's daily work volumes, the CapCell deployed up to ten underwriters into the teams that needed them (see Figure 10.3).

The underwriters, still a bit skeptical that the CapCell idea would work, were initially reluctant to share work. They felt protective of their clients and did not want to entrust work that they had previously done to a random underwriter from the CapCell who might not deliver the same level of quality their clients were accustomed to.

It did not take long, of course, for the work volumes to grow beyond minimum levels in some of the teams, so they had to share work with the CapCell—or start working lots of overtime and weekends. The challenge

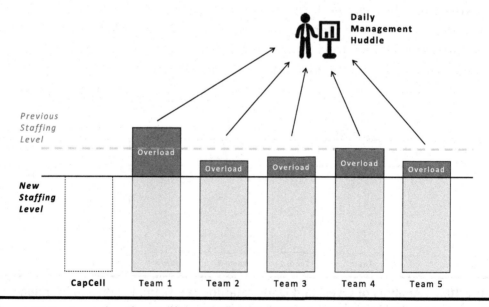

Figure 10.3   Lowering the Staffing Levels Initially Made Workloads *Worse*.

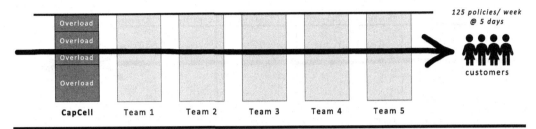

Figure 10.4   Balanced Flow Results from the Redistribution of Work. Customers Receive More Consistent Lead Times and Employees Do Not Feel Overburdened.

of finding work to share forced the sector-based teams to reflect on the nature of their work. After examining it closely, they discovered that they could share a higher proportion of the work with the CapCell than they had originally estimated. By constantly sharing and adjusting their workloads, the teams found that their workloads were a lot more balanced, with fewer peaks and valleys of demand, and predictable lead times for customers (see Figure 10.4).

There were spinoff benefits to this more leveled work that the directors had not even anticipated. On days when overall customer demand was below average, the CapCell underwriters were not all deployed to underwriting teams. To fill their days when not underwriting, CapCell employees worked on implementing improvement ideas, standardizing even more of the work and making it more shareable.

The leaders of the insurance group knew that the new design of the system and the implemented improvements were creating capacity gains, but they did not know exactly how much. They had a chance to find out when the IT project came knocking, five months into the CapCell experiment. The project's leadership asked for five people—full-time—and gave the insurance group a few months to figure out how they would meet this staffing request. Because of the capacity they had gained through their new workflow design, the leadership of the group did not need a few months. They felt confident they could support the project with 10% of their staff: they gave up four subject matter experts and a leader almost immediately. They suddenly went from 50 to 45 people, with seven people remaining in the CapCell and the other 38 distributed across the sector teams. And this 10% reduction in staff did not break the system: they maintained the expected customer lead time of 5 days without overburdening staff (see Figure 10.5). In fact, the net capacity gain was closer to 15%, because business volumes grew 4% year over year, and they were able to absorb this growth without increasing the 45 remaining staff.

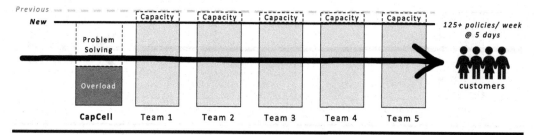

Figure 10.5 Improvements Carried out by CapCell Generated 10% Capacity Gains across All the Teams.

In addition to the gain in capacity, the CapCell experiment resulted in training more people across multiple sectors, adding more—not less—expertise and flexibility to the entire group. It gave the CapCell underwriters a greater breadth of experience from which to progress their careers. When there was turnover in a team, the group now had a pool of experienced people in the CapCell who could move to fill the role sooner, and they were able to reduce the gap of four weeks of short-staffing to one week of overlap—meaning there was no staffing gap at all, no client disruption, and a bonus week of side-by-side training for the incoming underwriter. Much to the surprise of the original skeptics, it was a win–win situation for everyone.

The CapCell experiment brought together a shared sense of purpose (find additional capacity to serve customers well with fewer staff) and a leadership team willing to challenge the status quo. The systemic usage of tools, like structured problem solving, standardized work, visual management, daily huddles, fluid communication, and a smart use of data all helped to make the idea into a workable system. Underpinning all of this was the development of people: expanding their underwriting skills and abilities to allow them to handle a much broader variety of work. Any of these elements on their own were not likely to have created better flow, but acting together, as an interconnected system, they did.

Three Main Takeaways

1. Unevenness in workloads eats up capacity. Look across the peaks and valleys of customer demand in a variety of related teams and then think about what you can do to level out the unevenness.
2. People will not naturally want to change the way they work. The desired behavior has to be designed into the system. In this case, the

new CapCell system forced underwriters to first find the parts of their work that were shareable, and then document and standardize them.

3. The usage of data analysis, structured problem solving, standardized work, visual management, daily huddles, and fluid communication worked together as a system to enable better work sharing, which produced the desired capacity gains.

Notes

1. Basically this takes the new demand level as a percentage of the previous level (100 policies/week 125 policies/week = 80%) and applies it as a percentage of the previous number of employees: 80% × 50 employees = 40 employees. This assumes lead time remains the same.
2. Leansters will also recognize this method as a variant of *heijunka*, or levelling-production.

Chapter 11

The Seven Gates of Hell

You are driving to a friend's house on your way to a holiday party, and you want to pick up some gum. Unfortunately, you do not know this part of town that well, and the only visible store for miles around is the Gargantu-mart in the nearby shopping plaza. You park and, once you are in the store, realize to your dismay that it is very busy. There are line-ups at every cashier. All you want is a pack of gum! Oh well, you grumble. You are already here. You decide you might as well just get in a line and wait. You line up impatiently behind the shoppers with their overflowing carts of merchandise.

The optimal way to handle line-ups, given a fixed capacity of checkout lanes, is actually to have one big snaking line that sends the first person in line to the next available cashier[1]. This is contrary to the way many supermarkets are actually set up, where there are separate lines for each cash and shoppers get to choose which to join. Additionally, the supermarkets often have an "express" lane, where shoppers with fewer than a specified number of items can be fast-tracked. Everyone, on average, would have a faster checkout experience if there were just one line, so why do supermarkets design their checkouts like this? Chalk it up to human psychology.

Individual customers do not like being treated as statistical averages. They have expectations about lead time (total elapsed time from request to fulfillment). If you only have a few items to buy, like one pack of gum, you expect to check out faster—or, at least, you feel *entitled* to check out faster because you are essentially demanding less time from the cashier than if you were buying a huge cartload of groceries for Thanksgiving dinner. In the latter case, you would expect to wait a little longer. The supermarket might reasonably think in the opposite way, where the higher revenue customer should get faster service.

Transfer this scenario into a workplace and it is the same thing: why do you have to wait nine months to get your IT Security department's ok just to download and try out a new software product on a free 30-day trial basis? It is because you are basically trying to buy gum but standing in a single line where most of the people in front of you have overflowing carts of requests to change or replace your company's IT systems and applications. Everyone, on average, will get the fastest service by having IT Security assess everyone's request in a first-in, first-out (FIFO) single queue system, yet you do not want average. You want *faster* than average because your request is *smaller* than average. You want (and expect) to get an answer quickly. Customers quite reasonably expect their lead time to be commensurate with the complexity of their request. How does Lean, being a customer-centric philosophy, deal with this notion of customer experience?

We saw in Chapter 9 that not only do we have the option of moving the right amount of people to the work (as the insurance group did in Chapter 10), but we can also move the right amount of work to the people. To achieve better balance, you can match the supply of labor with work demand, or vice-versa. So long as the result is more flow to the work, it does not really matter which approach you take.

A commercial lending group used to take up to six months to tell customers that they were *un*willing to lend them money. They processed potential loans sequentially, one department at a time, even though there were few dependencies between the expert functions that assessed the different aspects of the deal. This was akin to having only one checkout lane open in the supermarket, even though they could have opened more.

The lending process happened in two stages. In the initial stage, once an underwriter had a potential customer interested in a debt financing solution, he or she began a process of credit analysis and due diligence. During this stage, the underwriter would frequently have questions for the potential borrower and request more information from them as the need arose. This, of course, would lead to delays of varying duration, depending on how prompt the customer was at providing additional information. Once underwriting completed its process, the potential loan would move to a variety of different departments for their expert opinions. The legal department would opine, and then pass it to the environmental group for their assessment. After the completion of the environmental assessment, technical experts, such as engineers who knew the potential borrower's industry well, would get involved to analyze key risks in the borrower's operations. Finally, a risk analytics group would look at the deal from the perspective of how much the loan would add to the agency's overall portfolio of risk exposure. At each step there was often the need to go back and forth with the client to get more information, and there were no standards for how long each step should take. At any point in the process, one of the many expert functions in the long chain of events could stop the deal if there were elements of risk that they felt were too great for the firm to accept. After a number of weeks, if all the expert groups agreed that there were no unmanageable risks, the lead underwriter would issue to the customer a term sheet, indicating the price (interest rate) and a lengthy list of all the terms and conditions. Stage 1, complete!

A term sheet, however, is effectively a quotation, not a formal offer. It is non-binding. If the customer wanted to go ahead with the financing, Stage 2 would begin. The agency would then effectively repeat the entire process all over again, but this time doing a *deeper* analysis to ensure there were no significant risks left undiscovered in the first stage. Again, during this second stage of analysis, any of the expert functions could stop the deal if they found any risks too great to bear (see Figure 11.1).

Before the agency could start negotiations to reach a signed loan agreement with the customer, a risk committee had to authorize a formal offer (during the Authorization step at the end of Stage 2 in Figure 11.1). This committee was composed of senior-level executives who were, by design, disconnected from the customer and the day-to-day deal-making in order to provide independent, unbiased oversight of the company's risk exposure for amounts over a given threshold. So, even if all of the expert functions agreed to the deal—twice—and the customer was happy with the price and terms, the deal could still die a sudden death if a majority of the risk committee members did not like any aspect of the deal for whatever reason.

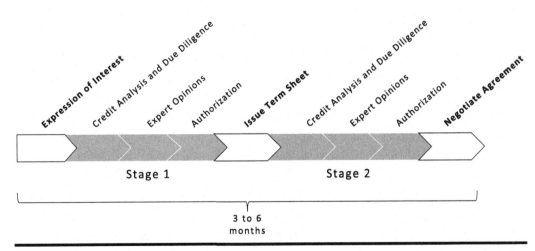

Figure 11.1   The Sequence of Process Steps Required to Complete a Signed Financing Agreement.

The committee did not have standard criteria for approving deals and relied on their experience and intuition. Underwriters found it intimidating to advocate for the approval of their deal because they found the committee's questions—and their decisions—unpredictable. One executive, a former underwriter, recalls that "it felt as though you had prepared very thoroughly for a History exam and then they would ask you questions about Geography".

If the committee vetoed a deal, the underwriter would have to go back to the customer to say "no". This was not a pleasant scenario. After making the potential borrower wait anywhere from one to 24 weeks, the firm would say, effectively, "we are not going to lend you the money". It was like asking the client to wait in line for twenty minutes to buy a pack of gum and then telling him, "Sorry, this cashier is closed!". This did not happen often, but when it did, it was a lose–lose scenario. It would frustrate the potential borrower for obvious reasons. Additionally, the agency had expended a lot of effort and time only to earn no revenue and annoy a potential customer. Underwriters nicknamed the entire process "The Seven Gates of Hell".

This lack of flow created, not surprisingly, additional work to do: the lead underwriter, not wanting the risk committee to reject the deal, spent a lot of time "socializing" the deal with all the relevant executives prior to taking the deal to the committee, trying to informally "get them on board". The larger the deal, the more time spent socializing.

Meanwhile customers continued to find the company slow and inscrutable.

Countermeasures

This lending group implemented numerous countermeasures to address this issue (with the help of a large, well-known consulting company). They delegated more authority to lower levels of decision-making, allowing relatively smaller deals to bypass the risk committee. They also set up daily huddles between underwriters and the expert advisory groups so that delays and other issues could be dealt with as quickly and as early in the process as possible.

One of the most effective countermeasures they implemented was that of setting up a triage point at the front of the process. They created a regular, daily meeting in which all the required expert functions would get together and make a joint decision on every new deal that came to the table.

The lead underwriter would write a brief, standardized overview of the deal (often in only a day or two) and then circulate it to the triage team a couple days ahead of the meeting. The expectation was that the advisory experts at the table would not only read the overview ahead of the meeting but also identify any abnormal risks, based on the limited information available, pertaining to their respective areas. They would then discuss any issues briefly during the meeting. Through consensus, the group gave deals a "green", "yellow", or "red" status. Green meant "go ahead" with the underwriting. Yellow meant there were some notable risk factors—requiring respective parties to gather further information and then bring it back for another assessment. Yellow was rework, but rework early in the process, to avoid much greater potential rework downstream. Red meant "no go". So, now, if they had to say "no" to a potential borrower, they could do so as early as possible, wasting as little of everyone's time as possible. Getting to the go/no-go decision now took 4 to 6 *days* instead of 1 to 24 *weeks* (see Figure 11.2).

The group of cross-functional experts sorted the green-lighted deals into separate "flight paths", based on complexity and expected time to process. They determined complexity by assessing each deal on three dimensions: credit risk (investment or non-investment grade); the size of the deal (dollar amount); and the type of deal (syndicated or direct[2]). Each flight path had a different target lead time (for customers) and a target amount of time and effort (from underwriters and others) to produce a signed loan agreement[3].

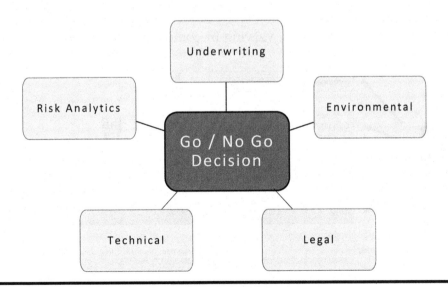

Figure 11.2   The Expert Triage Meeting.

Establishing target lead times meant that the analysis on the part of the underwriters, which, in theory, could go on forever, was far more aligned with customer expectations.

Managing Customer Experience

The system worked much like the way express checkout lanes work at supermarkets—except instead of having just one lane for 12 items or fewer, there were multiple lanes for various sizes of baskets. If you had very few items (low complexity) in your deal "basket", you would go to the fast lane. If you had a few more (medium complexity), you could go to the next fastest one, and so on. The most complex deals were the ones where customers had their baskets brimming with all sorts of different items (see Figure 11.3).

Now the simpler deals—the equivalent of those customers who just wanted to buy a pack of gum—did not sit unattended in a queue while all the complex deals consumed all of the underwriters' time and attention.

Just as the insurance group in Chapter 10 divided up the workforce and moved people to the work, the commercial lending group, in this case, divided up the work itself and moved it to the people dedicated to underwriting that specific level of complexity. Both groups increased balance in their workflows, but in slightly different ways.

Before implementing a systematic triage of the deals, the situation looked something like Figure 11.4, where there are, simplified for the sake of illustration, only three underwriters and six deals—two per underwriter—composed of three different types, varying in complexity and duration, with the

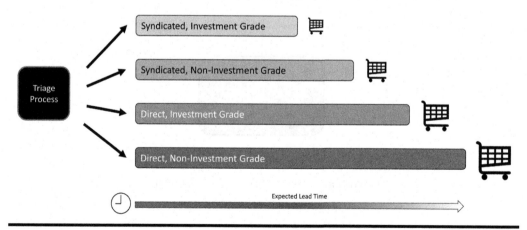

Figure 11.3 Triage by Complexity and Expected Lead Time.

largest square being the most complex, and the smallest square being the simplest. The underwriters process the deals in alphabetical order, from A to F, in a first-in-first-out fashion.

If we were to say that the small squares take one week to complete, the medium ones two weeks, and the large ones three weeks, then Figure 11.5 illustrates the order of deal completion.

We can then do some simple calculations on the touch time, lead time, and flow efficiency, as seen in Table 11.1.

The point to note here is that Deal F, the loan equivalent of a pack of gum, has a flow efficiency of only 25%, whereas the average across all 6 deals is 75%. The customer associated with Deal F is not likely going to have a very good experience.

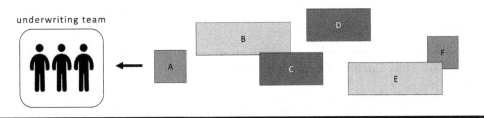

Figure 11.4   One Single Line for All Deals Regardless of Their Complexity.

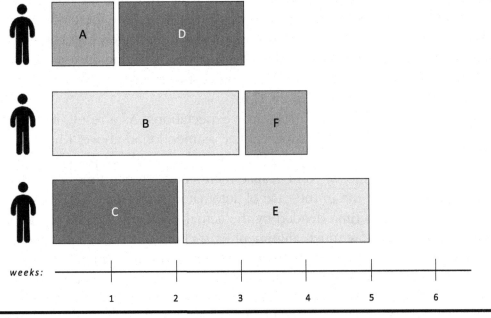

Figure 11.5   Individual Lead Times for Each Deal in Figure 11.4.

Table 11.1 Six Deals Processed in FIFO Order

Deal	A	B	C	D	E	F	Avg.
Touch Time (Weeks)	1	3	2	2	3	1	**2**
Lead Time (Weeks)	1	3	2	3	5	4	**3**
Flow Efficiency	100%	100%	100%	67%	60%	25%	**75%**

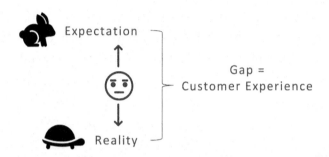

Figure 11.6 How Customer Experience Works.

In service industries, value includes customer experience—how a company treats each customer as a human being—just as much as it does the product or service being purchased[4]. Customer experience comes from the gap between a customer's expectations and what they actually receive. If the customer receives less than what she was expecting, the experience is poor. The bigger the deficit, the more disappointed the customer, just as the larger the surplus, the more delighted the customer is. Improving customer experience then comes down to either lowering customer expectations, improving actual service, or both (see Figure 11.6).

Complexity drives, in part, customer expectations. As a result, it impacts customer experience. At the supermarket, as mentioned above, I have expectations of speedier service when my cart is mostly empty compared to when my cart is mostly full because there is less "touch time" expected of the cashier (or of me in the case of automated self-checkouts). Flow efficiency, the touch time divided by the actual lead time, is thus is a good proxy measure of how much alignment exists between customer expectations (expected touch time) and reality (actual lead time). Since flow efficiency is 25% for Deal F, and 25% is very low relative to the service levels received by the other customers, we can say, with quite a lot of confidence, that the customer involved in Deal F has not had a good customer experience[5].

Managing Variation

Now compare this with a triaged system where the simple, medium, and complex deals have their own dedicated checkout lanes.

When there is dedicated staff working repeatedly on work of similar complexity, they become faster at completing it, and the scenario in Figure 11.7 would most likely produce some improvements in touch time. For the sake of illustration, let us assume each underwriter processes each deal in roughly the same time as before, and we come up with a scoreboard that looks like Table 11.2.

On the surface, it appears nothing has really changed. The average touch time, lead time, and flow efficiency is the same as in Table 11.1. But the *range of variation* in the flow efficiency has shrunk from a gap of 75% in Table 11.1 (lowest = 25% and highest = 100%) to a gap of 50% in Table 11.2 (lowest = 50% and highest = 100%). The triaged system depicted in Figure 11.7 is more consistent, predictable, and reliable from a customer point of view. Customers

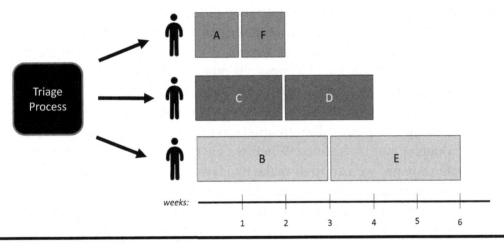

Figure 11.7   Same Amount of Work and Employees as Figure 11.5, but Now Triaged and Distributed Differently.

Table 11.2   Six Deals Processed by Complexity

Deal	A	F	C	D	B	E	Avg.
Touch Time (Weeks)	1	1	2	2	3	3	**2**
Lead Time (Weeks)	1	2	2	4	3	6	**3**
Flow Efficiency	100%	50%	100%	50%	100%	50%	**75%**

know what to expect. The longer deals actually do take longer (three to six weeks), and the shorter ones are actually quicker (one to two weeks). In the previous scenario, each deal, regardless of size and complexity, could take anywhere from one to five weeks—no one would really know. Now each lane has a far less variable rate of completion and we can estimate lead time with much greater accuracy[6]. Because customers cannot *see* their office work, their expectations are not informed by how many people are ahead of them "in line". They assume they are first in line. As a result, office people have to communicate lead times clearly and accurately. Establishing expectations ahead of time diminishes the gap between customer expectation and reality, improving customer experience.

This brings us back to our analogy of bucket brigades from Chapter 8. It would be easier for employees (although perhaps less interesting) if customers always requested the same thing. But they do not. Customers hand us different sizes of buckets, some of them leaky, containing different quantities of water. There is, in Lean language, *variation* in the process, as there is in all processes, and this variation creates a lack of balance, disrupting the overall flow. One effective way to manage variation, as we have seen, is to triage the inbound work into a manageable number of fixed categories (three to five is best), based on the expected time to complete, and then have dedicated staff for each category. In other words, sort and move the work to the right amount of people with the right skillsets.

While speed is important—and this is why we should always strive to design continuity into our value streams—so too is the consistency and reliability brought about by balance. When we have the basic stability of a balanced value stream, we can then make much more controlled adjustments and respond with more agility to changing conditions. For instance, after we have moved the work to the people (triage), we can move people to the work (workload leveling) based on the velocity required in each individual "checkout lane" (category or type) of work, much like the insurance group did with their CapCell system. To take our simplified value stream to the next level of performance, we would have to make the work shareable. This way we could handle the shortest deals first and the underwriters who finish their deals early could help out those working on the longer ones, shortening the lead time for both the simplest and more complex deals—see Figure 11.8 and Table 11.3.

When we look at the numbers between handling work as it comes in (see Table 11.1), triaging by complexity (see Table 11.2), and then adding in work-sharing (see Table 11.3), we see the average lead time go from 3 weeks down to 2.5 weeks and flow efficiency improve from 75% to 80%. But the

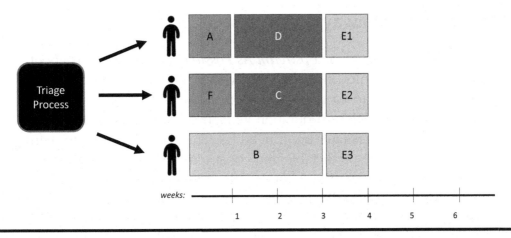

Figure 11.8   Work Sharing Enables Faster Lead Times and Less Variation in Duration.

Table 11.3   Six Deals Processed by Complexity with Work Sharing

Deal	A	F	C	D	B	E	Avg.
Touch Time (Weeks)	1	1	2	2	3	3	**2.0**
Lead Time (Weeks)	1	1	3	3	3	4	**2.5**
Flow Efficiency	100%	100%	67%	67%	100%	75%	**80%**

real improvement is in the *predictability and stability* achieved by moving the right amount of work in the right sequence to the right people with the right skillsets. Note the range of variation in the flow efficiency in Table 11.3 is now only 33% (lowest = 67% and highest = 100%).

Balance and continuity are mutually reinforcing concepts. We cannot have balance if we are multitasking between many different units of WIP, nor can we have continuity if the work we are handling comes in all sorts of different levels of complexity and duration. There will always be variation: on the inside—people, process, information, and technology are not always 100% rational, reliable, and predictable, after all; and from the outside—the volume and diversity of customer demand. But we can and should always strive to manage variation better by continuously working to implement more continuity and balance in all our value streams. Why? Because the resulting flow results in a win–win scenario: customers experience a faster, more predictable, and higher quality service, while employees, having fewer things to work on simultaneously, experience less overburden and stress. Creating flow is ultimately a way of respecting employees, customers, and shareholders simultaneously.

Three Main Takeaways

1. *Triage and Prioritize As Upstream As Possible*: make decisions about size, duration, complexity, risk, and whatever other considerations you feel are vital to sorting the work as early as possible in the process. Handle the shortest duration items first, if possible. The work can always switch lanes later on, if need be. The goal should be to manage variation to create predictable and consistent service for customers.
2. *Dedicate Staff*: have a fixed-but-flexible approach to staffing. That is, have everyone primarily assigned to only one lane, but cross-trained enough to help out in other lanes. You can more easily and reliably estimate lead time by having fixed resources and a more predictable duration to each unit of work in each lane. If lead time grows or shrinks in one or more lanes, adjust staff accordingly. Monitor daily and balance accordingly.
3. *Work in Parallel*: continuity is not just doing one thing after another but, in its most condensed form, doing things simultaneously. Determine what pieces of the work—pertaining to the same unit of value—can be done in parallel, as opposed to sequentially, and then do as much in parallel as possible. The speed gained will often outweigh any additional coordination required to pull the pieces together at the end.

Notes

1. Mele, Christopher. 2016. How to pick the fastest line at the supermarket. *The New York Times*, September 7, 2016: www.nytimes.com/2016/09/08/business/how-to-pick-the-fastest-line-at-the-supermarket.html (accessed May 24, 2019).
2. Syndicated meant the agency was one of a group of many lenders. Direct meant the agency was the sole lender.
3. The longest were the direct, non-investment grade deals. The shortest were the syndicated, investment grade deals, where credit risk was lower and the pricing and documentation were done by the lead financial institution of the syndicate, not the agency itself.
4. See Ross, Karyn. 2019. *How to Coach for Creativity and Service Excellence: A Lean Coaching Workbook*. New York: Taylor and Francis, especially Chapter 4, for further insights into the distinctions between manufacturing and service industries.
5. 25% flow efficiency would be exceptionally good because most of the time it is less than 1%. See Chapter 4. This is just an example, so the relative flow efficiency is what matters.

6. The math is simply Little's Law, which says that the Lead Time is equal to WIP × Average Completion Rate. WIP is easy to count—it is simply the number of items in the queue. But the *range of variation in the completion rate* affects how easily and accurately the lead time can be calculated.

THINKING
BEYOND FLOW

Chapter 12

Prerequisites to Problem Solving

Joe is a Senior Data Analyst with the Sales Operation Team at headquarters. He comes to work today ready to produce Fat Man. He has been thinking about it obsessively for his entire drive in to the office. Fat Man is the name he gives to the report that the Executive Vice President of Global Sales wants to see every November in preparation for reporting the year end results to the Board of Directors in January. It is the report that breaks down all of the company's revenue streams by geographic region, product type, and customer segment. It drills down to each office and every team and every salesperson in every region. It compares the growth from last year to this year and compares actuals to forecasts. Fat Man has been known to make or break Sales careers. It will contribute in no small amount to next year's strategy and will affect the size of the annual bonus for every employee in the company.

Fortunately, Joe has got a whole system in place to produce a flawless report almost effortlessly this year. He has a plan to extract the data from the DataTrak® system, run a macro to format it all, then feed it into the data visualization software program and design the multicolored graphs according to the company's brand colors specifications. The corporate finance and accounting group just gave him the green light yesterday that the data in DataTrak® is valid and consistent with their own. As he goes to run his query in DataTrak® this morning, however, he gets a pop-up window: "An unexpected error has occurred. If error persists, please contact your database administrator. Error code: 1jx-J%-BV4-7yR".

"What the *^&%*?" Joe blurts out at his monitor, struggling to keep his voice low. "How am I supposed to know who the freaking 'database administrator' is?"

He logs out and then back in. He closes and restarts the browser. He tries a different browser. He restarts his computer. Still no luck. He reluctantly calls the IT Help Desk, who suggest that he restart his computer. After 20 minutes of listening to bad hold music and being passed around to three separate Help Desk employees, each asking him to explain his predicament again from the very beginning, he resorts to shameless name dropping (everyone recognizes the name of the Executive Vice President of Global Sales). He finally gets a Systems Analyst called Alex on the phone. "Alex, my DataTrak® report is not working and I need you to fix it *now!*" he tells him, irritated.

A few days later, in a conference room seven floors up from Joe's desk, the Continuous Improvement facilitator is conducting a workshop on problem-solving methodology. She is encouraging a group of IT employees to write down problems on sticky notes that, if solved, would contribute to their team's strategic objectives for the year. The employees list whatever problem happens to be bothering them at that moment. Alex, the System Analyst, writes down his problem as "we need to automate the alerts when the servers fail to run their jobs overnight".

"Don't write your problems as solutions", the facilitator says to Alex, chastising him with a wag of her finger.

Alex is annoyed with her. He thinks to himself,

> she thinks she's smarter than everyone, but she doesn't really know anything about my work. If there's something that absolutely has to be done and is currently being done by a human and it can be automated … then it should be automated! End. Of. Story. Why should I write it out like a problem? That's just stupid!

Alex cannot imagine why automated alerts would not be a good idea. People like Joe are counting on their data being up-to-date for their latest reports. They are constantly pressuring him to reboot the servers and get the data up-to-date as soon as possible. To make matters worse, they know about the server failures before he does: he only becomes aware that the servers have failed to run their jobs when the business users tell him that there is a problem with their reports. "How could getting automated alerts be a bad solution?" he asks himself.

It might stop people from constantly giving me a hard time for a problem that I did not cause. If the alerts were automated, I would be able to warn the business users that their latest data is not available before they even tried to run their reports. At least our team would not look so incompetent. And I could even get to work on fixing the situation earlier so that the business users could be back to reporting as usual in far less time.

He begrudgingly rewrites his idea as a problem: "the problem is … we lack automated alerts when the servers fail to run their jobs overnight".

It never occurred to Alex that reducing the frequency of server failure might be a more worthwhile problem to solve.

Why not? Primarily because he is not looking at the problem from the customer's point of view. What does Joe, a customer of the server's daily job run process, truly value in this situation? It is not automated alerts to tell his IT department about failures faster. It is reliable, easy-to-access, always available, up-to-date, high-quality data. If someone were able to prevent the servers from failing in the first place, so that the desired data would flow to Joe without delay, Alex would not have the "problem" of needing automated alerts. Alex would not receive any angry phone calls from Joe. Everyone would be happy. Perhaps Joe could even spend time making enhancements to the reports, getting noticed and appreciated by the head of global sales. Alex could work on teaching other teams how to prevent their servers from failing instead of handling phone calls from angry internal customers all day.

Firms wanting to create a culture of continuous improvement often start with training everyone on the seven or eight types of waste and the "A3[1]" problem-solving method to eliminate it. Companies are often initially sold on Lean by the fact that a paint-by-numbers problem solving method is fairly easy for all employees to understand—after all, there never seems to be a shortage of problems at any workplace. Every business has infinite problems: money problems, technology problems, time problems, and, most of all, relationship problems with, and between, its employees, suppliers, partners, customers, competitors, shareholders, board of directors, the media, regulators, and all of its other important stakeholders. In fact, most people's full-time job seems to be about problem solving. Given the plethora of problems in every business, it is easy for most people to conclude that their firm needs to be better at problem solving.

This approach is a mistake. Yes, it is true that effective, daily, continuous, root-cause problem solving is deeply embedded in the culture of mature

Lean firms, and much has been written about such a culture at Toyota and elsewhere, but it should not come *first* or it will end up like the old suggestion box method—irrelevant, ignored, and forgotten. What needs to *precede* A3 problem solving and waste hunting is an awareness of—and appreciation for—the flow of value to the customer. Otherwise, almost everyone will start "problem solving" by simply coming up with the first solutions that come to mind that will relieve their current pain of being overburdened with work. And almost all of their solutions will involve hiring more staff or purchasing new technology—both expensive and, in the case of technology, often slow to implement. Moreover, these "solutions" may cause more problems than they solve: more people to manage; potentially more incompatible and glitchy systems to deal with. Instead of starting with problem solving, it is best to follow, in sequential order, the following five steps:

1. Define Your Customers
2. Understand Customer Value
3. Visualize Your Workflow
4. Create Flow
5. Solve Problems

Note these are simply an adapted version of Womack and Jones' original five principles of Lean Thinking[2]. It is the fifth and *last* step of Solve Problems (what Womack and Jones call "Perfection"), that establishes a culture of problem solving. It should *begin* with understanding customers and value. What is the purpose of your firm? Why does your firm exist, in your customers' eyes? What value do you provide them? Once that is clear, apply it at every level: what value does a given function, department, team, or individual role serve in the overall purpose of the firm? Who consumes the value that the function, department, team or individual produces and why? These fundamental questions are asked surprisingly infrequently. Knowing who your customers are and what value you provide to them—at all levels of the enterprise, top to bottom—is so fundamental that people are often too embarrassed to admit they do not know.

Step 1: Define Your Customers

Who's your customer? This question is more complicated than it seems. No matter what role you have in a firm, you always have at least *two* customers:

1. The next process step in the value stream *and*
2. The end (external) customer or stakeholder[3].

This is not always well understood. If you ask a salesperson who their customer is, they will probably look at you as if you have two heads.

"That's obvious", they will say. "My customers are the firms that I'm trying to convince to sign a contract with us!"

"Yes, and who's your *other* customer?"

Now they think you have three heads. They are genuinely puzzled.

"What about Operations?" you ask.

"Operations is not my customer", they will protest. "Operations *serves* my customers", the salesperson might say. "Now that I think about it, in a way, I'm *their* customer!"

But no, that is not true, at least not from a Lean point of view. Consider for a moment how value flows to a customer. Sales secures a contract with the customer. No one can dispute the value of this to both the firm and the customer. But Sales also provides vital inputs (information about the order/contract) to the next process step in the value stream, such as Operations. The accuracy, completeness, and timeliness of these informational inputs enable Operations to fulfill the promise Sales has made to external customers. Of course, Operations has to keep up its end of the bargain and deliver to the best of its abilities on its obligations too, but Sales often has a surprisingly large role in making the job of Operations easier or harder. If Sales is making the life of Operations harder, this can have a direct customer impact by prolonging lead times. It also has indirect impacts such as inflicting damage to the brand and causing customer attrition. And it also causes the company to consume more resources than necessary in Operations. So how much effort does Sales put into making the work of Operations employees easier? Usually Salespeople are measured and incented exclusively by the number of customers and/or the value of the contracts they pull in. Once the contract is signed or the order is placed, their job is done. Or so they believe.

If we were to look at the bigger picture, making the job of Operations easier would mean that customers would receive better service delivery. Over the long run, this better customer experience translates into more loyalty to your firm, making the customers more likely to deepen their relationship and purchase more products and services from you. How much is *that* worth to your firm? It is common knowledge that it is far easier and less expensive to retain and cultivate existing customers than to acquire new ones or beg old ones to come back by offering deep discounts (or hiring more salespeople). Moreover, if the job of Operations were made easier, fewer people would be needed in Operations. Could that freed up capacity be redeployed into Sales? What impact would that have on the growth of the business? So why does the Sales department typically not care about making the job of Operations easier?

To take an entire firm's performance to a higher level, it is vitally important for everyone—not just Sales, obviously—to think about how *both* their internal customers and external customers receive value through horizontal value streams. Vertical hierarchies persist because our resource-efficient thinking believes that dividing up firms into divisions and departments that isolate employees with narrowly specialized skillsets is the most "efficient" way of utilizing labor, just like on an assembly line! Unfortunately, in many ways, such silos act as a barrier to delivering customer value. In a Lean world, your boss is not your customer. If a firm wants to be truly "customer focused" it must think beyond getting to know the customer better or having friendlier salespeople. It has to also optimize *delivery* to the customer. Horizontal value streams begin and end with an external customer who is the unifying purpose that everyone in the value stream shares. And additionally, every process step in a value stream has its own specific, internal customer: the next process step (see Figure 12.1).

Thinking of both internal and external customers is, of course, a different challenge for different functional roles. Sales may find it relatively easy to think of the external customer as a customer, but harder to think of the next

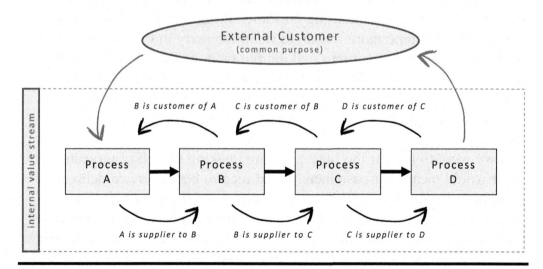

Figure 12.1   The Firm As a Value Stream.

downstream process step in the value stream as a customer. Conversely, internal roles like Accounting, HR, IT, Legal, or any other administrative or support functions may find it hard to think of any true "customer" at all, and, when pushed, they probably find it relatively easier to think of internal teams or stakeholders as their customers, and harder to connect their work to the external customer.

IT networks, absolutely necessary for doing office-based work, obscure from view our internal customers even more. There are one-to-many and many-to-one information flows with IT systems. That is, one person can save data in an application and many others can retrieve and update or consume that data in different locations and at different points in time. So too can many people work in the same application simultaneously, so that multiple records in the same collection of interrelated databases are being updated at the same time. In other words, there is no linear, one-to-one relationship between data producer and data consumer. In most scenarios in manufacturing or healthcare, it is fairly obvious where the widget or patient should go next once a specific process step is complete. In offices, an employee's "output" is frequently just newly updated data in an application. The employee often has no idea who will be next to consume that data, or why and when they might need it. Electronic data does not travel in any visible, physical sense. Hence the need to make the work visible is so crucial.

Leadership in every functional area of a firm has an opportunity to influence how each team thinks about its customers within the horizontal value stream, and then broaden this understanding. Enterprise-wide focus on a common external customer does not happen by itself, especially in non-customer-facing teams. Even less natural is thinking of the next internal process step as a customer. After all, internal customers do not pay the previous process step for their work. Leaders can start by simply asking employees to name who their customers are—and this will vary by process or product—and what each one values. *Once you are done with this work, where does it go? Who consumes it? Why? What do they value about it?* If employees do not have an immediate answer, how can they go find out? Who could they talk to?

Step 2: Understand Customer Value

No one wants to end up delivering the wrong thing faster to customers. Thus it is vitally important that company's start their Lean journey by defining value from the perspective of the external and ultimate end-customer[4] of the product or service. All subsequent efforts to design its internal value streams should be anchored to fulfilling this end-customer-specified value. When designing our value streams for continuity and balance we are creating flow, but we want to ensure we are flowing value, not superfluous stuff customers do not really need or want.

Sometimes external customer value is fairly obvious. If you have an existing product or service that customers keep buying again and again, and have been doing so for years, you probably know mostly what they value. But beware. What was yesterday's delightful new feature is now considered a basic standard. The original iPhone, released in 2007, was a phenomenal event. People lined up for hours. Now it seems as quaintly outdated as a Furby doll. Customers' wants and needs change over time, and will vary from market to market. If you are trying to launch a new product or capture a new customer segment, defining value is even less obvious and requires a lot more frequent feedback.

Because office employees do not naturally think of the next process step as a customer, they tend not to question or examine internal value creation. If you have an existing report that you keep producing again and again, and have been doing so for years, there is a high probability that it could be improved. But you need to ask your customer!

For existing products and services, it is best to start by asking your customers—internal or external—two questions: what are you getting that you do not want; and what do you want but are not getting[5]? Curiously, frontline employees are sometimes afraid of asking their internal customers what they want. Since internal customers are not paying (directly) for another team's labor, there is apprehension that they will ask for the moon. However, in my experience it is very helpful to learn what customers want, even if all their wants and needs cannot be fulfilled right away. It focuses a team's efforts on improving their delivery of only what the customer truly values and challenges them to find creative ways to meet customer needs. There is usually an immediate payoff: teams usually can eliminate some wasteful activities that the customer does not want, and free up some spare capacity to focus on the valuable stuff.

An additional and clever way to understand customer value is to take Clayton Christensen's Job-To-Be-Done approach[6]. Think about what "job" the customer has "hired" the product or service to do. This reframes the notion of value from the problem we are trying to solve for ourselves— which is usually some variant of "I wish I could make some aspect of my job easier"—to the problem we are trying to solve for our customers.

Christensen discovered that consumers were purchasing ("hiring") fast food milkshakes to relieve them of a long, boring morning commute by car. They could be held in one hand, were not messy or hard to handle in the car, lasted for a good portion of the long commute, and sated the driver's hunger until noon. Context matters. Competition, in this case, was not other milkshakes but fruit, bagels, coffee, donuts, and other snacks one might typically eat in the car on the way to work. What problem are you helping your customers solve?

When we focus only on our own internal "pain points"—as Alex the Systems Analyst did at the beginning of this chapter—and do not think about our customers, we often end up finding solutions that do not really solve anyone's problems. Conversely, by solving customer problems we end up solving our own pain points too. Think about it: if your customers stopped asking for so many things from you, would you have fewer "pain points"?

Step 3: Visualize Your Workflow

The third step to take prior to embarking on widespread problem solving is to make your work visible. This is especially necessary in office work, where the work is hidden from view. Fortunately, there are many ways to make work visible. Experiment with various tools and see which work for your own purposes the best. One of the most effective dynamic tools is the kanban board, which we saw in Chapter 7 and will see again in Chapter 14. By "dynamic" I mean a visualization tool that is actively used to manage the daily flow of work—it changes frequently. There are many important goals of dynamically visualizing the work, some of which are:

- To monitor and manage the daily demand of work versus the supply of employees and the availability of technology
- To prioritize new work and set customer expectations
- To find problems or abnormalities in the flow of work—and track accountability for solving them
- To communicate important information quickly (avoiding long meetings)

The classic value stream map is a static[7] tool, which is equally valuable, but for different reasons. Value stream maps are great tools for making discrete improvements to a process but are usually not used to manage the day-to-day work. Mapping aligns teams around a common understanding of how the work happens and, like more dynamic tools, makes problems visible. It also helps identify internal customers—something that can be difficult or simply not deemed important, as discussed previously. Often a value stream mapping exercise can satisfy the first three steps towards a Lean culture at once: identifying customers, identifying value, and making the work visible.

A value stream map should capture, at a high level, every major process step for a value stream, from customer request to receipt of the value fulfilling that request, so that all participants in the value stream are united around a common purpose. This customer "value" is not always about delivering an exciting new physical product or service, like a self-driving car or a music streaming app for your phone. It often involves the equally important, but quite mundane and administrative, aspects of meeting the needs and wants of *internal* customers/stakeholders. For instance, the corporate accounting department provides the CFO with financial statements every month. This report is of value to the CFO and her executive colleagues. How does the accounting team fulfill this value? What inputs (e.g. information, data, technology, and skillsets) are needed? How many people hours does it take to produce? What are the upstream and downstream process steps? By rendering visible and explicit the interconnections between people, technology, information, and processes (formal and informal) in the value stream, we can start to see problems in the context of producing value to customers. A simple, high-level map is all that is needed as a start (see Figure 12.2). The maps will become more detailed as more specific and focused problem solving is undertaken.

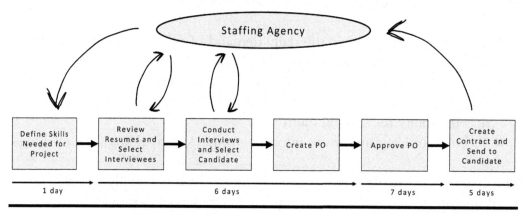

Figure 12.2 A Simple Value Stream Map of a Recruitment Process with Lead Times.

When there are multiple needs and wants of multiple customer groups (or stakeholders) in a process and value stream, it can be hard to know where to start. Who are the "customers", for instance, of financial statements: auditors, shareholders, the executive team, the board of directors, potential investors, or regulatory authorities? The answer is all of the above. As you look at your office processes, you will find that almost all of them have multiple outputs for multiple customers, and all or most of them will be dissatisfied with the process in some way or another. Teams typically choose a place to start by reaching consensus around where the most "pain" (for them) is in the process. Instead, a better way is to reach consensus around which *customer* is experiencing the most pain and with which product or service. Then, as we have seen in previous chapters, use data to measure the time-based performance (average touch time, wait time, lead time) of every major process step. With facts and data, we can cut through the ambiguity of opinions and feelings, and start to assess the real impact and scope of problems that face the customer.

Step 4: Create Flow

Once you know who your customers are, what they value, and how at a high level that value is currently delivered to them, the next step is to attempt to increase flow as best you can within the value stream. This was the focus of Chapters 4–11 of this book. Things get interesting (and fun!) when we try to create flow because we quickly discover that establishing and then consistently maintaining good flow is challenging. Our attempts at creating and maintaining better flow allow us to truly see what important problems currently exist in our value streams that prevent us from flowing value faster and better to our customers. That is ok. Problems are our friends. You have to uncover problems in order to have a chance at fixing them. Once we can see problems in the context of flow, we are ready to move the next and final step, Solve Problems.

WHAT IS PULL?

Womack and Jones define Flow and Pull as the third and fourth principles, respectively, needed to create a Lean production system. In manufacturing, a "pull" system is deployed to align the pace of production with real (as opposed to forecasted) external customer demand, to minimize overproduction and to be more responsive to changes in the market. For example, if customers are actually buying more of Product A than forecast and less of Product B, the pace of Product A production should go up and the pace of Product B production should go down. The increase in Product A demand "pulls" the corresponding increase in supply from the factory. In contrast, traditionally managed companies set the pace of production by inputting sales forecasts into a Material and Resource Planning (MRP) software program, rarely revising the numbers, and inevitably end up holding too much inventory of one product (overproduction), while selling out of another (lost sales).

The concept of Pull in a Lean manufacturing enterprise does not just comprise signals from retailers or distributors back to the shipping dock at the factory. It also extends throughout every step of a value stream *within* the factory. Every downstream process step signals to the one immediately upstream to produce another unit of work: e.g. once an outbound truck is loaded, the shipping department would signal the final inspection area to start to move the next pallet of finished goods to the shipping dock; the final inspection area would then signal the final assembly area to assemble one more truckload of widgets, and so on, all the way back to the purchasing of parts and raw materials. This effectively "levels" or "balances" the workload across all the process steps in the entire value stream so that no one step is overburdened with work, and "overproduction"—causing bottlenecks and excessive buildup of inventory—is avoided and work flows faster.

In service industries, production is always "to order". Companies do not make insurance policies, advertising campaigns, or custom software applications ahead of a customer asking for them. But the concept of balancing the work is still valid, since we want to avoid overburdening employees, reduce bottlenecks, and make value flow faster to customers. Since bottlenecks and overburdened employees inhibit Flow, I refer to the concept of Pull as "balance" and treat it as one of the two elements that contribute to Flow.

Step 5: Solve Problems

In a Lean enterprise everyone must think about how things everywhere, big and small, can be improved. And then everyone must run experiments, continuously and forever, in order to learn how to make a company's performance better over time. I have simplified this to "Solve Problems", which is equivalent to what Womack and Jones have labeled "Perfection" or what the

Shingo Institute calls "Seek Perfection". People frequently confuse *seeking* perfection with perfectionism. Seeking perfection is not *attaining* perfection (which is impossible). Seeking it is *pursuing* it. It is the pursuit that is important (think of the Lexus slogan, "The Relentless Pursuit of Perfection"). No one who continuously seeks perfection becomes complacent and says, "good enough" because they know nothing is ever perfect. Sometimes, of course, we have to say, "good enough, for now". We have to choose to focus strategically on improving some things over others in any given moment, since we can only focus on a limited number of improvements at a time. But everything can be improved, and you will never, ever run out of opportunities.

This attitude of perpetual problem solving may seem demoralizing to those who do not do it, like some Sisyphean curse where we can never reach the top of the mountain and get to put our feet up for a few moments of hydration and rest[8]. The problem is that business, like life itself, has a way of perpetually producing problems whether you like it or not. Time passes, nothing lasts forever, and the universe continues to expand. It is how you deal with this reality that matters. If you are not solving problems continuously, you are not progressing or even keeping up: you are falling behind. Falling behind feels demoralizing. Continuous progress does not. You get to the peak of the mountain, rejoice in your accomplishment, enjoy the view, take a sip of water … and then notice that there is yet another higher mountain on the horizon that you previously could not see. You embrace it as tomorrow's challenge to reach even better performance than today. Seeking perfection is optimistic.

Solving Problems the Slow Way

In every workplace, people will tell you that they solve problems all day. This constant problem solving/fire-fighting may give people some comfort of illusory progress and the occasional lucky break. The key difference—and it is a big one—is the root-cause approach. Lean companies take the time to frame and then solve problems to make sure the old problems do not come back. This leaves them in a much better position to both raise the bar on their current performance and to solve the problems that the future inevitably will hold. Most people at most companies solve problems in a reactive, break-fix way: make a quick patch here, or apply a Band-Aid there, and move on as fast as you can to the next problem. The attitude is: life is short, and everyone has got a billion things to do. Who has time for structured, slow, root-cause problem solving? What kind of bizarre company culture rewards people for being *slow and thorough* at problem solving? Don't things take long enough to get done around here as it is? Why should we do something deliberately more slowly?

Companies that are initially enthusiastic about Lean because it will make them "better" at problem solving usually lose their enthusiasm when they understand how slow, methodical, and scientific their thinking has to become to solve problems in a way that truly elevates a firm's performance. People are not naturally motivated to solve problems in a slow, "root-cause" kind of way. It challenges us to see and think about the problems we encounter all day differently. It often hurts our brains and tests our patience. It requires us to go see the actual work being performed with our own eyes, an action that is often perceived as time-consuming, uncomfortable, and intrusive by all parties involved. It is hard for us to appreciate the payoff of something so uncomfortable. A lot of time and effort is expended for an often meager-seeming improvement. We grow impatient and apply the quick fix.

People who have young children know well how challenging it is, when they are rushing to get out of the house, to teach their children how to tie their shoes. It is much easier to tie our children's shoes for them. And we do. Yet we always find the time, after school or on the weekend, to teach our children how to tie their own shoes. Teaching them is harder and more time consuming than doing it for them but we manage to find the time because it is a priority. We clearly understand the long-term payoff: we want our children to grow up to be self-sufficient and independent (and so do they!). Similarly, Lean companies always find the time to do root-cause problem solving because they clearly understand the long-term business value of learning and thinking in scientific ways. (Perhaps a Lean thinker came up with the idea of Velcro shoes).

The first four of the steps—defining your customer; understanding customer value; making visible how that value flows from request to fulfillment; and then designing the value stream for greater flow—provide the necessary context for people to see the long term purpose and impact of how slow, deliberate, structured problem solving is so important. Without these prerequisites, it just seems slow and tedious and annoying: *Problem solving? Why do I have to "learn" problem solving? I solve problems all day! I already know how!*

When people learn to see flow and the lack of it, they see problem solving as primarily being about learning how to remove the barriers to *the flow of value to the customer.* Effective root-cause problem solving becomes essential to the purpose for why a company exists. It is no longer just about removing personal pain points. It starts to be about improving outcomes for both customers and employees. You no longer have to choose between increased revenue and engaged employees. Lean eliminates the trade-off and creates a virtuous circle.

To summarize, do not start your "Continuous Improvement" program with an overly mechanistic A3 problem-solving approach. To profit from the long-term value of Lean, follow the five steps outlined above: look at the problem from the customer's point of view, and then ask, "how can we improve the flow of value to our customer?"

Three Main Takeaways

1. It is a mistake to start your Lean journey with problem solving. Start with understanding that you always have at least two customers. You have to know who they are and what both of them value.
2. Customer focus requires more than "getting to know" your customers. It also means delivering value to them. This happens horizontally. If a firm genuinely wishes to be customer-centric, it has to think in terms of value streams.
3. Problem solving is really learning how to increase the flow of value streams through continuous scientific experimentation. It is slow, frustrating, unconventional, and completely worth it.

Notes

1. A3 is a metric size of paper, approximately 11" × 17", that is favored at Toyota as a concise way of stating a problem, its cause, and its solution (and the story of how you got there) on one sheet of paper.
2. Womack James P. and Daniel T. Jones. 1996. *Lean Thinking: Banish Waste and Create Wealth in Your Corporation.* New York: Simon and Schuster. Their five principles are: Value, The Value Stream, Flow, Pull, and Perfection.
3. Non-customer external stakeholders can include shareholders, boards of directors, creditors, regulators, governments, partners, suppliers, and local communities. Please read the word "customer" to imply all of these other stakeholders.
4. By "end-customer", I mean the consumer of the final product or service, which is not your firm's paying customer in all cases. If you underwrite

insurance policies for brokers, it is the broker who is the paying customer but the end-customer is the consumer who purchases the insurance from the broker.

5. Scholtes, Peter R. 1998. *The Leaders Handbook: Making Things Happen, Getting Things Done.* New York: McGraw-Hill, p.67.

6. Christensen has a well-known talk about improving milkshakes to boost sales in a fast food chain: https://youtu.be/sfGtw2C95Ms

7. For learning how to do value stream mapping, look at: Martin, Karen and Mike Osterling. 2013. *Value Stream Mapping: How to Visualize Work and Align Leadership for Organizational Transformation.* New York: McGraw-Hill Education; and/or Keyte, Beau and Drew A. Locher. 2016. *The Complete Lean Enterprise: Value Stream Mapping for Office and Services, Second Edition.* Boca Raton, FL: CRC Press.

8. Sisyphus is a figure of Greek mythology who was condemned by the gods to repeat forever the same meaningless task of pushing a boulder up a mountain, only to see it roll down again every time he reached the top.

Chapter 13

Start with Standards

Early in my Lean coaching career, naïve to Lean's broader philosophy, I was a toolhead. I was once asked by an executive to lead a problem-solving session for a group of senior middle managers. They had all been seconded from a variety of functional areas to lead teams as part of a major technology project that was underway.

The project involved both IT and a principal line of business, and now HR was creeping into the mix as well. Executives were keeping their eyes close to this project, and the group of managers were under a lot of pressure to keep the project within its prescribed budget, scope, and milestone dates. They believed they needed more staff to do this, but they had a problem: they were running into frustrations about how long it was taking—and who was ultimately responsible—to decide to hire staff for the project. Typically hiring full-time, permanent staff for operational areas was the realm of HR, but this cross-functional project made it ambiguous who should decide what roles were needed, with what skillset, in what timeframe, on what terms, with who's budget, and so on. The company had never done a cross-functional project of this magnitude before, and there was no internal precedent for who should make the decision, nor was there a defined process to make it, and the territorial ambiguity and finger pointing was wasting time and leading to project delays.

The middle managers did not quite know what to do to solve the problem and keep all parties reasonably happy, so they had turned to the leader of the Lean Team to have a resident problem-solving "specialist" help them out. My boss chose me.

I was new to the company. Wanting to look knowledgeable, capable, and professional in front of this group of leaders, and to prove myself worthy to my boss as well, I was determined to display mastery of a genuine Lean "A3" problem-solving methodology.

Using my infallible Lean methodology, I would help them quickly and effectively solve their problem. I would be a hero. Unfortunately, this approach, so obvious in hindsight, was doomed from the start. There was simply no baseline standard to improve upon: no common agreement on who would make hiring decisions nor any process to follow; there was no consensus or precedent for how long it should take to make the decision (or recruit the new hire); and there was no agreed-upon budget for hiring, which made it vague even how many people to hire in the first place.

Yet instead of getting them to agree on a common course of action to establish some sort of standard that they could then improve later, I blindly marched towards my own failure, armed only with my meagre and inadequate method.

They politely went along with my approach. They all agreed on defining the problem as: "It's taking too long to make resourcing (staffing) decisions". I sheepishly did not insist on their defining a measurable, quantitative gap (mistake number one ... of many). I moved on to leading them through a mechanical Five Why[1] exercise:

Why is there so much delay in making resourcing decisions?
Because there is no consensus on who has ultimate authority to make resource decisions in this project.

Why is there lack of consensus about decision-making authority?
Because the executive sponsors of this project are expecting us to collaborate and make group decisions through cross-functional committees. No one person is allowed to make a decision.

Why is the group decision-making not working?
Because we each have our own distinct views of how we should resource the project, and there is no arbiter who can bring us to a common agreement.

Why is there no arbiter?
Because the executive sponsors are not aware that we are unable to come to agreement. They are not aware this is hurting the project timelines.

Why are the executive sponsors not aware?

Because it is part of our company's culture not to ask for executive help or disclose problems to them. And they are telling us to collaborate, not arbitrate.

I could have kept going with, "And so why is it part of our culture?", but I knew enough to have stopped there. The Five Whys worked as it should have in this case. Their impulse to protect executives from potentially negative information (and their untested assumption that the executives would react badly to it) was clearly a big part of the problem. Yet the delicate psychological and political aspects to this situation made these Five Whys somewhat futile—not useless, but futile, because there was no simple way to implement a countermeasure when the managers were not inclined to speak openly to the executive sponsors about the problems they were having.

At that point I did not know what to do. I was too bashful (at that time) to challenge their assumptions or to recast myself as mediator. I had booked the meeting room for 3 hours and we were already at an impasse after 60 minutes. Trying to kill time, I floundered around, grasping for random Lean tools, trying to get them to list out all the people who might need to be Responsible, Accountable, Consulted, or Informed (RACI) in a hiring decision. We ended early and noncommittally agreed to get together again to brainstorm what to do next, but we never did.

The group no doubt concluded that this whole "Lean problem-solving" thing was utterly useless. I do not blame them. I had blown it. No one in the room that day found the conclusion of our Five Why exercise helpful or practical. Certainly no one emerged from the room willing to go to the executive steering committee and tell them that they needed their help to make decisions faster. My problem-solving session had failed, and eventually, many months later, HR decided (notably without using any "Lean" problem-solving techniques) that a the project needed a single person to handle all the hiring into the project. HR had unilaterally influenced the senior executives sponsoring the project to hire such a person, give that person a budget, and empower them to make hiring decisions in consultation with the project leaders.

Reflection

HR did the right thing. There was no standard process and just establishing a defined role, budget, and decision-making authority was a big step in the right direction. Given a chance to do this one again, I would just ask the team of leaders to simply map the existing decision-making process at a fairly high level to expose its convolutions and structural delays. The visual map and any supporting data would have produced a more neutral, objective, blame-free tool with which to discuss the impact of the lack of timely decision-making with the sponsors. I would have had the middle managers consider a variety of potential alternatives to the current situation and map these out as well, weighing the pros and cons, as ways to "pitch" options to the sponsors. Once they had chosen and implemented a process for hiring for the project, they could then collect baseline data to measure the current state performance and improve upon it. But they had to have a defined process to begin with. I had come to help them improve their game, but they did not even yet know what sport they were playing.

As mentioned in Chapter 12, an office-based company should not start its Lean journey with A3 problem solving, but instead with four basic and prerequisite steps:

1. Define Your Customers
2. Understand Customer Value
3. Visualize Your Work
4. Create Flow

Creating flow will cause you to see problems all over the place, and then the time is right to engage in problem solving ... except there is another pre-requisite: root cause or "Lean" problem solving is about maintaining and improving process performance. If you want to do root cause problem solving, you need to have a baseline measure in place first.

Start with Standards

So, before you make the same mistake I did, and try to dive into the fifth step of problem solving without ensuring the previous four steps were in place, start with some basic measures. Here is a brief list of common "problem" situations you likely encounter at work and what to do *before* trying to find the root cause of anything.

■ No one knows who the customer is or what they expect: go find out.
■ Roles and responsibilities, basic process steps, and expected outcomes are not defined: define them.

- Everyone says they are overwhelmed with work but there are no measures for what is presently happening, including the volume of actual and expected demand and the average completion rate for various work items: start measuring.
- Everyone says things take "too long", but no one can say how long things should take: start measuring some more.
- High-level process steps not known (including upstream suppliers and downstream customers) or agreed upon: make them visible.
- Work is not sorted into categories, based on estimated complexity or duration (lack of balance): come up with criteria and sort it.
- There is no mechanism for prioritizing incoming work: come up with criteria and prioritize it.
- Work priorities are not coordinated (lack of continuity) between people or teams: coordinate it.
- There are no Work in Process (WIP) limits: establish some. Put all but the most urgent and important work in the backlog.

Once you have done the above, you will likely have a basic process defined and a measure or two in place to indicate how it is performing. Is the performance aligned with customer needs? (hint: go ask them). If not, what is your target level of performance? Your target performance level is your standard. You simply cannot know if a change is an improvement without standards.

Sadly, businesses implement changes (usually in the form of projects) all the time without any real evidence that the project made any difference. If things improve, project sponsors will, of course, attribute causality to their project; if things get worse, they will cite "other unanticipated factors". Most organizations are so rife with problems that someone with authority says, in exasperation, "something has to change!" and then everyone in the room launches multiple projects concurrently shortly thereafter. They throw as much at the proverbial wall as they can and see what sticks. Sometimes they get lucky and find something that works. Or, at least, it *feels* better. But was any business target achieved? Do customers notice or care?

Unless your firm has infinite money, time, and resources you might want to consider how wasteful this "spray and pray" practice is. Let's say you put ten project teams in charge of ten separate change initiatives (resource efficiency, anyone?) and your process improves slightly. You cannot really say which initiative caused the improvement, or whether it was due to a combination of factors, with any certainty. What you can be certain about is that

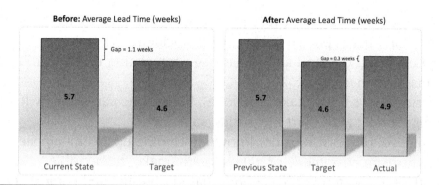

Figure 13.1   An Example of Using Measures to Learn and Improve.

nine out of ten teams basically wasted their time—not because they tried and failed, but because they tried, failed, and *failed to learn*. They failed to learn what did not work. Failure and learning is good; failure without learning is bad. It is bad because, in a few months, someone important and powerful, perhaps in a completely different department, will say, "something has to change!" and another ten teams will be set up and will try all the same things that did not work (and perhaps the one that did). And you wonder why your company has a capacity problem?

In order to learn from experiments, failed or successful, you have to have some kind of a measurable baseline and target. Otherwise, how can you know if a change is an improvement or not (see Figure 13.1)? As the great Tracey and Ernie Richardson repeat often, "No measure, no do!"

Note that in the "Before" version of Figure 13.1, the Current State is the baseline measure, and the Target is what the team thinks it can accomplish, given their analysis of the current state, but before they have actually made any process changes. The "After" version compares this target to the actual results after they made their changes. The Current State is now the Previous State. Note that the team did quite meet their target, but have nonetheless improved the lead time. Not meeting the target is acceptable so long as they reflect and learn on why they did not achieve their target. They may or may not decide to pursue closing the remaining gap of 0.3 weeks based on what they have learned. The most important element to measuring any process is to have both a target (future state) and actual (current state) and a gap because it is only by seeing and striving to close gaps that we can learn anything.

Many people will perceive collecting data as a tedious waste of time, but having a baseline measure will actually save you a lot of time otherwise lost to wasted effort, similar to my wasting the time of the middle managers who were trying to solve their human resourcing problems in the technol-ogy project I described previously. Using the rigor of facts and data and a structured problem-solving method—activities that are foreign to the culture of most office workplaces and therefore frequently resisted—actually saves tons of time in avoided meetings about how "solve" a problem. Next time you are in a meeting, see if the person speaking is framing the problem, guessing at the causes, or proposing a solution. You will likely note that they co-mingle all three. So does everyone else. Usually the highest-paid person in the room "wins", eventually, and many are glad that someone has made a decision, even if it is a poor and ill-informed one, because they are simply tired of the debate.

This happens too in paper-based A3 problem solving. I have seen too many people waste tons of time trying to figure out the "correct" way to fill in an A3 form because it is what their boss, barely familiar with Lean, told them to do: "We've got too many demands on our hands right now, Alan, and we can't plan our work effectively!" declares the boss. "Please do one of those A3 thingy-ma-jigs on this one".

Alan dutifully goes away and tries to write down what the problem is on an A3 piece of paper:

> The ABC team is having difficulty understanding the full range of work that its customers are demanding. This lack of clarity appears to be contributing to unexpected contention for resources and insufficient ability to plan and forecast. Demand for ABC's services is coming from multiple sources and varying points in the plan-ning and execution cycle. While some of that demand is direct and formally engaged, some of it is unpredictable and ad hoc.

While Alan's put down a lot of elegant words to paper here, and there is no denying he has a problem on his hands, there is *no existing measure* of how much work his team can handle and what it should prioritize first, second, and third. There is no measurable gap between what is happening (base-line) and what should be happening (target/standard). Poor Alan is trying to make up for this by stating a vague, unquantified problem (too much work for team to handle), guessing at a few causes (lack of clarity, inability to plan, unpredictability), and implying some solutions (if only we could plan and forecast to make work more predictable)—all in one paragraph! But because there is no measure in place, Alan is wasting his and his boss' time.

A better problem statement would be something like:

Currently there are 47 requests for ABC's services, coming from 6 different internal customer groups, all asking for delivery between now and the end of March. Our current staffing levels allow us to complete, on average, only 18 requests per month, meaning that we will likely be unable to service 11 requests within the desired time frame. Target state is to service all 47 requests before end of March, which will require us to complete work at a rate of 24 requests/month, without doing any additional overtime or hiring any more people. Gap to close = 6 requests/month.

In this example, the current state (performance measure of 18 requests/month), the desired state (new performance target of 24 requests/month), and the corresponding gap (6 requests/month) are clearly and quantifiably articulated. There is no speculation about what the cause is, or what the solution might be, since those will come later. This is a factual problem statement free of opinions, guessing, and wishful thinking. But such a problem statement requires that there be a current process defined and a current performance level (the 18 requests/month), against which to evaluate any implemented countermeasures as attempts to solve the problem. Target-Actual-Gap. This is rare in offices. Introducing it will usually elicit resistance.

The Challenge of Standards

Starting with standards is harder than it sounds. A big challenge with creating a culture of Lean problem solving in offices is that offices have far fewer standards compared to factory work. As author and consultant David Mann has noted, most factories typically have engineers on staff who are concerned about process design[2]. Even the most batch and queue, resource-efficient, conventionally managed factories have engineering specs that function as standards of what constitutes "acceptable" work. The workers may not be able to do the work to spec; or they might choose not to, and instead find workarounds (often improvements that they keep to themselves) to "meet their numbers". The presence of standards does not mean these are Lean factories by any means, but at least they do have some starting point from which to improve.

Offices, on the other hand, rarely have engineers (or anyone else) on staff concerned about process definitions, standards, and measures, never mind how to maintain and improve them. As a result, many office processes "have been left to evolve over time, usually with little examination[3]." Rarely does anyone measure the work in an office. Yes, of course, there are lagging measures in offices like financial results, but these look only backwards. The existing measures might tell you what your company, or even your team, accomplished last month but do not offer any guidance on what you are supposed to be doing *today* to meet customer expectations now or into the future. Why?

Everyone Hates Standards

Imagine you are in line for security at the airport. You are going to visit your sister. You bought her a hard-to-find bottle of her favorite wine and shoved it in your carry-on bag so that it would not break in transit. Now that you are in line, you suddenly remember the restrictions on liquids in carry-on baggage. "Crap! Maybe they will make an exception", you inwardly hope … but no luck: the security agent tells you that it is more than the allowable 3.4 ounces (100 ml). He informs you that you will either have to leave it behind or miss your flight. "But it's just a bottle of wine!" you are thinking to yourself, biting your tongue. "Who does this guy think I am, a terrorist? How could I possibly do anyone any harm with a 2012 Sonoma Pinot Noir?". You are really annoyed and disappointed, but you also know that the security agent is just following the standard procedures (aka the rules) and he is not going to make an exception for you. He has got a badge and a gun and there is no sense in arguing. You hand over the bottle.

As mentioned in Chapter 9, people in offices absolutely hate the word "standard". The words "standard work" evoke images of mindlessly repetitive work in a Dickensian factory. Office professionals are about as sanguine about following "standards" as they are about handing over an expensive bottle of wine to an airport security official.

STANDARD WORDING

Ask office workers for words that come to mind when you say "standard" and you will get a bunch of synonyms for authoritarian rigidity and inflexibility. After all, we supposedly hire knowledge workers for their brains, not their brawn, and they feel entitled to a large degree of professional autonomy to think on their own. It is a deeply entrenched cultural norm to feel entitled to this sort of "autonomy", which, in their minds, is largely equivalent to "freedom from standardization". Thus both frontline employees and leaders usually prefer a laissez-faire leadership style in a knowledge work environment[4]. In general, leaders leave their people alone to figure out on their own how best to do their work. Yes, a few of these smart people *love* standards—and they are also the ones who typically want to join the internal Lean team, suffer from borderline OCD issues, or both. But most normal people interpret the suggestion of standardizing what they do as "just shut up and follow the rules". Standards to them mean top-down compliance: no exceptions, no judgment, no thinking … just robotic, mindless bureaucracy.

If you hate the word "standard" since it connotes a highly-regimented, assembly-line style of working, choose a different word! The following is a list of suggestions of what could be used instead:

- Measure
- Method
- Job aid
- Guideline
- Process Document
- Code
- Knowledge Article
- Target Condition
- Norm
- Reference
- Framework
- Requirement
- Rule
- Specification
- Procedure
- Checklist
- Template

Or make up your own! It does not matter what they are called. The point is only that they have to help, not hinder, the employees doing the work.

Many will try to hide their visceral reactions against standardization with pseudo-rational justifications. They will quickly proffer that because of the highly "creative", "variable", and "custom" nature of their work, it cannot be standardized in any way; "My work changes every hour. I never do the same thing twice". Standard work might apply in mass production environments, they will quickly concede, but is neither applicable nor helpful to their type of work ("I don't work on an assembly line … you can't standardize what I do!"). Their work is "different". It is "thinking work[5]".

The greatest Lean thinkers, on the other hand, most of whom have only practiced Lean in manufacturing environments, love to quote Taiichi Ohno's observation that "there is no *kaizen* [continuous improvement] without standards[6]". So where does this leave office work? If offices have few or no measures (or any other types of standards), and there can be no improvement without them, does this mean that we can never improve office work?

Brace yourself (deep breath): standards can very much improve office work too! The big difference between the way standards work in Lean companies (in *any* industry, offices included) and traditionally managed companies is the fact that standards are, in Lean companies, created bottom up and horizontally. Just as contracts exist between buyers and sellers *for the benefit of both parties*, so too do standards in Lean companies join internal supplier and customer teams in mutually agreed-upon operational definitions of what "good work" looks like. Management can check how closely the work is to "good", but it should not create nor impose standards on anyone unless they pertain to human safety (such as at the airport) or regulatory/legal requirements. Standards are simply internal agreements or contracts, freely and willingly entered into, that ensure both parties live up to their responsibilities and obligations to each other, while making everyone better off.

Eight Big Misconceptions about Standards

To help you implement standards in your office workplace, it might be worthwhile to dispel some common misconceptions about them.

Misconception #1: Standards Are Coercive

Frontline employees who are closest to the customer and the value-adding work should always create the standards. A leader's only role in standardization is to encourage, promote (and, yes, sometimes insist) that the team create, follow, and improve standards for the benefit of customers. Other than that, the inmates should get to run the asylum. The reason most people hate standards is because they have experienced them only as top-down rules imposed by management. This is not how Lean uses standards.

The people who benefit from rules tend to be those who make the rules. If we want customers, first and foremost, to benefit from standards, the standards have to *help* the people who directly create value for the customer. In other words, standards should make a frontline team's work *easier*, not more cumbersome. When standards work well, they create consistency and predictability for employees and external customers. When they do not work well, the frontline teams who created them must change them.

Misconception #2: Standards Are Always Very Precise and Detailed

Do not standardize everything! If the output has to be very precise and consistent, such as when flying airplanes, performing brain surgery, or transacting large amounts of money, the standards are going to have to be more precise. This does not mean they have to be long and detailed. Do not think of standards as those dreaded 500-page Standard Operating Procedures in three-ringed binders, and please do not create any more. Office work rarely needs to be this precise, and is often customized to specific customer needs. A standard could, for instance, be as loose as "confirm the accuracy of the documents detailing the terms and conditions of the long-term debt swaps within 48 hours of the transaction" or "resolve the customer's problem to the best of your abilities on the first call, regardless of how long it takes" and it would still be very effective. Standards do not even have to be in written form. The most effective standards are often simple and visual in nature (think of instruction booklets from IKEA—no words!). A standard is a target we are striving for—to meet customer needs and expectations.

In "thinking work" we rely a lot on conversations as the medium for transferring knowledge, communicating ideas, and coming to agreements. Yet often people leave a meeting room with different interpretations about what was agreed or said. Newly received information merges with our existing knowledge before we form our conclusions. Could standardization help something as fuzzy and nebulous as communication? Yes, absolutely. If we make it a standard to make our tacit knowledge, thinking, and assumptions as explicit as possible, it helps create a shared understanding and avoids conflicts down the road. We can also standardize who should communicate, how often, about what topics, and for how long. Standards lead to better communication without ever dictating its content.

Misconception #3: Standards Only Apply to Highly Repetitive Work

Every job (or task, process, or project) has some repeatable elements and some unique, improvised elements. Just as humans are all the same and all different, at the same time, so too with work. Every commercial contract, for instance, is the same in many ways, and also different in as many ways, *simultaneously*. Strive to standardize the repeatable, tedious, error-prone and/or annoying aspects of all your jobs and projects. The intertwined nature of the truly repeatable work and the truly "thinking" work makes it hard to sort out. What appears to be a "unique" process probably has many standard aspects to it when analyzed closely. It involves asking a lot of questions to make a person's thinking process explicit.

Determining what to standardize and to what level of detail should be left to, as always, the people who have to use the standards to help them do their work. Some standards can definitely be *too* precise or rigid to be useful—for instance, in a lot of service roles, you have to be able to absorb and respond to high variation in volumes and complexity of customer demand—you cannot just set a standard of "serve an average of 18 customers/day" in an ice cream shop because on cold days you might have no customers and on hot ones you might have 468. Yet other standards can be too vague. So how can you know what the "right" level of standardization is? Simply ask: would more (or less) standardization of this process make the work easier, better, faster and/or cheaper for you, the customer, and/or the company? How can we try it out and to learn if we are right?

Misconception #4: Standards Need to Be Created and Enforced Centrally

Centralizing standards is a bad but potentially seductive idea. It appeals to technocrats who dream of clockwork and managing a company as if it were a top-down, people-free machine, with standards and rules for everything. In reality, companies are not machines (and never will be), but complex adaptive systems. Employees in such a system will ignore or resist any unreasonable rules or standards imposed on them by management. (They will, of course, begrudgingly follow them if their livelihoods depend on it). Centralized rules thus will always create additional work, like conducting inspections, audits, and similar "police" work, to enforce them. Not only will this police work consume additional organizational capacity, but it will also make the workforce passively antagonistic to the company's ambitions, and generally make for a very unpleasant place to work. Centralized rules will not suit customer needs either (one size does *not* fit all).

Misconception #5: Standards Kill Creativity

There is only so much room in your brain for creative thought. Time spent thinking about what to do, when, for how long, and with what approach— the logistical stuff—often crowds out your time to think creatively at work. Standardization of the logistical stuff reduces the headspace you need to devote to this sort of work and frees up capacity for your brain to be *more* creative, not less. When employees have to figure out what to work on, and then figure out what the boss' expectations are, before they actually *do* the work, they waste a lot of time and mental energy prioritizing and making decisions about logistical, administrative stuff. Would not that brain power be better off spent on actually doing and improving the work?

Knowledge workers often store much of the knowledge of how to do the work—including their unique and creative approaches—in their "wetware": the brain. This is problematic because it means we all have different models of how things work and what the best approach to doing the work is. We have to share our thinking in order for people to agree to it, as well as to help improve it. It is also problematic because unshared knowledge will leave the building when the person does.

If we make our tacit knowledge, thinking, and assumptions as explicit as possible, we can then share our logical frameworks with others. This allows others with less experience to learn from us faster. Having the score to a piece of music does not make us play like a famous concert pianist, but it certainly allows us to learn how to play the music faster than if there were no musical score, and we had to figure it out "by ear" (which is how many office workers and managers learn most of their job). Standardize (through words, pictures, recordings, etc.) as much of your thinking as you can so that others can become creative virtuosos.

Because much of the value-adding work office workers do is based on judgment and decision-making under situations of ambiguity and uncertainty, we should try to *reduce* the amount of judgment, ambiguity, and uncertainty we have to deal with every day. This sounds paradoxical, but the more we can turn our existing work processes into a repeatable formula, the more time and brain power we can devote to new challenges or the non-repeatable aspects of the existing work. We should not have to think about the basic who, what, why, when, where and how of our work. For instance, we should have a standard system for how to evaluate, prioritize, and sequence all incoming work so that we do not have waste time guessing whether we should start working on Project A or B next. Further, we should generally know the basics of what we need to do, and for approximately how long, when we start working on Project A or B. In operational work, we want to focus on the quality of the work we are doing (something the customer cares about) and not to have to focus on figuring out what to do next and how to do it (which the customer does not care about).

The work of corporations, over time, follows the same trajectory. A corporation also wants to devote more of its workforce to innovation and discovery. The most creative, innovative companies standardize whatever they can, as fast as they can[7]. They make the "unpredictable predictable, and the exceptional repeatable[8]". This essentially frees up more collective corporate headspace to devote to the more unfamiliar stuff: new products, new markets, and new ways of operating, by reducing the time it takes to think about the old and familiar stuff. You want to devote your company's collective mind to driving the car faster to new destinations, not figuring out how to get into second gear. The faster a company can standardize, and move on to tackling the new unknown stuff, the greater its competitive advantage.

Misconception #6: Standards Are Not Customer Friendly

When I worked in the shipping industry, the customer service teams documented standards on the specifics of each of their large customers (the so-called "strategic" or "key" accounts). These were above and beyond the standard process to make a booking (exports) or release a container (imports)—which was simply basic training. The customer-specific standards would help customer service agents understand the nature of the customer's business, their specific transportation needs, their primary destinations, commodities, routings, documentation requirements, contractual pricing, levels of urgency, preferred frequency, and mode of communication, and so on. It got to the level of "if it's electronic equipment coming in to the port of Long Beach and destined to the Midwest, it is urgent and must make the first available train. If it is fold up lawn chairs discharging in Tacoma, it is less urgent between June and January, and can dwell at the port for up to three days—in Feb through May, only two days is allowed". These standards also helped train new hires to make them productive sooner. It allowed CSRs to go on vacation or take sick days without worrying about the risk of their clients experiencing inconsistent service levels. Most importantly, customers loved it. Standards should ultimately help make customers happy. If they do not, improve the standards!

Misconception #7: Measurements Are Not Standards

Not all measures are standards. Many measures are descriptions of past performance or arbitrarily chosen internal targets (e.g. revenue, margins, customer volumes) that have nothing to do with creating customer value more predictably. Not all standards are measures (they can be, for instance, a standard set of steps to take in response to a type of incident or problem). But standards can be measures, and measures can be standards.

Typical quantitative standards (aka measures) that help in offices are things like estimated vs. actual amount of work completed per time period, Work in Process (WIP) limits, estimated vs. actual completion times, backlog volumes, prioritization criteria (e.g. decision-trees) and daily work schedules. This is what Jim Benson calls an *appropriate* level of standardization that allows teams enough structure to deliver consistently to customers, and to improve upon this delivery, while also remaining flexible in response to changing customer needs[9]. In fact, the more you can standardize appropriately, the more flexible you can become.

Qualitative standards that help are behavioral in nature. What behaviors do we want to see? What behaviors will make us like our work more? What behaviors will help us get our work done faster and better? What behaviors will make customers love us? Leaders can standardize some of the behaviors they want to see into their Leader Standard Work. This can include standard floor walks or huddle attendance, but also what standard questions to ask during one-on-one employee meetings. Leader standard work, done right, is a very powerful tool to change the culture of an organization towards becoming Lean.

Misconception #8: Standards Are Inflexible and Can Rarely Be Changed

Just because standards create stability does not mean that they should never change. On the contrary: they *must* change. Frontline employees must be able to change the standards they created at any time, so long as there is consensus among them. Only standards involving high-risk situations should require managerial approval. Standards must change because: (1) there is always a better way; (2) customer needs and business conditions change all the time; and (3) employees are more engaged with their work when they can improve their work in a meaningful and measurable way.

Agile practice is full of helpful standards, despite its manifesto saying that people are more important than processes[10]. Consider Scrum, for instance: backlog prioritization, sprint planning, daily stand-ups, sprint reviews, retrospectives, etc. are all processes that involve standard tools, structures, roles, and behaviors. Standardization is largely why they are effective.

Summary

Root cause A3 problem solving and the similar Kata methods are very valuable and powerful activities for any firm. It not only solves problems to increase the performance of the business, but it also serves as a way to coach and develop the problem-solving capabilities of employees. But, to reiterate: do not *start* your office Lean journey with problem solving and continuous improvement tools. Start with understanding who your end customer is and what value means to them. Articulate to all employees how they themselves would benefit from improving the flow of this customer value. Then map the value stream. Make the work visible and, as much as you can, gather data about time (e.g. touch time, waiting time, lead time) in all process steps to understand your current flow of value. Study the system: is it capable of consistently and sustainably meeting the customer's needs? Why or why not? Where and how could you implement standardization to improve flow? Only once you have taken these steps to understand the work and then standardize it where appropriate and necessary—and at the right level of structure and detail to be helpful to both employees and customers—can the problem solving for true improvement begin. Indeed, there can be no continuous improvement without standards. Yes, even in customized knowledge work.

Three Main Takeaways

1. Before a process can be improved, it needs to have a current and a target performance level (standard) and a gap between them. Do not try to solve problems without such standards in place or you will be wasting your time.
2. Offices have a longstanding culture of having very few standards applied to their work. Office workers feel entitled to a high degree of autonomy and are not accustomed to having to follow a standard. As a result, there is much cultural resistance to implementing standards, even though this resistance is founded on a lot of misconceptions.
3. Standardization frees up capacity for employees to be more creative and innovative at work. Companies that can standardize their repeated work faster and better gain competitive advantage.

Notes

1. The Five Whys is a popular Lean tool used to uncover the root cause of problems.
2. Mann, David. 2015. *Creating a Lean Culture: Tools to Sustain Lean Conversions* (3rd Edition). Boca Raton, FL: CRC Press, p. 146.
3. Mann, David. *Ibid.* p. 146.
4. Bob Emiliani has astutely pointed out that the higher you go in an organization, the less empirical the decision-making tends to be. There is more reliance on *de jure* (intuitive) reasoning and less *de facto* (fact-based) reasoning. Since office workers tend to be found in head offices, co-located with executive leaders, the culture norm tends to be much more *de jure*. See Emiliani, M.L. "Bob". 2018. *The Triumph of Classical Management Over Lean Management: How Tradition Prevails and What to Do About It.* South Kingstown, RI: Cubic LLC.
5. It is worth noting that many craftspeople opposed mechanization in the early 1800s. For instance, the original Luddites were skilled textile workers in England who felt (rightly) that automated textile machinery was threatening their jobs and wages. The introduction of these machines allowed factory owners to replace skilled workers with cheaper, lower-skilled workers. Standardization can, understandably, be threatening. It has a long history. Yet it did a lot for improving productivity and the British economy. The trick is to not layoff anyone for standardizing or improving their job.

6. This is quoted everywhere and has been passed down by people who worked with Ohno as something he repeatedly said. It has entered the Lean folklore. See an example by Shook, John. 2018. Standardized Work or Kaizen? Yes. *The Lean Post*, December 12, 2018: https://www.lean.org/LeanPost/Posting. cfm?LeanPostId=986 (accessed December 29, 2018).

7. See Martin, Roger. 2009. *The Design of Business: Why Design Thinking Is the Next Competitive Advantage.* Boston, MA: Harvard Business Press.

8. Ballé, Michael, Nicolas Chartier, and Pascale Coignet, et al. 2019. *The Lean Sensei: Go See Challenge.* Boston, MA: Lean Enterprise Institute, p. 65.

9. Benson, Jim. 2018. Optimize when you can, standardize if you must. *Medium. com*, August 23, 2018: https://medium.com/whats-your-modus/optimize-when-you-can-standardize-if-you-must-94571edbd455 (accessed May 22, 2019).

10. Kent, Beck, Mike Beedle, Arie van Bennekum, et al. 2001. Manifesto for Agile Software Development: https://agilemanifesto.org (accessed May 22, 2019). To be precise, the manifesto says that it values "individuals and interactions *over* processes and tools" (my emphasis). This can be misinterpreted to mean *no* processes and *no* tools, which is not only a perfect recipe for chaos, but also not, I believe, what the authors meant. How do I know? Because the authors explicitly wrote "while there is value in the items on the right [processes and tools], we value the items on the left [individuals and interactions] more"—*both* are necessary and valuable!

Chapter 14

Using Standards to Create Flow

The manager of a team of software developers wanted to solve the seemingly simple problem of knowing what his team's productivity was or, as he put it, "knowing what was going on". This was not a case of his being removed from the daily work in a closed-door office, or sitting on a different floor than the four employees who reported to him: he sat alongside them in an open-concept work space. He knew his people well, and could see they were busy and working hard all day ... but what were they really accomplishing? Probably quite a lot, he suspected, but he was never exactly sure.

He was already doing what most managers do to know what is "going on": he held weekly meetings, and the team did a round-table of verbal status updates. He also met with each person one-on-one for 30 minutes every two weeks as part of his leader standard work. Whether in the team meeting or one-on-one, his employees would, by turn, declare what requests (to change or enhance a software application in some way) they were working on, and what status they were in (e.g. just started, blocked, almost done). They would talk also about other projects and initiatives they were working on. In effect, they described that they were all busy and working hard. They certainly were, and employee performance was not an issue, but the manager was still dissatisfied.

The manager wanted to know what was actually being *achieved*—from his customers' point of view—from all this busyness and hard work. He was frustrated that he did not know, or was unable to keep track of how much work was actually crossing the finish line and at what pace. Dissatisfied, he continued to seek out an effective way to better understand his team's work output.

The manager decided to use visual management in the form of a simple Kanban board[1] to establish a standard Work in Process (WIP) limit and gain visibility to what tickets were being worked on by whom at any given time. He designed a whiteboard with a simple set of columns of their process flow as well as an important "On Hold" column to not lose sight of items that, for one reason or another, could not currently advance. The rows consisted of the names of the developers (see Figure 14.1).

The system worked using the following standards:

1. When a user or developer created a ticket, it went into a backlog. The backlog was sizeable because, as is often the case, the demand for work exceeded the supply of labor (developers).
2. The team of developers conducted an initial triage within seven calendar days of the ticket input date to determine whether the request was actually feasible. If it was, they would make a rough estimate of the time needed to complete it (small, medium, high, or "project-sized" effort).
3. In an agreement with the managers of the internal customer teams, each customer team maintained a priority ranking of the tickets they had created. By having the various customers prioritize their own tickets, the developers could align their priorities with those of their customers. Interestingly, when the customers sat together to discuss

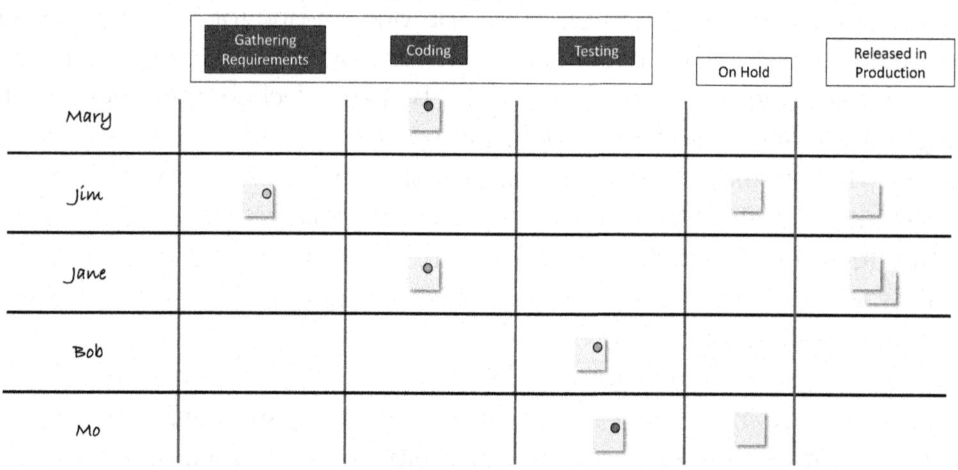

Max WIP = 1

	Gathering Requirements	Coding	Testing	On Hold	Released in Production
Mary		●			
Jim	○			□	□
Jane		●			□
Bob			○		
Mo			●	□	

Figure 14.1 The Visual Board That the Team Used to Manage Their Work.

priorities, they were more understanding of *other* teams' priorities and did not demand that all attention be focused on their team.

4. When a developer finished a ticket, she would "pull" the next top priority one from the list. She would then estimate a target completion date and begin to work on it. She would not start work on a new ticket until finishing the current ticket or hitting a roadblock (e.g. more information needed from customer) that required the ticket to be put in the "On Hold" column.

5. The developer would then move the ticket through each of the stages of work until completion. A colored magnet (red, yellow, or green) would indicate whether the target date was still realistic.

6. At the weekly staff meeting, the team stopped doing round-table status reports and did not discuss tickets with a green magnet. They only discussed tickets with a yellow or red magnet. They also discussed tickets in the "On Hold" column to find out whether a colleague or the manager could help the situation. Finally, if someone had more than one ticket going at the same time, the manager would seek to understand why.

Importantly, there was no blame assigned for a yellow or red ticket. If a ticket was yellow or red, the ticket owner was asked to briefly explain why and to implement countermeasures if it was something within their control. The leader enforced the rule that they could only work on *one ticket at a time*. They could only take on a new ticket if the previous one was no longer in the development phase.

Many of the staff were skeptical at first. Was this system too mechanical? Could it really work in a "knowledge work" field like software development? Their leader insisted that they try it out despite their doubts.

One employee in particular felt unclear about the whole system and for a while, continued to work on multiple tickets at the same time. The manager persisted and the employee gave the one-ticket-at-a-time concept a try. A few weeks later, the employee personally thanked his manager for putting such a system in place. He said he had never felt less stressed and yet more productive in a long time. The leader was pleased too: the system seemed to be producing the behavior he had hoped for.

The immediate result was that their weekly "look how busy I am" status report meetings shrunk from 1 hour to less than 30 minutes. They no longer had to speak about what they were working on, what stage it was in, or if it was on track or not, because the information was all there in front of them, for all to see in an instant. They only spoke about yellow or red tickets and what they were doing to get them back on track (which could include asking for help from one's colleagues).

They applied the notion of limiting WIP at the team level too. Previously the team would release an updated version of the software only once they had enough tickets to justify creating a "build" (release). Now they formally targeted a minimum of two releases per month, even if it sometimes resulted in fewer tickets per release—in other words, they reduced their batch sizes. The team had already developed the habit of releasing new code into production quite frequently, but the explicit target allowed them to track their accomplishments throughout the year and create more predictability to their schedules.

They also trained everyone in the team on the production release process, which formerly had been the domain of only one employee. This training allowed the team to increase the number of production releases because they did not have to wait for the people with a specific skillset to be available to run the process. Because all staff could now run the process, if someone was absent, a colleague could take over and the flow to the customer would not stop. With fewer tickets but more frequent builds, the system was easier to test, debug, and fix, and the number of "failed builds" that never made it into production decreased. The reduction in rework more than offset any additional work associated with more frequent releases. As a bonus, the training required the team to document the process. As they documented it, they realized there were small improvements that they could make.

In the year before the cross-training and changing the production release schedule to a minimum of two per month, only 46% of builds made it to production without rework. After the changes, that rate increased to 76%. In one year, the number of production releases went from 18 to 34. Interestingly, the number of closed tickets stayed the same. The customers received a comparable amount of enhancements as the previous year, but received them faster and more frequently. And no one had to work any harder or faster. In other words, the team improved its flow.

Obviously, this team did more than just implement standard work: they devised a whole system for managing their work more effectively. But the standard work (prioritization, estimated durations; WIP limits; routines to keep the board updated) were the fuel that kept the system running. One of the great aspects of this team's system was that it balanced structure with autonomy: it gave some form and shape to the work without dictating how it should be done. Everyone knew exactly what he or she was working on, and what he or she had to work on next, and the target for approximately how long it should take.

The system, once it became habitual, was almost entirely self-regulating. The leader did not have to tell anyone what to work on, or check-in on people to see if they were getting stuck or overwhelmed. He could now focus on other projects, coaching his people for personal development (not correction), and take vacations without any worry. Even better, customers knew where their tickets were in the queue and when they could expect them to go into production. If they missed the latest release, they knew they could catch the next one in two weeks or less. As a result, there was far less political jockeying between the business customers and the leader of the team to have their ticket expedited into the next release (at the expense of some other customer) because it was a predictable, stable system.

The standards that structured the system meant it was organized and efficient, not a tool to punish employees or make them work harder. When one of the team's employees later left for a higher-paying job outside the company, he wrote to the manager a few weeks afterwards, "I miss the highly organized, non-micro-managed environment of my previous job".

Three Main Takeaways

1. Limit WIP: work on only one thing at a time. Make sure that one thing is your highest priority. Do not start any new work until you absolutely cannot advance your current work any further and it has to go on "hold".
2. Involve customers in prioritization: ask customers to rank order their priorities. While not everything they want done will be done right away, at least their highest priority items will be, and they will have reasonable expectations about the lower priority items. Predictability is often just as valuable, if not more so, than speed.
3. Systems Drive Behavior: visual management, prioritization, estimated durations; WIP limits; routines to keep the board updated, cross-training, and release schedules were tools or subsystems that all coalesced into a system for flowing value to the customer. As systems become more robust, they become largely self-governing, freeing up the leader of the group to do more value-adding work.

Note

1. Very much in the style used in Agile methodologies like Kanban and Scrum. The manager in this story was originally inspired by Benson, Jim, and Tonianne deMaria Barry. 2011. *Personal Kanban: Mapping Work, Navigating Life*. Seattle, WA: Modus Cooperandi Press.

Chapter 15

Lean Thinking and the Digital Age

In the prehistoric days of 2014, getting a coffee at a coffee shop meant you had to go to the store, wait in line, order and pay, wait again (while they made your coffee), and then you received your coffee in a cup with your name misspelled on it. If you were to map this out from the customer's point of view, it would look a lot like Figure 15.1.

Nowadays, I can order and pay for my coffee while riding the bus into the office. I order it at the stop before the one where I get off, to allow the shop sufficient time (about 5 minutes) to receive the order, put it in the queue, pour my coffee, and put it up on the counter (and with Ken, not Cam, written on the printed label). I get off at my stop, walk two minutes to the shop, grab my coffee, and go to my office across the street (see Figure 15.2).

When we digitize a process step in a value stream almost completely out of existence, as the coffee shop has done here with the "order and pay" step, we often overlook the more important fact that we also eliminate the waiting time upstream from it. Yet this is one of the primary reasons why digitization holds so much promise: we are condensing the value stream and

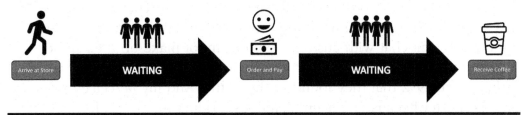

Figure 15.1   The "Old School" Way of Ordering a Coffee from a Coffee Shop.

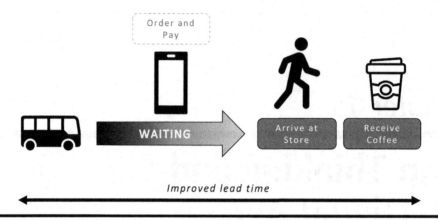

Figure 15.2   The Redesigned Process Based on the Digitization of the "Order and Pay" Process Step.

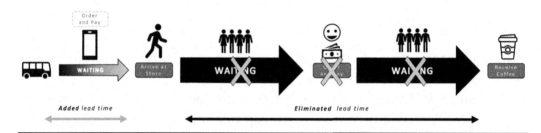

Figure 15.3   Automation Eliminates all the Original In-Store Waiting Time and Adds a Little at the Front End. The Net Waiting Is Dramatically Reduced.

creating continuity! My relatively recently acquired ability to order my coffee through an app on my phone means that I entirely eliminate the time that would be previously consumed by waiting in line (see Figure 15.3). It also speeds up and adds reliability to my ordering process (if I order the wrong thing on my phone it is hard to argue that it was the barista who misunderstood my order), and virtually eliminates the process of paying, both of which are nice perks, but it is avoiding waiting in the long line-up that is the real selling feature for me as a consumer.

From the coffee shop's perspective, this digitization also shortens their efforts devoted to the ordering and payment process. They can reallocate this saved time to making the coffees rather than taking orders and making friendly chit-chat with customers who cannot make up their mind, then change their mind, and then decide to pay entirely with a jar of nickels from 1992 that they found in their attic. And my *perceived* wait time is shorter because I am simultaneously riding the bus (a form of transportation waste associated with my job that is not easily eliminated in the short-term, and so something I have to do in any case, with or without the existence of a coffee-ordering app on my phone). So long as the coffee shop does not raise their prices for my using it, this technology makes me better off without making anyone else worse off: the lead time for me, both actual and perceived, is shorter. The coffee shop is also better off from an operational perspective (elimination of the order and pay process), but also gets the important but intangible benefit of building my consumer loyalty by making my life easier when interacting with them. Everybody wins[1].

So, What Do We Mean by Digital?

As with trying to define Lean, if you ask ten random people what "digital" means, you will likely get ten different answers. Generally, I understand it to mean two main things:

1. IT has moved to the "front-end" of the business, becoming a big part of how consumers interact with a company.
2. Data and predictive analytics are allowing companies to gather real-time feedback on customer behavior to improve both their products and services, as well as the marketing of these.

The first dimension refers to the fact that IT is no longer a generic, supporting tool for administrative "back office" functions. Fifteen to twenty years ago, many aspects of IT were considered to be a commodity service, and it caused a lot of companies to offshore large portions of its IT functions, assuming they could be done by nearly anyone anywhere. Now IT is moving to the customer-facing side of the business, meaning that technology is a big part of (or entirely) the interface between external customers and a firm. Think of all the electronic purchases we make—both in our personal consumption and as business procurement: our first experience with a company or brand is almost always a digital one. We might see an ad online, then click to go to the website or download the app. Initial customer contact, previously handled almost exclusively by sales and customer service staff, is now mediated digitally through our personal phones, tablets and laptops 88% of the time[2]. Sometimes *all* customer contact is handled digitally— have you ever spoken to a live person at Netflix, Amazon, Uber, or Google? Companies are now thinking a lot more about the "digital experiences" they are creating for their customers, and how their brand is managed in the digital sphere across a wide variety of channels and platforms.

The second dimension means that digital businesses are able to capture real-time (or near real-time) feedback about consumer behavior. While companies used to collect customer feedback data through time-consuming and expensive surveys, market research reports, and (occasionally) direct observation, now they can do much of this more quickly and affordably with data. The erosion of the privacy of individuals is a very valid concern, but nonetheless, on the positive side, the analysis of these consumer behavior data allows a firm to improve the value of its offerings and improve its marketing approaches to different customer segments.

The human ability to compute large sets of data is limited. Computers, not so much. This is how Spotify knows what song you might want to listen to next; how Netflix knows what you might to want to watch next, or how Amazon knows what you might want to buy next. It is how Siri, or Alexa, or customer service bots know the answer to your questions—at least some of the simple ones. Firms are using data to try to identify which customers might be ready to spend more, so they can nudge them along a little faster through targeted and timely marketing; and which customers might be at risk of leaving for a competitor, so they can take remedial actions to retain them[3]. Medical clinics can use real-time data to predict probabilities of patients having strokes or heart attacks and take preventative measures before such an event can occur[4]. Artificial intelligence will likely change the nature of work quite drastically, but it will not replace humans. It will just put a premium on the things that computers do not do well, like thinking, judgment, and problem solving.

"Digital" is not just limited to the front-end of the business. It also means enhanced automation and connectivity between *every* part of the firm, including between the firm and its external partners and suppliers, who may be half-way across the world. This is basically the continuation and expansion of the traditional "back office" role of IT, only it is becoming much more powerful, affordable, and wider in scope. With application program interfaces (APIs), we can effectively and securely exchange real-time data with many different stakeholders, including entities outside the firm itself, like suppliers and customers, regardless of geography or time zone. We can also remotely monitor the performance of our productive assets—whether these be industrial machines or stacks of servers—because we are connected to them digitally in real-time. Exciting new capabilities are being enabled almost every day in the areas of Artificial Intelligence, Robotics, Distributed Ledgers (aka blockchain), Big Data and Analytics, Cloud Computing, 3D printing, Virtual Reality, Internet of Things, and so on. So, taking advantage of the newest digital capabilities has become a priority in all industries and will continue to be even more so into the future.

As a result of so many new capabilities becoming available, offices are becoming essentially data factories. In the data factory we use software and human knowledge as our primary tools to add value to data and transform it into meaningful patterns of information and knowledge: what we commonly call our products and services. Our products and services are simply value-added information—the right information, at the right time, in the right amount—that customers are willing to pay for. Even money or software, if that is what you are selling, are just arrangements of structured information (stored on servers) that have value to customers.

What can be confusing about office work is that while we *sell* information-based products and services, we also *buy* information and knowledge as the "raw material" to produce them. We also use process-related information, as all industries do, to run the data factory day-to-day: information tells us when to work on what, and (later) how well we are doing at it. The information we buy, transform, and sell (e.g. financing contracts, policy analysis, marketing strategies, permits and tickets, legal advice, etc.), and the information we gather and use to manage the work, are best understood as two distinct classes. If we made toasters for our external customers, we would naturally want to use information (e.g. how many toasters/hour we should be producing, how many defects we have, the costs of labor and materials, etc.) to run and improve our business operations internally. It is easier to conceptually separate physical toasters from operational information flows in a toaster factory, but it is exactly the same conceptual division that needs to happen when we produce information-based widgets in the data factory—we produce info-widgets for external customers, and we gather and use information to learn about how well (or poorly) we are producing our info-widgets. Flow is essential to both.

So, what does any of this have to do with Lean? Most offices lack good management systems—what many call "operating models" —to run the data factory. As we search for better models, which model of factory operations are we going to want to copy and adapt, Toyota's or GM's?

To help you decide, here is a passage from a blog written by Amazon's Chief Technology Officer, Werner Vogels, in late 2017:

> We should ponder how we can organize the 'production' of data in such a way so that we ultimately come out with a competitive advantage. We need mechanisms that enable the mass production of data using software and hardware capabilities. These

mechanisms need to be lean, seamless and effective. At the same time, we need to ensure that quality requirements can be met ... A company that wants to industrialize 'software production' needs to find ideas on how to achieve the same kind of lean and qualitatively first-class mass production that has already occurred for industrial goods ... the first place to look will be lean production[5].

Vogels goes on to argue that a successful digital business model will use continuous improvement, experimentation, standard processes, and high-quality standards for the production of data. He implies that successful firms will have to develop a business model where their software developers—regardless of whether they are employed in house or through outside supplier firms—deliver highly relevant, value-producing software solutions to business operations. And *quickly*. In other words, software developers have to flow value to their *internal* customers in business operations better and faster, so that the operations can, in turn, flow their info-widgets to the *external* paying customers.

In an office, we can draw the parallel between our computer hardware and the capital equipment traditional factories use, while our software is like a die that an industrial machine might use. The legendary thinker Shigeo Shingo came up with the revolutionary concept of the single-minute exchange of dies (SMED) at Toyota, where they learned to switch over a line to produce a different model (of car, in this case) with minimal downtime. SMED has the benefit of making the company far more responsive to changing customer demand by limiting overproduction and not holding excess inventory. They were able to make changeovers 94% faster: down from 90 minutes to less than 5[6]. It is done largely by careful preparation and then rapid swarming. They practice, prepare, and rehearse before carrying out the exchange. They use a large team of people and everybody knows their role and responsibilities, so they execute rapidly and precisely. As a comparison, it can often take one average person 20 minutes to change a single tire on a car, but NASCAR pit crews can do this under 15 *seconds*[7].

Vogels is basically advocating for a similar SMED approach to the deployment or enhancement of software, the capital equipment of the data factory. The typical "industrial" way of implementing and upgrading software in offices is to create a giant, multi-million-dollar program that promises to only take a couple of *years*. Of course, these heroic projects, in the best of cases, take twice as long and cost three times as much (and usually do not deliver anywhere near what was promised). Vogel's Lean/Agile approach advocates instead that internal software releases happen frequently and quickly to minimize disruption and continuously increase the flow of info-widgets and external customer value. Do not think it can be done? Have you ever seen a NASCAR pit crew in action?

Lean First, Automate Second

Because of the glacial pace of change typically associated with traditional enterprise software applications, Lean advocates tend to promote Lean inter-ventions as being technology-free. We are keen to point out that we need to get rid of the waste in the process *before* automating it. This makes a lot of sense. Compared to large-scale technology deployments, tech-free Lean improvements are relatively cheap and fast. For instance, Jean Cunningham, a former CFO, and presently the Executive Chairman of the Lean Enterprise Institute, writes: "IS [Information Systems] should not drive the change. It is the last thing to change AFTER the [non-IS] changes to the actual process have been designed, tested, and agreed on[8]". John Seddon, the great cur-mudgeonly systems thinker from the UK, reiterates that technology must come *last* in any business improvement efforts[9]. This is very good advice. We can probably all think of numerous examples in our workplaces of underwhelming software deployments that have reduced delay and rework in one area, only to have created an equal or larger amount somewhere else. In hindsight, some Lean thinking prior to deciding to purchase, configure, and implement the software would have helped.

Homer Simpson once proclaimed, beer in hand: "To Alcohol! The cause of … and solution to … all of life's problems[10]!" The same proclamation could sadly be made about software. Because all our problems appear to be caused by software, we perversely assume all of our problems will be solved by it. Good software can do amazing things for us, but we are often far too quickly seduced by the shiny allure of new software without think-ing very much about what constitutes good software. "New" and "good" are not necessarily the same thing. When thinking about introducing new software into a value stream, we forget to ask: what customer value is the value stream *currently* producing? How is the value stream performing at *currently* delivering value? How will value production and delivery be *bet-ter* because of the new software? If we cannot specify the gap between what we are giving the customer now and what we would like to deliver to the customer in the future, we can end up delivering (perhaps even using

Lean/Agile methods) well-designed, great-looking, intuitive software that is really good at helping us do the wrong things faster. The unintended consequence is that we pollute our value streams with bad software (optimized for vertical silos), and employees, customers, and results suffer.

So, yes, we should always try to improve our processes *before* automating them. We definitely do need to first understand value from the customer's point of view, study its flow, map the value stream, identify and eliminate/reduce the non-value adding steps as much as possible, and then—and only then—begin thinking about how technology can improve the value stream even more. To modify Peter Drucker's phrase: there is nothing so useless as digitizing that which should not be done at all[11].

But why does Lean thinking have to stop short of technology implementation? Limiting Lean to the technology-free realm short-changes an enterprise of the full value Lean thinking has to offer. The "streamline first, automate second" approach implies you can get a process (or value stream) to an ideal state where it simply cannot get any better without investment in technology (and that you would know when you were there). This sort of perfection is, of course, impossible. All processes—wholly automated, entirely manual, or somewhere in between—will forever contain some degree of waste. There will always be waste. You will never get to a point where you can say, "Now that this process is perfect in its analog state, it is time to digitize". Nor will we ever get to a point where we can say, "Now that we've completely digitized our process, it cannot be improved any further". The point is, as always, to continuously expand our organizational capability to improve the flow of customer value, electronic or otherwise, in response to perpetually changing business conditions. Since value stream flow can benefit immensely from technological automation, the Lean community should be thinking about technology far more than it currently does.

IT is really important. IT is as fundamental to an enterprise these days as electricity or caffeine: we cannot do our jobs without it. And, like it or not, digital innovation is going to continue to march forward into the future at an increasingly fast pace. All our office value streams already contain human, analog, and digital elements to varying degrees. The digital elements—data and the corresponding technology required to process them—will continue to grow disproportionately to the others, but the purpose of the larger business system remains that of creating value for a customer. So why not use Lean thinking to improve our *entire* value streams, digital elements included?

Lean ideas, applied to software production (aka development), have already proven very successful in the Agile movement. Agile increases the speed and flexibility of software delivery, while also reducing the risks. It is hugely helpful. Unfortunately, these benefits of Agile come *after* the decision to develop the software has already been made. Agile does not necessarily ensure that we choose to develop the right software for the right process in the first place. That, I believe, requires a broader value stream analysis (which, to be fair, many Agilists do appreciate). Lean thinking can help IT and business leaders maximize the benefits of digital tools by simply applying the two design principles for flow that we've already discussed—continuity and balance—when considering where, how, and why to deploy technology initiatives within existing value streams.

Automation and Continuity

We saw above how digitization can create more continuity in a simple value stream for buying a cup of take-out coffee. What makes for an instructive thought experiment is to imagine how this same digitization might have been done differently. What if the mobile app enabled me to *order* remotely and ahead of time (e.g. while on the bus), but not *pay*? This would be like partially automating the "Order and Pay" process, which is the 2nd process in the original value stream (see Figure 15.1). I would arrive at the store but still have to line-up to pay. Meanwhile, the order process has been moved upstream to the bus, so some additional wait time has been introduced, just as before. The resulting process is slightly improved, but not much, because a lot of the wait time has not been eliminated. There is not as much continuity to the value-adding process steps (see Figures 15.4 and 15.5).

The lesson here is not that we have to automate every process entirely out of existence or not at all. While partial automation typically does not produce dramatic time savings for the customer, it can still be worthwhile

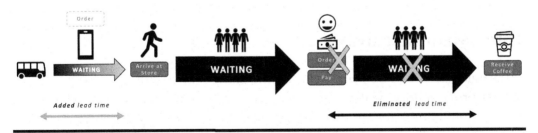

Figure 15.4 When Only the "Order" Portion of "Order and Pay" Process Step Is Eliminated through Digitization, the Waiting Time Before the Pay Process Is Not Eliminated.

Figure 15.5 The Redesigned Process, after Partial Automation. Lead Time Remains Only Slightly Reduced.

if the cost of implementation is reasonable (and it does not make anything worse for the customer). If we can free up an hour out of someone's day, that hour can be used productively to produce an hour's more value: maybe by figuring out a way to automate the part of the process that is still being performed manually.

Lean thinking simply guides us to create more flow in our value streams by compressing the process steps and creating more continuity between value-adding activities. Prior to making any regrettable and irreversible changes, we should consider how our proposed process improvements, digital or otherwise, are expected to impact the white spaces and, ultimately, the customers, in our value streams. Just as we can create more flow with "analog" tools and methods like standard work schedules, cross-training, and cross-functional collaboration, so too can we create much greater flow with thoughtfully implemented digital automation.

A caveat is needed, however: no matter how thoughtfully digital improvement creates continuity and flow, the value stream will become unbalanced, even if it was previously well-balanced. How to avoid this pitfall is addressed in the next chapter.

Three Main Takeaways

1. Digitization can be seen through the same lens as any other type of process improvement. To the extent that it compresses the value stream, eliminates the waiting time, and creates continuity, the more it improves flow.
2. Contemporary offices are becoming data factories, fulfilling the electronic orders of customers. If we want to copy a method for how to run a factory well, we already have a model of excellence: Lean.

3. Lean thinking can help us understand and optimize the whole value stream before deciding to implement technology, so that we avoid making large technology investments that do not improve the flow of value to the customer.

Notes

1. There is the issue of information privacy—the coffee company can track my buying behavior with their app, which clearly has more payoff for them than for me. So, I pay for convenience with my personal information. One could also argue that consumers lose the short, cheery verbal interactions that happen between cashier and client (who are generally strangers to one another). This is not something that I personally value over the convenience of avoiding the line because I currently get plenty of social interaction in other aspects of my life. However, it is important to recognize that there are many people in society, particularly senior citizens, who value even small bits of social interaction more than speedy service. I do not think that friendly cashiers are the best or only countermeasure to this deeper problem of loneliness—the root cause of which deserves to be examined more thoroughly—but I am glad there is still a non-digital ordering option.
2. PYMNTS. 2018. Consumers Are Increasingly Researching Purchases Online. PYMNTS.com, January 9, 2018: www.pymnts.com/news/retail/2018/omichannel-ecommerce-consumer-habits/ (accessed May 22, 2019).
3. Agrawal, Ajay, Joshua Gans, and Avi Goldfarb. 2018. *Prediction Machines: The Simple Economics of Artificial Intelligence.* Boston, MA: Harvard Business Review Press, pp. 32–33.
4. Agrawal, Ajay, Joshua Gans, and Avi Goldfarb. 2018. *ibid.* pp. 44–45.
5. Vogels, Werner. 2017. Rethinking the 'production' of data. *All things distributed* (online blog), December 20, 2017: https://www.allthingsdistributed.com/2017/12/rethinking-production-of-data.html (accessed February 20, 2019).
6. The "single-minute" in SMED refers to single digits.
7. Vorne Industries Inc. SMED (Single-Minute Exchange of Dies). Leanproduction.com: www.leanproduction.com/smed.html (accessed January 27, 2019).
8. Cunningham, Jean E. 2018. *The Value Add Accountant: An Indispensable Partner Supporting Strategic Improvement Efforts.* New York: JCC Press. p. 151.
9. Vanguard Consulting Ltd. Vanguard-method.net: https://vanguard-method.net/2014/10/it/ (accessed May 22, 2019).
10. Jappana. 2010. To Alcohol! The cause of … and solution to … all of life's problems. YouTube.com: www.youtube.com/watch?v=hUVwR0rw5fk (accessed May 22, 2019).
11. Drucker's actual phrase is: "There is nothing so useless as doing efficiently that which should not be done at all". Peter Drucker Quotes. BrainyQuote.com, BrainyMedia Inc, 2019. www.brainyquote.com/quotes/peter_drucker_105338 (accessed May 22, 2019).

Chapter 16

Automation and Imbalance

Digital technology is so promising because it can drastically accelerate the rate of task completion through automation. Yet it does not always optimize the value stream. You may recall Bob the Bottleneck from Chapter 8. Figure 16.1 presents a simpler version of the same concept.

Let us say you are the CEO of this company again. As is typical in most offices, no one has any idea of the throughput rate for each process step, never mind the overall rate that customers experience, and you, as CEO, are probably the least likely of all to know this. All you know is that more than a few of the customers you have been speaking with recently are disappointed in the service levels for this product. It has become acute enough that you feel you need to get involved. When you asked your VP of Human Resources to see if the processes were understaffed, she produced some data showing that people in Process 2 and Process 3 have been quitting their jobs at an alarmingly high rate.

You convene a meeting with the VPs of Processes 2 and 3, and ask them to present their ideas on what to do to fix the situation. The VP of Process 3 says that, despite his resolute efforts to squeeze every last drop of

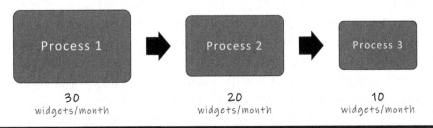

Figure 16.1   An Unbalanced Three-Step Value Stream, Prior to Automation.

productivity from what is left of his team, they simply cannot keep up with the volumes, and he is desperately trying to backfill the vacant positions as fast as he can. He asks you to augment his allocated staffing numbers, claiming that, unless he has an adequate number of "buffer" employees, the area will always be overworked and continue to lose people due to the stress.

The VP of Process 2, in contrast, produces a slick PowerPoint presentation asking for a technology investment of half a million dollars so that she can fully automate her process within six months. You consider both proposals and quickly decide the best course of action is to invest in the automation software that will speed up Process 2. As consolation, you tell your VP of Process 3 that you understand the pressure he is under and that you fully believe he is capable of leading his team through these difficult times. You add that you will consider hiring more people in the next annual budget planning cycle once the automation of Process 2 is complete and the resulting cost savings have offset the investment in the new software.

You are pleased at your decision. The new automating technology will have tremendous computing power. It can process four million (!) widgets/month, at least according to the PowerPoint. You are convinced that this will exceed all of your customers' delivery expectations, while also saving the company money, and so will be well worth the investment.

A year later, after a project that took 50% longer and cost twice the amount estimated, Process 2 has been fully automated for three months. There was much fanfare at the official launch, but you are now looking at the financial results for the quarter and things are not exactly ... better. Sales are down. Customers have been leaving you for the competition. And the employee turnover rate in Process 3 remains as high as ever, despite having replaced the former VP with one of your best leaders. The automation did free up some cash due to the headcount reduction in Process 2, but now that the revenues from this product line are projected to be below expectations, you cannot justify hiring more people in Process 3.

Remember from Chapter 8 that the second rule of bottlenecks states that the end-customer receives value at the rate corresponding to the *slowest* rate of production of all the steps in the entire value stream. Process 2's rate has improved due to the automation—since it now has near infinite capacity, it will always produce at whatever rate Process 1 can feed it—but Process 3 remains unchanged. Process 3 is still producing 10 widgets per month and so the customer experiences *no improvement in lead time* (see Figure 16.2). Speeding up Process 2 with automation has created an even bigger bottleneck in front of Process 3. The people in Process 3 are busier than ever, and

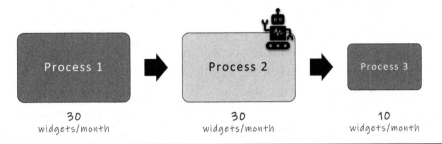

Figure 16.2   Customer Still Gets Only 10 Widgets per Month.

yet nothing ever seems to get done any faster. This is because automation, when applied to any single part of a value stream, will always unbalance the whole value stream. Automating a process without considering the upstream inputs and downstream impacts often leads to disappointing results. What you think is going to be a digital miracle of automation turns out to just be an expensive project with little or no customer impact.

There are at least two ways in which Lean thinking can help us work better with this unbalanced scenario. Both ways require knowing the throughput rates of each process step and making them visible to all the value stream's participating teams.

■ *Approach A: Balance Processes 1 and 3.* The first approach is to find a way to increase Process 3's throughput rate so that it can process at approximately the same rate as Process 1, ideally prior to, or simultaneously with, the implementation of the automating technology in Process 2, to minimize disruption to the customer. The most obvious way to do this is to use the freed-up labor from Process 2 and reallocate it to Process 3. The best scenario will minimize job loss and allow the same people who formerly worked in Process 2 to migrate to Process 3 with a bit of retraining. This may not always be possible, depending on the skillsets required for each process, but it should be the first option. If automation is perceived as job loss, your next technology implementation will be met with a lot of resistance.

You might also want to consider reallocating some staff from Process 1 to Process 3, thereby *slowing down* the throughput rate of Process 1. After all, customers were getting their widgets at a rate of only 10/month before the automation of Process 2. You might be able to satisfy customer volume and lead time expectations with a throughput rate of 20 widgets/month, which is still twice as fast as before. Such an improved performance might help generate sales growth, and more staff could be added incrementally to both Processes 1 and 3, in equal amounts, in tandem with the increase in revenue. In either case, if Process 1 is *balanced* with Process 3, neither group of employees will suffer undue overburden. And, ideally, no one will lose their job to a robot either (see Figure 16.3).

■ *Approach B: Implement automation at the last step, then balance Processes 1 and 2.* A second way to approach the imbalance seen above is to automate the *slowest* step in the process (presuming it is possible to automate it). In this case, it would be Process 3. This may seem like an obvious thing to do based on the illustrations presented here. In the real world, in can be more challenging to know what the slowest step is: bottlenecks are invisible; there is no data being collected on the throughput rate of each process step; there are often more than three process steps in the value stream; and there is a lot more variation in the duration and content of work that moves through each step.

In our example, automating Process 3 would improve the customer-felt lead time to the next lowest production rate—namely that of Process 2, or 20 widgets/month, which is twice as good as before (see Figure 16.4). The

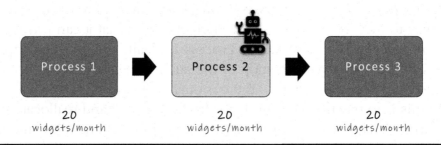

Figure 16.3 An Improved Process 3 so That It Is Balanced with Process 1. Even Though Process 1 Is Now Slower Than Before, the Customer-Felt Lead Time Is Twice As Fast.

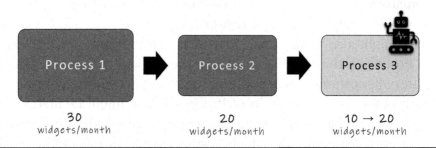

Figure 16.4 Automating the Slowest Process Step.

value stream remains unbalanced so long as Process 1 continues to produce at 30 widgets/month, but no more so than it was prior to automation. To increase flow even more, and relieve Process 2 of overburden, one should, of course, try to improve the throughput time of Process 2, perhaps by redeploying the labor saved in Process 3. Or, if the rate of 20 widgets/month is sufficient to satisfy current customer demand, Process 1 could even slow down by effectively allocating less time each month to that process (and more to another) until its output is roughly 20/month. In either case, we should continue to strive to balance the value stream.

DATAPHOBIA

People have been conditioned over most of their lives, starting in their early school days, that measurement is a tool that those with authority over them will use to evaluate and then punish/reward them. Bosses, teachers, and parents use measurements in the form of report cards or performance reviews as tools to coerce behavior. Hence many frontline employees are demoralized by having someone measure their work. When employees feel that it is not within their total control or ability to make the numbers reflect well on them and their work, they will often try to discredit the measurement system, game the numbers, or both. The threat of undesirable consequences if one does not "meet the numbers" can make good people do bad things. The Wells Fargo account fraud scandal that became well known in 2016 is only one example of many.

Unfortunately, the lack of reliable measures exacerbates value stream performance for everyone. In the absence of good facts and data, upper management is often left to make decisions based only on anecdotes, opinions, and PowerPoint presentations. These are frequently not the best decisions. If you are a leader and want to make better decisions informed by data, focus first on eliminating the fear and consequences associated with measurement and data collection. Data should not be tyranny by numbers, but a doorway to understanding. Think about the times when you might have used data differently than as a way of purely understanding a situation, without any judgment. Have you ever used data as a way to reward some employees and punish others, e.g. setting an unrealistic target and then holding everyone "accountable" for meeting it? Did everyone have 100% control over the outcome? If not, the measure probably demotivated many people and pleased a few lucky ones. As a general rule, do not ask your employees to do anything you would not do yourself. If you are not comfortable with someone measuring the speed at which you complete tasks, do not expect others to be any more so. If you are comfortable with it, make the data visible to all, so that everyone can emulate your behavior.

Offices rarely possess reliable throughput data on their processes. In these cases, there are two rules of thumb that will usually work when considering automation:

1. Automate the *final* process step.
2. Automate the *slowest* process step (if obvious).

Accelerating the final process step—the final delivery of value to the customer—in any value stream is rarely a bad thing. This is especially true when delivering intangible, electronic outputs because there is no monetary cost for the receiving customer to store them. And customers usually want the things they have paid for as fast as possible. Nevertheless, one should always ask the customer on the timing they prefer. If the final step is already automated, work backwards to find the closest step to the end of the value stream that has not yet been automated.

Accelerating the slowest process step can be relatively easy when the slowest step is so obvious that data is not necessary. This happened in a cash management team. This poor team had the unenviable task of taking electronic requests to transfer funds from a variety of different and unrelated systems throughout the corporation, all with their own unique formatting conventions, converting the formatting into a standard format understood by the international banking system (SWIFT) and then manually inputting these data into this same system. Their work was important: without them, customers and suppliers would not get their money in the right amount, in the right currency, at the right time, in the right bank account. The various internal systems did not "speak" to the banking system and so a human "interpreter" was required. Because of the manual input, this process was not only slow, but had the risk of human error. A simple typo can cost a lot in banking transactions. The other aspects of the process were already automated, and so it was very easy to detect which was the slowest process step (see Figure 16.5).

The remedy, quite obviously, was to automate the manual part of the process. What was needed was an IT system that would take the information from each business value stream, convert it automatically into a standard format, and then transfer it directly into the banking system. With relatively little effort on the part of IT, this is exactly what happened. With all of the steps automated, the process was balanced, and the information flowed flawlessly. Despite how obvious this solution might seem in hindsight; it took many years to convince the various upstream teams to allow it to go ahead. Mistrustful of technology, the upstream teams all feared that there would be costly glitches, and were initially reluctant to allow the automation project to happen. Happily, this technology implementation was done well (no glitches) and saved the cash management team two and half hours of tedious data entry per day (see Figure 16.6).

Unlike more analog improvements, where task completion rates are at a human pace, technology typically accelerates task completion so radically that it is disruptive. The word "disruption" has acquired a positive connotation recently, referring to situations where a new technology (think Uber or Netflix) has allowed smaller startup firms to displace the larger incumbents and achieve rapid market dominance in an established industry. The small tech firms have essentially unbalanced the market in their favor. Internal to any firm, however, imbalance and disruption are far less desirable.

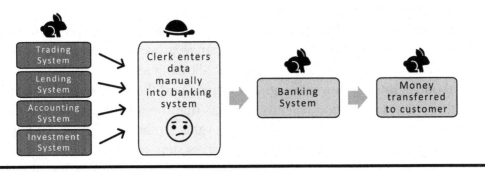

Figure 16.5   An Obviously Unbalanced Process.

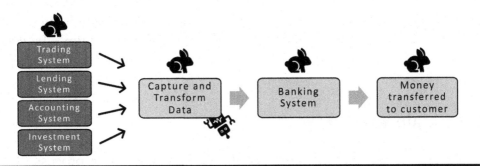

Figure 16.6   A Balanced Process after an Automation Project.

Without a sense of how technology can unbalance a value stream, companies will almost always suffer unintended negative consequences of implementing what could otherwise be very promising technology. Since the importance of establishing and maintaining a balanced flow across functional areas in a value stream is not well appreciated by most leaders, and they are not usually incentivized to care very much about the workloads of those outside of their own vertical silos in any case, employee dissatisfaction after large system implementations is often just considered "unavoidable", and attributed to "resistance to change". Sadly, entire departments may be unnecessarily overburdened with excessive workloads for months (or even years!) after technology has been deployed upstream. Only after undergoing mandatory "change management" workshops, org chart redesigns, team building events, pizza lunches, birthday celebrations, and maybe even some process improvements, teams that were once overburdened usually crawl their way back to some state of equilibrium. Relief, in the form of additional staff or new technology is eventually bestowed upon the areas that complain the loudest or those that have the most influential PowerPoints. But it is often too late: a cynical attitude has developed on the part of employees. They feel that management does not care about their workloads and is using technology only to reduce staffing expenses.

Digitization, despite its huge potential to create time savings for customers and employees, rarely turns out to be the panacea everyone wants to believe it will be. Lean thinking can help. It helps by allowing leaders who make decisions about technology investments to evaluate and then minimize—or avoid altogether—the unintended negative impacts that the implementation of digital tools will almost always cause. Conducting value stream analysis, including measuring the throughput rates at each process step, and from the end-to-end perspective of the customer, should be a mandatory requirement for all technology projects prior to being started. Technological advancement should be a great thing. From the wheel to the internet, technological progress has, over the long run, improved the lives of humans immensely. Lean thinking allows companies to enhance productivity and shorten customer lead times by taking advantage of technology, while fully respecting its employees at the same time.

Three Main Takeaways

1. Because it radically increases the throughput rate of one process, automation will always cause the entire value stream to become

unbalanced. This means that, without thoughtful ways to restore balance, customer outcomes may not improve and some employees will become more overburdened than before.

2. Understanding the end-to-end value stream and knowing the throughput rate of all of the major process steps is essential to avoid the negative consequences of automation while still benefiting from the positive ones. Armed with this knowledge, plans can be made ahead of technology implementations to reallocate labor and restore balance.

3. In the absence of good data to guide us to where to automate first, two rules of thumb can be used: 1) automate the last process in the value stream; or 2) automate the slowest process (if obvious). Rebalancing will still likely have to be undertaken in most cases.

Chapter 17

Lean Leadership and Strategy

Creating value for customers is the primary purpose of a Lean organization. Of course, companies cannot create this value at the *expense* of shareholders, employees, suppliers, or any other important stakeholders, but customers must come first. The basic logic is: please your customers and your profitability will follow. Lean leaders must embrace this logic in words and actions.

Much has already been written about Lean leadership and so, consequently, I do not have that much to say about it. Lean leadership is often described as "servant" leadership because value creation—in every business, in every industry—happens only at the frontlines. Lean leaders exist to serve the frontline flow of value creation. The job of leadership is to ensure the frontline workers have the right environment, information, technology, skills, knowledge, and coaching support to do the best work they can in every moment ... for their customers. To the extent that there are gaps, and there always will be, continuous improvement seeks to close them.

This egalitarian and democratic approach to leadership is at odds with the more classical mental model of a leader being a charismatic and powerful commander. But asking leaders to care about the success of the frontline workers should not be misunderstood as asking them to join in socialist solidarity with their proletariat comrades. It is about revenue. Frontline employees are the only people who make the products and deliver the services that produce all the firm's revenue. They—not the leaders—are the cash generators of the company. If leaders want to please customers and generate more revenue for their company, they can only do so vicariously, through the work of their frontline employees. Lean leaders know that it pays, quite literally, to be concerned about the welfare of those who create the value.

What happens in traditional management is typically just the opposite: the higher up you go in the chain of command, the more distance there is from the details of frontline operations. There are strong socio-cultural norms and expectations of executive behavior that create and reinforce this distance. For instance, one of the conventional rituals of executives is to spend a lot of their time in meetings. Most would say it is not a choice: it would be socially awkward (if not career-limiting) to choose not to attend such meetings in favor of, say, spending time studying the work of the frontline employees. This is not to say that all meetings are bad or unnecessary. But one feature of meetings is that they tend to substitute clean, abstract representations, such as spreadsheets and slide shows, for first-hand knowledge of the messy and chaotic business operations on the "shop floor"—even when the "shop floor" is a carpeted office space full of keyboards and screens. When abstract representations of operations become a more frequent source of knowledge than actual interaction with people at the frontlines, frontline employees and the value-adding work they do tend to become, well, abstractions. Thus, higher-level leaders lose sight of their company's actual capabilities to meet customer needs. The thinking is: meet the numbers; do not get caught up in the details; I have people working for me who's job it is to monitor the frontline capabilities. Yet when other people are tasked to bring analysis of frontline capabilities to leadership, it becomes indirect, abstract knowledge again. This abstraction is more consistent with a view of the firm's primary purpose as creating value for owners, not customers.

The management style most typically associated with classical, resource efficient, industrial-era leadership is commonly referred to as "command-and-control". This style, at its worst, assumes that workers have no inherent desire to work and, if left to their own devices, will naturally shirk all responsibility. Therefore, the logic goes, they need to be perpetually supervised. Back when factories had extremely low wages and horrible working conditions, there was probably a great deal of validity in the assumption that workers disliked their work. Not surprisingly, a big part of management's job in the industrial era was to keep workers utilized, often using the expeditious (but short-lived) mechanism of fear and coercion. Similarly, when poorly educated and semi-literate laborers made up most of the workforce, it arguably made more sense that decision-making would be the exclusive dominion of management.

With the decline of industrial manufacturing in advanced economies, and a shift to a more highly educated population and a service-oriented economy, the preferred management style that tends to dominate today's modern offices is laissez-faire. The operating philosophy of laissez-faire is to "hire smart people and leave them alone"—what the smart person of Tom Davenport (a writer and consultant) has acronymized as "HSPALTA[1]". Despite Einstein's adage that "we cannot solve our problems with the same thinking we used when we created them", when HSPALTA management does not yield the desired results, leaders frequently come to the same conclusion: they just need to hire some *better* people (and continue to leave them alone).

Lean leadership, in contrast, distinguishes itself from both command-and-control and laissez-faire management styles by its intense focus on daily operations and the development of frontline employees.

Development of People

When it comes to the development of frontline employees, Lean leadership is neither the "do what I say" of command-and-control, nor the "do whatever you want" of laissez-faire, but somewhere in the middle. Lean leaders go to where the value-creating work happens and actively provide guidance, support, and coaching to the employees there.

"Developing people" in a Lean context does not mean simply sending people to industry conferences and training programs. It does not mean being overly nice to employees either. The crux of developing people is *challenging* them. It means setting difficult targets and then challenging employees to figure out how to meet them (and without telling them how to do it). It means promoting those who prove themselves capable of solving increasingly difficult and vexing business problems. Developing people means pushing employees to be a little better at thinking through business problems tomorrow than they are today. It is the continuous improvement of people. Not providing such a challenge is a waste of their human potential. Being a Lean leader is analogous to the personal trainer who pushes her client to run that extra mile or lift that extra ten pounds. As the client (employee), you do not necessarily enjoy it in the moment, but you know it is good for you, and you appreciate it afterward when you look back on what you have accomplished.

While traditional leadership is usually all about personal, individual success, Lean leadership is about bringing out the best in *other* people. When a leader's direct reports all achieve good results, the leader is much more successful than he is trying to achieve results on his own.

Connecting Functions and Systems

Complementing a Lean leader's focus on developing people is an intense interest in how the frontlines are performing the value-creating work. Another way of thinking about it is that frontline employees work *in* the system, while leaders work *on* the system[2]. Lean leaders are thus responsible for creating, maintaining, and improving the management systems that govern the value-creating work of all the frontline employees within their span of control. These systems typically include prioritization systems, workflow systems, measurement systems, communication systems, visual management systems, problem solving systems, and reward and recognition systems. The fact that leaders are responsible for working on the systems does not absolve frontline employees from having to improve their work, but one can only expect people to improve the work over which they have a fair amount of control. So, yes, frontline employees must continuously improve their work— and so must all leaders, at all levels. Lean is not simply something that can be delegated downwards and forgotten about because someone needs to build, maintain, and improve the systems governing the frontline work.

Management systems are nested within one another. The end-to-end value stream of a specific product or service family is the "master" system and all the sub-systems within it work towards the common purpose of creating and flowing value to external customers. The more *connected* the subsystems, both vertically and horizontally, the more the system will produce the desired outcomes. It is not enough to create and monitor the systems, they need constant tending, like a garden. After establishing the initial systems, leadership's job becomes primarily concerned with cultivating these connections.

Vertical connections are typically more robust in most companies because most companies are organized in some form of vertical hierarchy. Still, there can often be a tendency to hide problems from one's boss and there can be confusion about priorities. Consequently, leadership has a responsibility to remove the fear of problems and clarify priorities along the vertical dimension.

More challenging, and far more important, are horizontal flows. Since value can only flow to a customer horizontally across different areas of a

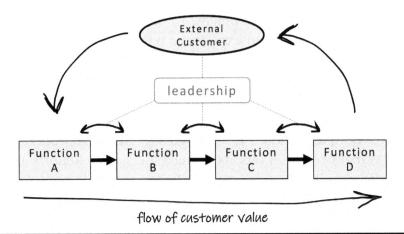

Figure 17.1 The Connections That Create the Horizontal Flow of Value to the Customer.

company, it falls uniquely to leadership to promote cross-functional coordination and collaboration. This does not happen on its own in a vertically organized company and requires leadership effort to displace the inertia of top-down territorialism and functional myopia. After all, why should anyone care about their next downstream process step when this internal customer is not paying them anything? Unifying around a common goal of serving the external customer is necessary in overcoming these internal barriers. And if leadership does not do it, no one will (see Figure 17.1).

Go See

What unites a Lean leader's devotion to developing people and improving the flow of the daily work is a deep customer focus and a compulsion to "go see". Since the frontlines create customer value, developing the frontline staff who create this value becomes an obvious way to improve it. This may, on some level, seem obvious, but traditional thinking tends to believe that customer value is almost exclusively a function of better product design (new product development or "innovation") and clever marketing strategies. Operations, it is assumed, just needs to follow orders: make to spec and deliver according to schedule. This view fails to acknowledge the immense impact Operations has on customer experience. To the extent that Operations takes care and pride in its work, customers experience better quality products and services. To the extent that Operations is more productive, customers can enjoy a better price, or the company can deploy more people into Research and Development. To the extent that Operations can shrink lead time, customers can experience reliable, quick, on-time delivery. While innovation and marketing are hugely important, a customer-focused firm cannot allow its leadership to be laissez-faire about Operations: they must go to the frontlines and develop the management systems with them, shoulder-to-shoulder.

Similarly, a Lean leader does not rely exclusively on abstract representations and verbal or written reports to make decisions. Reports and data are valuable to running the business, but Lean leaders do not fully trust second-hand information—in part because we learn so much more from direct observation; in part because information tends to get distorted as it filters its way up from the frontlines to higher levels of management. Hence, they must go to gather facts about operations through direct observation to supplement their indirect information (all those data and reports). They "go see" things with their own eyes, and listen with their own ears, to understand the true nature of the work. In Lean manufacturing lingo, this is called a *gemba*[3] walk, and frequently anglicized as a "floor walk". Do not misinterpret "floor walk" as simply walking around randomly and socializing with employees. In a sedentary office context, it should really be labeled a "sit with": leaders need to sit with frontline colleagues and see, with them, on their computer screens, the problems they are encountering in the flow of their daily work.

T-Shaped Leadership

Leaders who feel uncomfortable coming down to the level of the frontline work often protest, "but I can't be everywhere at once!". And this is true. There is an expectation, as noted above, that leaders attend a lot of meetings. They barely have any free time in their calendar. This fact, however, does not diminish the importance of going to see the frontlines regularly. This is why, in part, leadership is challenging. They have to manage with both breadth of vision *and* depth of understanding—what is often described as "T-shaped" skills[4]. Conventional leaders become increasingly biased towards the "horizontal" breadth (the top of the "T") as they move up the ladder and away from the frontlines. To gain more breadth of understanding of all the activities within their scope of responsibility, leaders quite understandably resort to using more heuristic thinking—cognitive short-cuts that rely on experience and intuition rather than facts and data. They use abstract representations of the "big picture" as substitutes for concrete facts and knowledge about daily operations. As an unintended consequence, they lose depth of understanding of the challenges the frontlines are facing. It is not any individual's "fault": the cultural norms of leadership behavior encourage and reinforce this.

Lean leadership, in contrast, maintains a balance between the vertical depth and horizontal breadth of the "T"—they zoom in and then zoom out. Lean leaders are not always at the frontlines—leaders truly cannot be everywhere—but devote far more time to it than traditional leaders do. They accomplish this depth of understanding through floor walks. Lean leaders do not seek to be everywhere but seek out deep understanding at the frontlines in brief but frequent visits. The details of operations in one area are only a sample, but, by doing floor walks frequently enough (e.g. daily), the sample becomes sufficiently representational of the health of the entire value-creation system. The facts gathered at the frontlines make for better strategic decisions—more informed of the existing frontline capabilities of the firm— when zooming out and managing along the horizontal axis of the T. And better strategic decisions lead to fewer meetings, amongst other benefits.

Operations *Is* the Strategy

By staying in the comfort zone of spreadsheets and slide presentations, uninformed of the current realities of the frontlines, leaders put themselves at far greater risk of making poor strategic decisions. This is essentially why "brilliant" strategic ideas so often fail to materialize: an idea that seemed great in the boardroom fails in "execution" because those who came up with the idea had no deep knowledge of the current capability and willingness of those who were being asked to execute on it. One can easily blame the feckless frontlines (and/or the consultants) for these strategic blunders, but the reality is that a poorly executed strategy is just a poor strategy. A good strategy needs to take into account the firm's ability and willingness to execute. If a football coach comes up with a "great" strategy before the game but the players cannot execute it on the field, and so lose the game, should it really be considered a "winning" strategy[5]?

Most companies think a lot about their outward business strategy: deciding what to make, whom to sell it to, at what price, in which geographies, through which channels, and so on. They think about their "footprint" and assess market power asymmetries[6]. Strategy as outward footprint evolves into a plan to gain market power over competitors, suppliers, and customers, thereby being able to leverage this power to gain wider margins, larger market share, or both.

All companies in competitive industries must think about the market forces surrounding them, of course, and Lean companies do so just as much as traditional ones do. Yet *all* companies think about these things in much the same way, and thus it confers little, if any, long-term competitive advantage over pure luck (which predicts, after all, that 50% of the time you will make above average returns compared to your industry peers). Lean companies distinguish themselves not by ignoring market forces, but by thinking with equal or even greater intensity about their internal operations. This is something to which most traditional companies give far less serious thought and attention[7].

The typical internal "strategy" or "plan" at traditionally-managed companies is simply for executives to compel everyone reporting to them to execute on the external "footprint" strategy. Operational execution becomes a series of top-down projects, realignments, and enforced compliance with new priorities. Internal competition dominates over cooperation. Frontline employees and middle-managers become demoralized by their lack of agency. As Michael Ballé and Jeffrey Liker write:

> Day after day, people react to management edicts and to mounting problems that never really get solved by complying, which quickly replaces their ability to think. Therefore, they feel powerless to fix even the most glaring problems in front of them[8].

To a considerable extent, Lean turns strategy on its head. Ballé and Liker call it an "outside in and upside down" strategy[9]. Instead of thinking of how the firm can use its market position to conquer others, a Lean company starts with customer needs and looks inwards, asking "how can we better help customers—and potential customers—solve their problems?" The desire to solve customer problems leads to solving pragmatic, operational problems at the frontlines. This is the outside in, customer-centric aspect. Then, to better solve customer problems, leadership goes about improving internal capabilities from the ground up, through setting operational targets, developing people, and improving the systems of value creation at the frontlines. The corporation recognizes leaders who develop the frontline employees the best. It flips the conventional power pyramid upside down.

A company's Lean strategy is really an internal, operational strategy that complements its external business strategy. It involves a company deciding to do what so few other companies do: focus strategically on internal operations and frontline staff. It is not hard, conceptually, to understand, but uncommon in practice, because it is 180 degrees from traditional management culture. While there is a different focus at different levels of leadership, a Lean strategy implies, quite simply, three dominant leadership behaviors: setting the direction and operational targets for the few most important things to achieve; working diligently to establish and continuously improve the management systems so that there is greater flow of value to customers; and caring deeply about the development of people (including leaders and future leaders) so that they can do their best value-creating work every day.

Three Main Takeaways

1. Leadership in a Lean enterprise is predicated on the foundational notion that a company exists to create value for customers. Following from this principle, leadership is about supporting those who create the value: the frontline employees.
2. Support of frontline employees means setting the direction and targets, challenging individuals to meet these targets *and*, most importantly, establishing and improving the management systems that govern the flow of frontline value production. The stronger the connections—both vertical and horizontal—between the systems within the value stream, the more robust the value stream will be in terms of flow and respect for people.
3. A Lean strategy is both bottom-up and outside-in: focused on operations more than market position, and customer needs more than competitors.

Notes

1. Davenport, Thomas H. 2005. *Thinking for a Living: How to Get Better Performance and Results from Knowledge Workers.* Boston, MA: Harvard Business School Press.

2. This notion of working *on* the system is taken from an IEX Whitepaper: Institute for Enterprise Excellence. 2016. Systems By Design, September 2016: http://instituteforexcellence.org/wp-content/uploads/2019/05/systems-by-design-4-28-19.pdf (accessed May 22, 2019).

3. *Gemba* means "the actual place" in Japanese. In practice it means where the value is being created. This is the shop floor in manufacturing. It is sometimes spelled *genba*. The actual practice of going to see with one's own eyes is known as *genchi genbutsu* in Japanese and jokingly translated by some Anglophones as "go get your boots on".

4. See Wordspy.com. T-shaped: https://wordspy.com/index.php?word=t-shaped (accessed May 22, 2019)

5. See Martin, Roger L. 2010. The Execution Trap. *Harvard Business Review*, July–August 2010: https://hbr.org/2010/07/the-execution-trap (accessed May 22, 2019).

6. Ballé, Michael, and Jeff Liker. Why lean thinking challenges our assumptions about management. *Planet-Lean.com*, October 14, 2016: https://planet-lean.com/liker-balle-lean-management-upside-down/ (accessed May 23, 2019).

7. E.g. a quick search for books on Amazon.com yields over 40,000 results for the key words "business strategy" and yet just 6000 for the key words "operations strategy" or "execution".

8. Ballé and Liker, *ibid.*

9. Ballé and Liker, *ibid.*

Conclusion: Work Is a Human System

We want to not only show respect to our people, the same way we want to show respect to everyone we meet in life, we also want to respect their humanity, what it is that makes us human, which is our ability to think and feel—we have to respect that humanity in the way we design the work, so that the work enables their very human characteristics to flourish

–Fujio Cho, former Toyota President and Chairman[1]

A friend of mine was talking to me recently about how she discovered Lean while working as a customer service rep at a payroll company. Payroll can be complicated and, since payroll specialists are human, mistakes can occasionally happen. And when they do happen, people get upset. She described how everyone had a box of tissues on their desk to wipe away the tears after particularly difficult calls. She implemented Lean in her office as a tear-reduction initiative.

People should not be made to cry at work on a regular basis. Work simply does not have to be like this.

People often misperceive Lean as some sort of sinister management plot to turn them into "a monkey with a keyboard", as one person in my office put it. Adherence to schedules and standards, the collection and analysis of data, the visual display of metrics and daily stand-up huddles, cross-training staff and the use of structured problem-solving methods... the sheer rigor and discipline of it all might seem overly technical and cold, lacking any regard for the human side of work.

This is perhaps the greatest paradox of Lean thinking. Lean respects people by not blaming them. Lean seeks to fix the management system, not the people in the system. Note this is very different from not caring about people. Lean's focus on management systems may appear to be coldly scientific and impersonal, but it is very caring and people-centric.

Traditional management thinking, in contrast, focuses almost exclusively on people in an overly simple, cause-and-effect, reward-and-punish way. Good results are attributed to good people; bad results are attributed to bad people. This unscientific, resource-efficient thinking disrespects all people. If we believe that people are the singular source of all of our successes and failures, we will consistently try to use carrots and sticks to "improve" people in the hope of making the "bad" ones good and the "good" ones even better. We all know about the sticks: "these are my performance expectations for you". (The unspoken but implied part is "Meet them... *or else!*). The use of carrots, implying that we have to bribe effort out of our people, can be equally patronizing and disrespectful. Our modern corporations offer its employees pay-for-performance bonus plans, behavioral coaching, professional training opportunities, career advice, table tennis in the rec room, free yoga classes, catered lunches, motivational posters, recognition ceremonies, and so on. These well-intentioned, well-meaning carrots do little harm... but is there any real evidence that these activities produce more engaged employees or significantly better business results? This mechanistic, resource-efficient thinking is better suited to an era of industrial mass production. It is time to shift our thinking into the 21st century: sustained success in a digital economy is not about good people, it is about good systems.

W. Edwards Deming, one of the great systems thinkers of the 20th century, famously said that "a bad system will beat a good person every time"[2]. Even the best people cannot thrive in a bad system. We focus so much on hiring "good" people but exert so little effort toward creating good management systems. As a result, our companies are mostly filled with good people working in a mediocre (or worse) system—and while the system produces cyclical results that vary from year to year, over the long-term, the average is, well, mediocre. When this mediocrity cycle is in a downturn, we tend to mistake the poor results that are caused by random cyclical variation as a one-time special event that must have a distinct cause. And that cause is, in a resource-efficient world, always people. Once we make faulty assumptions about the causes of our problems, we make a bunch of bad decisions to solve them: we eject the "bad" people from the system and then try to hire more of the "good" people into the same system. Results soon improve, due to the random cyclical variation over time, and we attribute this to all the new people we hired... until the next downturn, when those formerly "good" people suddenly turn into "poor performers" (similar to our politicians—we love them when they get elected but hate them by the next election). The eternal cycle continues: results go up, results go down; people are praised, people are blamed. Is this really an effective way to create long-term, sustainable success?

Yes, occasionally there are truly toxic people in the company and these people should be removed from the organization as fast as possible, because a good system will not make a truly bad person much better. But the fact of the matter is that most of our people are good. Deming estimated that 94% of problems in the workplace were problems with the management systems[3]. That means that 6% of problems are due to other factors like, possibly, people. Does it not make sense to focus more of our attention on the 94%? If we want to get good results from the good people we already have, we have to improve the system, not the people. A good system with just average people will outperform an uncoordinated collection of individual superstars every time.

If we truly care about people, we need to build better systems. A people-centric culture is only obtained through improving the systems in which people work. Throughout this book I have used analogies of work being like serving meals in a restaurant, passing buckets in a fire brigade, managing traffic on a highway, or optimizing lineups in a grocery store in an attempt to get you to conceive of work as a system. The Lean tools and routines that improve the system may seem cold and technical when you read about them. But their deeper purpose is a profoundly humanistic one.

Work supports us in so much more than financial ways. It helps us find balance in the highs and lows of our lives. It should not be a place that routinely makes us scared, upset, or demoralized. But asking individuals who are behaving badly to be better than they are is not a viable way to bring about change in an organization. We have to establish systemic solutions the elicit the right behaviors. Work is a human system and Lean is a way to design more humanity into the system.

We can see genuinely people-centric management systems at places like Toyota, in their auto plants around the world, but also in newer, digital businesses like CI&T in Brazil, the REA Group in Australia, LesFurets.com in France, or Menlo Innovations in the USA, to name just a few. Such great workplaces can and do exist. It is possible, and this is what we should be striving for in all of our workplaces.

When I advocate for the design of management systems that create more continuity and achieve more balance in the flow of the work, I am not doing so for the benefit of unscrupulous managers, so that they might impose a dehumanizing management system on their employees for the purposes of enriching only themselves and shareholders. On the contrary, I am doing it because we, frontline employees and leaders alike, are so chronically busy at our office jobs and yet nothing ever seems to get accomplished. I see so many people suffering needlessly at work: being abused by stressed out bosses and customers; being frustrated by dysfunctional hardware and software; being bored and unfulfilled by having to do mindlessly repetitive tasks; being exhausted from overwork; and feeling completely powerless to use their creative ideas to improve the system. I have been there. I want to change the system that produces that kind of needless suffering.

People are important because they are needed to build better systems. Companies do not exist to make the people who do the work happy; nor do they exist to make the people who have invested in the company rich. Companies exist to create value for customers, plain and simple, and to survive over the long-term. To be sure, a sustainable system of customer value creation depends on having both satisfied employees and shareholders, but the external customer has to be the guiding purpose. And creating and maintaining such a system is not easy to do. So long as we all have to work for a living—and most of us do—why can it not be made better for *all* stakeholders? Why can work not bring joy to employees *and* customers, while also bringing good financial returns to shareholders? I believe it can. Continuously striving to flow more value to customers—using a management system we call Lean—is the best currently known way to do this.

Notes

1. From a 1997 speech, as translated and cited in Shook, John. 2008. *Managing to Learn*. Cambridge, MA: Lean Enterprise Institute. p. 53.
2. The W. Edwards Deming Institute. W. Edwards Deming Quotes. Deming.org: https://quotes.deming.org/authors/W._Edwards_Deming/quote/10091 (accessed May 23, 2019).
3. The W. Edwards Deming Institute. W. Edwards Deming Quotes. Deming.org: https://quotes.deming.org/authors/W._Edwards_Deming/quote/1538 (accessed May 23, 2019).

Appendix: Value Stream, System, and Process: Understanding Three Fundamental Terms

There are three foundational terms—Value Stream, System, and Process—that are often confused and misunderstood because they are defined in multiple ways by different authors in different contexts. A primary source of confusion is that they are, all three, sometimes—but not always—*synonymous* with one another. In an attempt to reduce confusion, I define them, at least as they are meant to be understood in this book, below. These definitions should not be radically different from what you might encounter elsewhere in Lean and related Process Improvement literature, although they may differ quite a lot from how other business writers with different models employ them.

Value Stream: *The path that information (and physical material, if relevant in your work) travels, from the point of an external customer request/ order to the point of fulfillment of that request/order. It is composed of multiple process-steps that transform inputs into outputs by adding value to them. The final output is, ideally, exactly what the customer requested, delivered exactly when the customer wanted it, in exactly the right amount, at a price the customer was willing to pay. To the extent that the final output is not the ideal, there is room for improvement within a value stream.*

Value streams are mental models of our work. Talking and writing about value streams is a way for humans to construct a useful model to explain the way work functions. To make our mental models easier to analyze and understand in teams, people usually share them by representing them visually as "maps". Maps are not the same as the actual work, but are the tool by which we attempt to understand and improve it. A good value stream map is an extremely helpful tool in improving business performance and customer outcomes.

The word "value" in value stream usually implies that the customer is willing to pay money in exchange for this value received, but sometimes the payment for services rendered by entities like governments, non-profits, and healthcare providers is paid through indirect mechanisms (like taxes or insurance companies). The value stream model of work, however, is just as valid in these sectors. The customer (or citizen or patient) has a need, and values the fulfillment of that need. The organization or institution fulfilling the value does so through a value stream.

Since a typical office has many, many different value streams, it is sometimes hard to decide what belongs together in the same value stream and what merits a separate or distinct value stream. Value streams are usually identified by the type of value they deliver (e.g. different products/services, or a family of related products/services), and/or by the different customer segments. For example, buying a mortgage (i.e. buying a house) and buying a stock are both ownership investments, but, for individual investors with average incomes, these are different in magnitude, and are done to fulfill different needs. A customer's desire to purchase stock and her desire to purchase a mortgage would be fulfilled by different value streams, even though they both, at a certain level, have similar characteristics.

In some cases, the same types of products may serve different needs for different customers. For instance, a bond issue might serve a small, start-up company looking for debt-capital to grow and expand its business, but for a large, mature company a bond issue (of a similar type and amount) may serve only to improve short-term liquidity needs. So if you underwrite bonds, you might well have a "growth capital" value stream and a separate "working capital" value stream, even though nearly identical products would move through both. In the case of non-physical goods and services, it is possible to slice and dice value creation in a thousand different ways, but an understanding of customer value, and what problem you are trying to solve for that customer, should be the guiding direction. Value streams begin and end with a customer—so where a company demarcates the precise beginning and end of its value streams depends on both the sequence of activities involved in the creation of specific products/services *and*—more importantly—the type of value its specific customers want and expect from these products/services.

It is helpful to think of principal or primary value streams as distinct from internal or supporting value streams. Primary value streams are the ones that create and deliver the main products or services to the *external* customer. They are the ones without which there would be no revenue and no business. In manufacturing, these are known as "production" value streams. If you make only toasters, then your toaster production value stream is your main one. Similarly, if you underwrite loans to medium-sized, privately owned businesses, that is your main value stream. You can have one or many primary value streams, depending on the array of different products or services your firm provides to external customers, and the variety of customer segments you serve. A big company like General Electric or IBM would have many, many primary value streams.

Enabling the primary Production value streams are many internal (aka "supporting" or "sub-") value streams in every enterprise. Like external value streams, they begin and end with a customer, only the customer is a different stakeholder group (e.g. internal teams, suppliers, creditors, or shareholders). Some supporting value streams, such as procurement and financing, involve the exchange of money (with external suppliers), yet many do not pay. In all other respects, they have the same characteristics as the principal value streams.

There can be, in theory, an infinite number of sub-value streams within an organization. If I send you an email asking if you want to go for lunch, you might have a "Respond to Ken's lunch request" sub-value stream. As a general rule, try to stay at a higher-level of detail in your value stream mapping exercises before getting into the micro details (such as responding to my lunch invitations). Go to the micro-level only when it is necessary to help you solve an important problem in a larger value stream.

Sometimes the concept of a supporting value stream is confusing to people. Most people can grasp how HR and IT value streams support an enterprise's primary value streams with people and technology, respectively, but other internal processes are less obvious. For instance, in which "value stream" should you classify activities such as strategic planning, or the production of annual financial reports?

Womack, Jones, and Roos, in their landmark 1990 book *The Machine That Changed the World*, identify five principal categories of value streams.

I find them to be very helpful, so I am paraphrasing the five categories here in terms that are more generic and less specific to the auto industry:

- Production (or Service Delivery)
- Research and Development (of new products and services)
- Procurement
- Sales and Customer Support
- Managing the Enterprise

In the cases of strategic planning and financial reporting, they both squarely fit into the last one: Managing the Enterprise. There is still value being delivered, even though the recipient/customer is not paying for them directly. Key stakeholders of the firm, like employees and shareholders, certainly do find them valuable.

Production value streams, as discussed above, are your company's primary, main value streams. They only exist because you have (or will have) paying customers. The Research and Development, Procurement, Sales and Service, and the Management of the Enterprise value streams only exist because there is (or will be) a Production value stream. These four non-production value streams are equally vital to the functioning of the enterprise, but, nevertheless, they are *supporting* value streams because they support the Production value stream. The value they create is often (but not always) provided to the internal customers in the Production value stream.

The typical "Lean 101" course tells you that Lean is all about "waste" and that "value" is only "what the customer is willing to pay for". That is a bit like teaching medical students that human health is all about the heart, and that the rest of the vital organs do not matter. Yes, the external customer is only "willing to pay" for the value-adding steps in the Production value stream, and perhaps a little for Sales and Support too, but it takes an entire collection of supporting value streams across the whole enterprise to enable production or service delivery. The heart is vital, but so are the brain, lungs, blood and bones, and all the other organs and systems in the human body. One is not any "better" or more important than any other. All the parts are necessary, but not sufficient on their own, to the healthy functioning of the whole system.

Often the supporting value streams employ more people than a firm's Production value streams. Thus, the bulk of improvement opportunities within an enterprise is often in non-production areas. We should not ignore supporting value streams. There is a vast amount of interdependency between a firm's main Production value streams and the functions like HR, Marketing, IT, Procurement, and Accounting that support them.

System: *a system is a group of interconnected, interdependent parts that act together as a unified whole, toward a common purpose. The behavior of systems is governed by underlying principles and procedures, which may or may not be well understood.*

Systems, like value streams, are mental models. Nearly everything in the universe, large and small, can be explained as a system. You do not have to know anything about systems theory to comprehend the basics of how systems work, just as you do not have to be a physicist to understand the basic properties of gravity. The basic characteristics of systems, which I outline below, are not hard to grasp.

It is important first of all to understand that the word "system" in a business (and Lean) context does not refer exclusively to electronic information (IT) systems. The world is filled with an infinite number of systems, like the traffic system, our cardiovascular system, or the solar system. We live within and around an infinite number of systems. Our bodies contain systems, but our bodies, in turn, are contained in larger systems. In business systems, the component parts usually include three basic elements: people (actors), technology (physical/electronic tools), and information (both as the material of production and general communication).

Value streams are systems too. More specifically, they are complex, adaptive systems that have a social component (people and relationships) and a technical component (processes, information, and technology). Value streams, like all systems, contain many component parts (process steps) that can be further broken down into smaller systems. The "production system" of a company is a collection of primary and supporting value streams.

All value streams are systems, but not all systems are value streams. A "visual management system", for instance, is a subsystem that supports the management of a larger value stream. Systems differ from value streams in that they can be both bigger and smaller than value streams, and do not necessitate a customer (or other business stakeholder), nor do they need to have the purpose of creating customer value, at least not in a commercial sense. For instance, the solar system provides value to humans by providing us with a habitable planet, but, as far as I know, no one owns the solar system and it cannot be monetized; it just exists.

Just like value streams and their component parts, there are, in theory, an infinite number of systems and subsystems. You can have sub-atomic particle systems and inter-galactic systems, and everything in between. Smaller systems (sometimes called subsystems) are nested in larger systems. As work systems and their related subsystems get progressively smaller, we tend to refer to them as processes (see below), and processes can be further broken down into methods and steps. When does a system or value stream become small enough to be called a process? There is no precisely defined line. To quote the great systems thinker Peter R. Scholtes, "when does a ship become small enough to be called a boat?"

Because of this fuzziness between systems, processes, and value streams, it best to make our thinking and assumptions about the system we are trying to describe explicit, so we often use diagrams (like maps) to share and communicate our models.

Process: *a process is a sequence of steps or activities required to transform inputs into outputs.*

Processes are like value streams and systems—they are humanly constructed mental models to comprehend and describe how work works. Processes are usually smaller than value streams, but not always. Think of a value stream as a big process, composed of a number of smaller process steps. Primary value streams typically begin and end with an external customer, whereas processes do not necessarily end with a customer, not even an internal one. For instance, software on servers processes data and the output, say a table of updated data, may be consumed only by other IT systems or devices. The internal employee never consumes the table of data directly but accesses elements of it through an application interface. Similarly, you may be the supplier and consumer of your own process. If you are producing financial analysis in a report, you might do some analysis in spreadsheets as an interim step—this process produces an output for no other customer than you. This output then becomes an input into your creation of the final report.

Processes, like systems and value streams, are potentially infinite in number. You can decide where they begin and end, and what level of detail they will contain. They can begin and end anywhere, but there is usually a logical basis for where they start and stop. For example, the process for making your morning coffee might begin by filling your coffee maker with the right amount of water to produce the desired number of cups... or, it could start with a farmer picking the berries from a coffee bush in Indonesia. Like all models, the optimal scope and level of detail depends on what you need to use the model for.

The word "process" is frequently used in common parlance to mean only the formal, procedural information about how to perform work that is repeatable and predictable. This formal knowledge is mechanical (algorithmic, in the language of cognitive science), and usually codified in writing and diagrams. As a document, it can be variously referred to as a standard, a policy, a guideline, a manual, a procedure, a job aid, a standard operating procedure (SOP), or some similarly officious and administrative-sounding term. The word is often used in a negative way to connote inflexible bureaucracy, such as "we have too much process around here". Thus it is not uncommon for Lean people to implement more explicit and standardized processes in areas where there are none, and then to simplify processes in areas where there are too many.

You might hear people around your office say things like, "Most of what we do is 'thinking' work, not 'process' work". The subtext of such a statement is that processes only pertain to clerical and administrative work, and that the "real" value-adding work is somehow perceived to be above this lowly and profane world of mere "process" work. It may horrify them to learn that processes involve rules of thumb, professional judgment, and decision-making with incomplete information too. These processes are sometimes referred to as "heuristic" processes. Thinking, too, is a process.

In reality, process is not inherently negative. There are good processes and there are bad processes. If we think of "process" as merely a description (not a judgment or evaluation) of how work moves between teams, maybe the word might regain its neutral connotation. Many Lean tools, like value stream maps and the data contained within them, are helpful in large part because they help de-personalize process analysis, removing a lot of the fear that people might initially have, and replacing it with objectivity and neutrality.

Getting employees comfortable with process analysis is a foundational first step, because—like it or not—*all* business outcomes are the consequence of a process. Many of your most important and complex processes are not documented or formalized—but that does not mean it is of no value to think of your work as a process. Just the opposite: if you want to improve business results, you have to understand and improve the processes that created them. If people in your office do not like the word "process" because they think it implies that they work in a meat packing factory, use the terms "value stream" or "system" instead. They are all effectively the same thing: useful models for understanding and improving work.

Generally Speaking

- Value streams are larger than processes. Systems can be smaller, equal to, and larger than both value streams and processes.
- All processes are systems, but not all systems are processes.
- All value streams are systems, but not all systems are value streams.
- All value streams are (large) processes, made up of smaller process steps.
- Not all processes and not all systems are value streams because, unlike value streams, systems and processes do not have to begin and end with a customer or create value for some stakeholder.
- Systems and processes have no scale—they can be sub-atomic or galactic, whereas value streams are almost always at the scale of human work enterprises and the business systems and processes contained within them.
- Value streams and processes are usually visually depicted in a linear sequence, whereas systems are usually depicted visually as a networked web of nodes and connections (interactions/relationships).

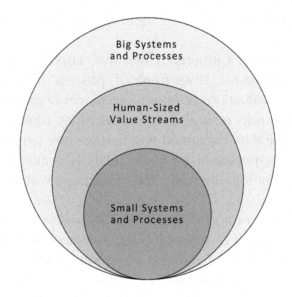

Index

Page numbers followed by "*n*" refer to notes.

Printed in the United States
by Baker & Taylor Publisher Services